The Dangerous World of Butterflies

The Dangerous World of Butterflies

The Startling Subculture of Criminals, Collectors, and Conservationists

PETER LAUFER, PH.D.

The Lyons Press
Guilford, Connecticut
An imprint of The Globe Pequot Press

The Lyons Press is an imprint of The Globe Pequot Press.

Editor/Project Manager: Holly Rubino
Text Designer: Sheryl P. Kober
Layout Artist: Kim Burdick

Library of Congress Cataloging-in-Publication Data is available on file.

ISBN 978-1-59921-555-6

Printed in the United States of America
10 9 8 7 6 5 4 3 2 1

With love to

Sheila, my

flutura
fertito
hu die
kupukupu
pinpirin
Schmetterling
papalló
chou
sommerfugl
buttorfleoge
papillon
parpar
lepke
farfalla
drugelis
pürpüruk
borboleta
bábochka
mariposa
titli
leptir
buom buom
vlinder
skoenlapper
rama-rama
psyche

butterfly

Contents

A Relentless Quest for Tranquility

"WHAT'S YOUR NEXT BOOK GOING TO BE ABOUT?"

Without fail, when I read to audiences in bookstores, when I'm interviewed on radio and TV about my work, even when I'm introduced in a purely social setting as an author, that question comes up. It's as predictable as migrating Monarchs.

I'm a journalist. I deal with the news, and in case you're lucky enough not to notice, there's some pretty bad news going around. I report on earthquakes, fires, and floods, along with wars and other man-made disasters. My books include a study of Americans rotting in prison overseas. I traveled around the world for that one, to twenty-one countries, checking in on Americans locked up in some of the most miserable conditions imaginable. I've written about a sordid and infamous rape case in New Jersey. I've written about the rise of neo-Nazism in Germany. My book about migration from Mexico to Gringolandia introduces the reader to the selfish hate spewing from American flag–waving vigilantes parading along the border, and the ghastly death-defying trail our economy's laborers tread as they commute to their underpaid jobs.

The news often is grim, of course.

As the Iraq War debacle continued, I wrote *Mission Rejected*, a book profiling American soldiers who returned from the Iraq War opposed to it, and those who refused deployment to the Middle East to fight it. And although I try to convince readers that it is—after all the blood and guts—an optimistic book because these soldiers risk their freedom, their careers, and their reputations when they follow their consciences, theirs are sad, sad stories.

One day up in Fairhaven, Washington, at Village Books, a vibrant independent bookstore overlooking the Bellingham Bay, I heard the query again.

"What's your next book going to be about?"

The audience packed the ground floor of the store, jammed onto folding chairs and standing around the bookshelves. It was a hot summer night, and I had been up at the lectern reading from the Iraq book and answering questions for over an hour. I was wearing a suit coat that I could not take off without ruining the video of the event CSPAN was recording because the microphone cord was snaked inside my jacket and the microphone was clipped to my lapel. I was sweating under the hot lights the camera crew insisted were needed for a good picture, and the store was not air-conditioned.

The give-and-take with the crowd was spirited, but I was ready to call it a night when the predictable question provided my exit strategy.

A woman raised her hand and called out in a desperate-sounding voice, "I find myself getting mired in this war. How do you get perspective so you can be effective?" Of course she wasn't just asking me for my opinion. It was much more of a collective plea, a plaintive howl of, "What should we do, what can we do, what must we do?"

Behind me was a huge banner reading THIS WAR IS UNWINNA-BLE & IMMORAL. In front of me were rows and rows of anti–Iraq War activists and Vietnam War–era veterans, all—it seemed—as crazed as I was about the tragedy of the Iraq War, consumed by a desire to try to figure out what to do to stop it.

"Fatigue sets in," I finally said about the overwhelming sadness about the war that permeated the room. "It's so depressing, and it's really hard to fight against it all the time. There have to be laughs. We have to find some relief. And yet our work against the war is unending because the machine is extraordinarily pervasive." I paused and smiled, and I used a line I'd come up with a few weeks before at another reading in an attempt to end the evening with some relief from all the grief. "That's why my next book," I announced, "is going to be about butterflies and flowers." A predictable titter rippled through the crowd, and I waved good-bye. As I signed books for the audience, we agreed we were exhausted by the trauma of war.

When CSPAN broadcast the Bellingham event, the network posted my Web site on the TV screen, and the next day I was on the receiving end of an avalanche of email, with about half of it in support of the anti-war soldiers and the other half in favor of the attack on Iraq.

Some of the incoming notes were predictably nasty, but often with a comic turn of a phrase, like these words from a fellow named Nicholas Troiano: "I am currently watching you on CSPAN. You sicken me. Please, stay in Canada. You disgrace this country. As a young American who aspires to be a future politician, you really disgust me." And then the entertaining closing line, "Feel pleased I took the thirty seconds to acknowledge you, Nick."

Some of the criticism was just sober disagreement, such as these words from a J. E. Harrington. "Hello, Mr. Laufer. I have to say I think you are as far off the mark as one can be. I believe your public position on the war gives strength to our enemies. If we had listened to the weak and those who did not want to fight in World War II, I would have heard you deliver your message in German." And then a gracious salutation, "Regards, J. E. Harrington."

Warren G. MacDonald saluted what he called my "very impressive" journalism credentials before he slammed me with "your left-leaning ideas in *Mission Rejected* bring dishonor to our wonderful men and women serving to protect you in your right to say such demeaning commentary."

From an anonymous correspondent came: "What is immoral, sir, is the likes of you and your ilk defending tyrants and dictators worldwide. Are you really that out of touch with reality? The sixties are over, Pete. Learn to deal with it a little, buddy! When tyrants and dictators speak, they quote you and yours. There is blood on your hands, sir. Like it or not, that is a fact." It was (bizarrely) signed with a hearty, "Good day!"

Of course there were letters of support, too. But mixed in with the radio talk show–like barrage of strident attacks and embraces was this surprise:

> Hi,
>
> I watched your book talk on CSPAN from Bellingham, Washington. I am impressed with the antiwar movement, but dismayed that things move so slowly. I was a young bride of a draftee during Viet Nam and I never understood why the antiwar movement did not recognize or sympathize with the antiwar soldiers. It was a very tough time for all but it led me to our butterfly reserve at the same latitude as Udorn, Thailand, where we spent the war.
>
> Jokingly, at the end of your talk you said your next book was going to be about flowers and butterflies. Let me offer one of our rustic bungalows to you when you seek a respite. It is a very beautiful and peaceful place. It is also good to be reminded what civil war does to a country. The scars in Nicaragua are not very deep.
>
> —Jane Foulds
>
> P.S. This is a serious invitation. Good luck to you. The world needs a good butterfly book. Peace and tranquility await you at Nicaragua Butterfly Reserva. Come visit us.

What a delightful counterpoint to what my old colleague in the radio news business, David McQueen, used to refer to as "the dismal details of the daily downer." I reread the note, smiled, and went back to work. But a day or so later I went back to the message and read it again. I dropped a quick email to this Jane Foulds and asked her if it really was a serious invitation. She answered immediately. "I am serious," she wrote, "and the *reserva* is beautiful. Your only decision is: Do you want to be on the farm amid the birds and butterflies and camp life, which is hard. If you want a more comfortable hotel in town, all levels of accommodations are available in Granada."

I had not been back to Nicaragua since I covered the Sandinista–Contra War in the mid-1980s. I'd never been to Granada, but knew of its reputation as a treasure of Spanish Colonial architecture. I showed the correspondence to my wife. Her reaction was immediate: "Let's go!" I started to tell the story to friends and colleagues—about the throwaway line, "My next book is going to be about butterflies and flowers," the CSPAN broadcast, and the immediate invitation to the *reserva*. Every single friend and colleague I told responded in chorus with my wife, "You must go!"

It did seem serendipitous. Kismet at work.

I wrote back to Jane, asking for more details. She called the camp "rustic," and reported that she is comfortable there, but that she's hosted visitors who didn't handle the lifestyle well. "This is five kilometers from town on a bad road in a Third World country that is tied with Haiti to be the poorest in our hemisphere. It is a country that has serious problems; episodic electric and chronic water problems." But then she offered the flip side. "Our *reserva* is beautiful. We have worked very hard to get the wow factor. We have a 70,000-cubic-foot butterfly enclosure with 200 butterflies of perhaps 50 species. It is planted with the host and nectar plants each species requires. Our 10 acres are planted with flowers and trees, and we have great birds including the motmot and oreopendola."

The motmot and the oreopendola? Fantastical images were coming to me, along with the lure of the unknown and a new adventure.

But then back to reality. "There are also snakes and mosquitoes. The native food is pretty much chicken and hamburger and beans and rice—very little green. We have a twenty-year-old Toyota Land Cruiser that breaks down regularly because of the shaking it takes on the road and the problem of inferior Chinese replacement parts." Don't worry about malaria, she wrote, but "there are rumors of cases of dengue, and parasites are common. We worry most about snake-bites, but probably cars are the biggest real threat." Drivers in Nicara-gua are notorious for recklessness. Jane reiterated that she thought a spell at the *reserva* might be a healthy respite from what she referred to as my "normal life."

But as I read and reread her email messages, the invitation to the *reserva* started to move in my mind from a passing flutter to an adventure story. I bought the *Lonely Planet* guide to Nicaragua and ordered a stack of butterfly books from my local library.

I realized I was searching for a much-needed break from the bleak.

Where the "butterflies and flowers" line had come from, I didn't know. Butterflies and flowers just flew into my mind and blossomed there as an automatic metaphor for peace and love, relief from misery, and happiness. I certainly had no particular affinity for or knowledge of either butterflies or flowers when I started using them as potential book fodder, just a passing affection and appreciation for them over the years, and maybe some vague memories of catching butterflies back in grammar school, putting them in jars filled with formaldehyde, and sticking pins through their dead little bodies to mount them on . . . what? A board for a science project? Or maybe that was in Cub Scouts for a merit badge.

But as I was weighing Jane's invitation, I remembered that there are butterflies in my Sonoma County backyard. Bodega Bay is a wintering haven for migrating Monarchs. Several years before the Iraq War, I had wandered over to their hangout, a grove of trees in

Bodega Dunes State Park, and I barely remembered them only as blackish leaf-like things, hanging in masses from trees in a far corner of the park.

I began seeing butterflies everywhere. Not in flight, it was almost winter. But on billboards, for example, as graphic displays in advertisements. It reminded me of when I bought a jalopy Studebaker, I think it was a 1952. Suddenly I saw Studebakers everywhere, when prior to owning one they had seemed a rarity.

When the library books were due, I renewed them, and they sat on the bookshelf unopened while I thought about butterflies and flowers. Was the Jane Foulds invitation a gift from the muse, or a distraction to file and forget? My eyes are always on the lookout for subject matter. To me, journalism is an all-or-nothing calling. A real journalist is a journalist to the grave. He may stop writing or broadcasting. She may open a restaurant. But for a real journalist, the nose for news never stops sniffing. We see stories perpetually and everywhere. We're drawn toward the sirens. We never stop asking questions. We're never off duty.

I pulled a thin volume out of the stack of library butterfly books. It was one of the Rudyard Kipling *Just So* stories, *The Butterfly That Stamped*. I read it aloud to my wife and one of my sons. It was the Sunday after Thanksgiving and we were sitting in front of the fireplace, enjoying a roaring fire on a cold, rainy night. Our peaceful scene and Kipling's language retelling the tale, "O my Lady and Content of my Heart, I shall continue to endure my fate at the hands of these nine hundred and ninety-nine Queens who vex me with their continual quarreling," lured me to a fantasy land far from my usual diet of bad news stories. (By the way, the butterfly is the hero; he inadvertently saves the king's peace of mind.)

Another of the butterfly books was *An Obsession with Butterflies*. In its first few pages, the author, Sharman Apt Russell, questions if butterflies could be "beauty without cause or consequence" and warns, "Some of us become obsessed with butterflies." That sounded promising. I'm sure my obsessions are what motivate me. I flipped through the pages to learn there are about eighteen thousand different butterfly species. That sounded promising, too. Plenty of material to work with in this new world I was stumbling into. And then this intriguing question and answer: "Of what use are butterflies? Less than you may think." Although they can provide a tasty morsel for hungry birds and lizards.

Nabokov's Butterflies was next on my stack, hundreds of pages of Vladimir Nabokov's writings, edited by Brian Bird and Robert Michael Pyle, including a line from Nabokov's autobiography regarding his lifelong love affair with butterflies. "Few things indeed have I known in the way of emotion or appetite, ambition or achievement, that could surpass in richness and strength the excitement of entomological exploration." A pretty decent recommendation for accepting the assignment from Jane Foulds to write my butterfly book.

The illustrations in *The Spirit of Butterflies* furthered my intrigue. Author Maraleen Manos-Jones collected images of butterflies adorning sculpture, mosaics, paintings, illuminated texts, jewelry, fashions, postage stamps, advertising, and the biceps of tattoo artist Huggy Bear Ferris. The book shows off a Panamanian *mola*, the layers of colored fabric cut and sewn into a butterfly motif. There is a butterfly Hopi *kachina* doll, a butterfly mosaic from Pompeii, a Chinese bridal robe, a Picasso collage featuring a dead butterfly, and an Absolut vodka ad made up of butterflies forming the shape of a bottle. At this point I was definitely seeing more butterflies than Studebakers.

I started checking out fares and schedules to Managua, and wondering about the origin of the clichéd butterflies in my stomach. I embraced the intoxication that comes with a new assignment. Jane's offer, my brief foray into butterfly literature, and my natural wanderlust combined to seduce me into a quest. My journey into the dangerous world of butterflies had begun.

Chapter One

OFF TO NICARAGUA AND AN INTRODUCTION TO LEPIDOPTERA

THE CONTINENTAL FLIGHT FROM CALIFORNIA IS HEADED SOUTH TO Central America on a sunny winter day. I lose track of the guy I'd seen in the airport waiting room pulling *Spanish for Dummies* out of his bag. I had wanted to suggest he conceal it behind a newspaper page. Instead I'm chatting up one of the stewardesses.

"Where are you going?" she asks.

"Managua," I tell her.

"I don't go there anymore," she says, looking genuinely concerned about my choice of destination. "I was there the week of the elections." She's referring to the November 2006 elections that brought Sandinista Daniel Ortega back to the presidency. "We were forced to stay in our rooms by corporate security. We heard gunfire at night." She clearly wants to tell the whole story of her last trip to Nicaragua; it seems she wants to warn me. "I slept under my bed." Is she joking? It appears not, but how do you fit under a hotel room bed?

"We were told not to order room service because that's how kidnappers got into a crew room the month before. They forced the crew into a van and stripped them. Pointed machine guns at their heads. Stole everything. It was terrorism."

This is the same stewardess who, moments before, introduced a passenger to the rest of us via the intercom, announcing he was just returned from Iraq "serving his country." She organized a round of applause for him from the cabin.

I

Managua looks almost as grim and scruffy as when I was there last. Damage is still obvious from the 1972 earthquake that wiped out downtown. Grand tracts of the old city near Lake Managua's shore lay empty. The earthquake-damaged buildings were either bulldozed and the lots left barren or they remain unrepaired and decaying, further ravaged by passing time; the city has been diluted to Los Angeles–like sprawl spreading for miles. Placards left over from the election campaign decorate the traffic circles: huge photographs of Ortega, signed "Daniel" and captioned *¡La solución!* At the time *La solución* was still fighting charges from his stepdaughter, Zoilamerica Narvaez Murillo, that he had molested her since he was first elected president in 1979, back when she was eleven.

I spent the night at the new-to-me Holiday Inn (no gunfire, and I slept in—not under—the bed). When I was last in Managua I stayed in a *pension* a few blocks away from the "landmark neo-Aztec pyramid," as Lonely Planet calls the luxury hotel that was headquarters for business, government, and the international press during the Sandinista–Contra war years. It's always a good idea to avoid spending the night at the most likely target.

There is nothing new about Americans acting out their dreams and fantasies in Nicaragua. Jane Foulds was preceded by a long list of expatriates, and there were plenty of her contemporary fellow Americans seeking their Nicaraguan fortunes while she was busy developing her *mariposario*—U.S. soldiers building a clinic and a school at the invitation of the government, investors looking for a cheaper tropical alternative to Costa Rica, surfers searching for the perfect wave, and plenty of graying military pensioners seeking the companionship of *chiquitas* happy to help them spend their Yankee dollars. One of the oddest of the earlier bunch was William Walker. He and his private army invaded Nicaragua and managed not only to occupy

Granada, but to get himself elected president. Back home (Walker hailed from Nashville), his president, Franklin Pierce, quickly and officially recognized the rogue regime. Walker's Nicaragua unsuccessfully attacked Costa Rica, and Walker went home to Nashville in defeat, only to return to Central America and try to rebuild his empire. His last adventure was an invasion of Honduras, but rather than elect him president the Hondurans stood him up against a wall in front of a firing squad. He was executed in 1860. The U.S. Marines spent much of the first few decades of the twentieth century occupying Nicaragua, an operation attacked repeatedly by forces Augusto César Sandino led with his original Sandinistas.

I hail a taxi that looks in good enough condition to make it down the Pan American Highway the hour or so toward Granada, reputed to be the oldest European city in the New World, founded by the Spanish in 1524. Jane's husband Gerry picks me up with the old Land Cruiser, looking in better shape than she described it in the email. I've been hanging out at Kathy's Waffle House across from the fading blue *Convento San Francisco*. Kathy's is another gringo dream: Sandy Perkoff founded the café with his Nicaraguan wife Kathy, she a couple of generations younger than he. In Granada I met several other crotchety American graybeards sporting nubile Nica wives. Sandy and I sit on the crowded porch of Kathy's, a prime meeting spot for Granada's landed gentry and its tourists, he ogling young Nica women promenading the *Calle Cervantes* and me securing his patter into my notebook, including why he likes living the ex-pat life in Granada. "I don't have to follow my dog with a baggie." He points to the church, "He just goes across and shits in the courtyard." He employs a long litany of other reasons life far from his American roots suits him just fine, from cheap real estate to pretty women.

Daniel Ortega wasn't the only headliner in trouble with the law at the time. Eric Volz, another American from Tennessee, was on trial for murdering his girlfriend. Unlike William Walker, he didn't invade to control land, he traded it as a real estate agent, selling coast-side Nicaraguan properties to retiring Yankees. He barely escaped a lynch mob before being found guilty and sentenced to thirty years. "I am in prison, but the prison is not in me," he told the *Washington Post.* "I have learned that I can endure." Endure he did until an appeals court overturned his conviction and he was released several months later, and left Nicaragua. Good thing, says Sandy Perkoff from his perch at Kathy's, calling Central American prison time "the same as dying, only slower." He knows, he says, from his first-hand experiences in solitary in Costa Rica on marijuana possession charges.

Perkoff is a restaurateur and a real estate agent; selling real estate to gringos is big business. The spur off the Pan American Highway that leads to Granada is lined with teasers, billboards for real estate offices—in English. At the Managua Holiday Inn developers have been holding a trade show. "Live Your Dream," suggests Gran Pacific Nicaragua, with a slick full-color brochure that promises, "Nicaragua emerged from the dark cloud of civil war that ended in 1989 to become a beacon of success . . . easily accesible [sic], safe, beatiful [sic], inexpensive, and business opportunities are timely." Especially for copy editors.

As I look around the neighborhood Jane Foulds calls home, it and its characters appear to me as pages out of Graham Greene. Including Jane. Perkoff knows her. "Oh, yeah," he says, "the Butterfly Lady."

Gerry Foulds and I head out of Granada. I should have paid better attention to the route when he hit the dirt road past the cemetery; it might have prevented me from getting lost the next day when I was traveling back to the *mariposario*, the butterfly reserve. We bounce a couple of miles toward *Laguna de Apoyo* and pull into his and Jane's driveway past a subtle marker that reads, *Quinta de Gringa*, the gringo lady's country house. A multicolored butterfly flag flutters from the side of the main house, which is set far back from the dirt road. Jane had warned me it was, as she called it, "rustic." But she looks comfortable settled in a caned rocking chair on the porch, wearing a bright blue tie-dyed T-shirt adorned with the image of a big blue butterfly. After just a quick hello, Jane and Gerry take me on a tour, she carrying a huge butterfly net, the pole easily three feet long.

We stop at a trap of rotting fruit under netting. Gerry pokes around the netting looking for catches.

"It is fermenting fruit," Jane corrects me when I call it "rotting."

"If fermenting and rotting are something different," adds Gerry. The two of them talk in alternating phrases, finishing sentences and completing thoughts. They've been married since 1968, just after Gerry was drafted in the Army and was sent to the Thai–Lao border as an interpreter. Jane did not stay home in Pennsylvania, but joined him in the jungle. When the last of their three children went off to college, they picked Nicaragua to retire to because it reminded them of Southeast Asia.

"They come and go," says Gerry about the butterflies he's trying to lure to the traps with the fruit. "We usually have the same locals, the habitual drunks. But every once in a while we get different ones that come through, and then it's a thrill."

The strategy behind the trap is for the butterflies to eat the fermented bananas and get drunk.

"They come into the trap and they usually fly up into the netting, and we'll catch them and put them in the butterfly farm," says Jane.

"If they're something different we'll put them in the farm," Gerry adds. "If they're just the normal, regular ones that are around here all the time, we just let them go. We catch them over and over again. It's like throwing them out of the bar drunk and they come back the next day. They're getting drunk and we get entertainment." He smiles.

"It's a good lesson for the tourists," says Gerry. The drunken butterflies are easily accessible for visitors to pick up, hold, and inspect. "They see that they're not so delicate that you can't grab hold of them. You don't crush them, you just grab them—gently—and then you let them go." And he's demonstrating while we talk.

Next Gerry tells me the males of some species mate before the females break out of the chrysalis. An introduction to drunken butterflies and stories of butterfly rape and pedophilia, all after just a few minutes on the *reserva*.

When I returned to the States after my Nicaraguan interlude I followed up on Gerry's observations and checked in with one of the world's leading entomologists, Dr. Thomas Emmel, zoology professor at the University of Florida in Gainesville. He provided some graphic details about the rapes, and explained how this behavior can be beneficial to the species.

"Most butterfly males have to be out as adults, out of the pupae, for about twenty-four hours or more before their sperm cells are mature," Emmel tells me, but there's no such waiting time for the females. "She's ready to be mated as soon as she emerges because she has eggs that are maturing and are ready to be fertilized by the sperm." The males of most butterfly species patrol for virgin females. They court them and try to mate with them shortly after they emerge from the chrysalis and begin to fly about. But not all the males court and wait for an invitation to start a family. "In some of the *Heliconius* butterflies they've advanced this calendar to the point where the males sit on pupae that may be one or two days away from hatching that are going to produce females," explains Emmel, and he describes the one-sided act the males perpetrate next. "They'll sit on that pupa as it darkens and the butterfly inside starts to wiggle and split the skin. Then they get excited enough that they will actually puncture the pupal skin with their external claspers at the end of the male abdomen and mate with the female butterfly inside—before she emerges. Because she doesn't have any choice in the matter, it's been termed 'pupal rape.'"

Not that the female doesn't play a definitive—if inactive—role in this earlier-than-most-butterflies mating game.

"The female pupa emits a pheromone, an external hormone, an odiferous hormone, that attracts the males. Literally two, three, five males may be flying around this pupa and landing on it. The strongest and biggest one, or at least the one that's most aggressive, pushes the others off and gets to mate with the female."

Sounds like a bar in Gainesville, I suggest. The scientist doesn't argue the point.

"One of the best males, probably the best male, gets to mate," says the professor, and the pupal rape, as offensive as it is if we anthropomorphize it, is productive for the species.

"When the female hatches," he's referring to a raped female, "it can then take to wing and start laying eggs right away—within the first hour, not having to wait for a male to find it. That's an advantage because female butterflies, like males, can get attacked by a bird at any point in their life and the earlier they start laying eggs, the better. They're getting some of that next generation out and safely in the egg stage before being attacked."

If the rape victim survives predators, the potential exists for her to become a butterfly baby machine. Unlike most temperate butterflies that live only a week or two, *Heliconius* adult butterflies can live several months, if they manage to avoid becoming bird food. Over a lifetime of four or five months one female could produce as many as five hundred eggs, laying about twenty a day.

"But the earlier they get started, the better," says Dr. Emmel, "because one never knows when a windstorm will come or a heavy rain or a lizard will make a mistake and grab that butterfly and smash it before it realizes it isn't tasty to eat. All of those chance events could happen and the butterfly, if it can shorten the length of time between hatching and egg laying, is at a great advantage."

Like it or not . . . Rape. Windstorms. Heavy rain. Lizards, birds, dragonflies. It's a dangerous world for butterflies.

"The butterfly has its heart in its hands every hour, I'm sure," Emmel agrees, "because there's something that's going to grab it or eat it. All sorts of things can happen."

Finding a specialist who studies drunken butterflies proved more problematic. Informal confirmation of the story Gerry Foulds tells about his tipsy butterflies is easy to find, but not scientific proof. Finally, at the University of California at Berkeley, a smiling Dr. Robert Dudley, professor of integrative biology, offered an academic nod to the notion. Dudley specializes in animal flight dynamics, but he figures he may well have seen his share of drunken butterflies. The drink of choice? Ethanol. "A lot of butterflies feed on fermented fruit on the forest floor," he points out, "and there are a couple of anecdotal accounts, but it's never been systematically investigated. No one has ever really worked on that systematically, and that's a shame because comparative biology of ethanol exposure is really interesting." One of the many fascinating aspects, I learn fast, about butterflies is how much about them remains unknown.

"Do you believe they are drunk?" I ask the researcher.

"They behave as if they are drunk," he answers carefully. There are a lot of other compounds in those fermenting fruits. "That's the problem with the drunken animal story." Nonetheless, there are anecdotal stories about butterflies being attracted to beer. "That's one way to make a good butterfly trap: stir up some bananas in beer, and you'll get both moths at night and butterflies during the day.

They're not seeking out the ethanol per se, they're going after the whole nutritional package. I would assume they're drunk, actually, because there's enough alcohol in the fermentation product. There may be some other things going on, but I do not see how you could exclude the effects of alcohol."

Dr. Dudley smiles and agrees the idea of drunken butterflies adds to the fun of studying them.

"Pupal rape and drunkards," says Gerry Foulds. "Not the oohs and aahs tourists think of with pollinating butterflies."

We tromp toward their butterfly enclosure, a funky rig of netting on posts, what the Foulds call their flight house and what their live butterfly collection calls home.

"These are local ones," Gerry says, stopping to show me what he calls "Crackers, the only ones that make noise." Jane and Gerry are refreshingly new at this butterfly business, amateurs and self-taught. Gerry points at the Crackers and says, "They're *Hamadryas*, which means something like sending up to the virgins. It's Arabic." We listen to the cracking sound. "They'll attack you," Gerry says. "They'll buzz people. They're territorial. They're mean." Gerry says no one knows the purpose of the sound.

He's correct, I learn later. *Hamadryas* are known as Crackers, and they make the cracking noise that we heard with their wings. But scientists at the University of Florida Institute of Food and Agricultural Sciences have found another noise-making butterfly, the Blue-and-white Longwing, *Heliconius cydno*. The *Heliconius cydno* make what researcher Mirian Hay-Roe calls a faint and hard-to-hear clicking sound, noise she is convinced is used for communication between the Longwings and used to scare other butterflies from the Longwings' home turf and food supply.[1] She is the first scientist to record the call of the Longwing.

Hamadryas make a much louder noise then *Heliconius cydno* and were first noted by Charles Darwin, who hypothesized that their easy-to-hear clicking is a mating call. Other scientists suggest it is designed to scare predators. Jayne Yack, a colleague of Mirian Hay-Roe, working with others at the Carleton University Biology Department in Ontario, believes the *Hamadryas* clicks are made with a single wing, not wings colliding, and that the butterflies are equipped with a hearing organ at the base of the forewing, adding to the theory that these insects are communicating with each other.[2] Amazing.

But virgins? Arabic? There is a Hamadryas baboon, and hamadryas in Greek and Roman mythology refers to various nymphs. Nymphs, baboons, virgins.

Jane holds a Cracker butterfly for me to photograph. Her thumb is poised just behind the *Hamadryas* head and she's trapping the butterfly against her forefingers, forcing the wings to spread so I can see its coloring and full wingspan.

"You're not hurting it?" I ask.

Her candor is refreshing. "That's a difference of opinion, but it doesn't seem to." She explains that the order butterflies belong to is called Lepidoptera because the wings are all scales. *Lepid* is the Greek word for scales; *ptera* is Greek for wing. "All the color comes from the scales," she tries to instruct me. "There's no pigment in them. It's all refracted or reflected light." The Cracker looks like a stained glass window, with circular patterns adjacent to irregular rectangular shapes, a variegated brown, black, and ecru.

Because she knows my butterfly knowledge is minimal, Jane offers me this primer: "The difference between a butterfly and a moth is that moths in general fly at night, butterflies in the day." The antennae differ, she says, identifying moth antennae as bigger, with more hair, "and they're uglier."

"So go ahead," Gerry says as we pass another trap, "reach in and grab one."

"What do you mean, 'Reach in and grab one?'" I say, looking at the captive butterflies.

"Just take it out," he says.

"I'll squash it," I say, worried.

"You're not going to squash it," he says.

"Just get it by the body," instructs Jane. "They're stronger than they look."

I grab it, and it does seem I am not harming it, although it looks extremely delicate.

"They're not delicate," Jane says, dismissing my concern.

At their request I let it go, and it flies off, seemingly unhurt.

"See? There's no harm done to it," says Gerry.

We're walking past plants raised as butterfly fodder. "Each butterfly has only one or two plants that it likes," says Gerry. "The mama butterfly will deposit the eggs on a particular kind of plant so that when the eggs turn into the little, tiny caterpillars they'll eat it, and they'll just eat it down to nothing. That's why most of our job is to constantly grow stuff." That takes a lot of water, and water is in short supply on their tract outside of Granada.

It is hot and sticky as we wander toward the butterfly enclosure. "C'mon, Barney," Gerry yells for their dog. But Barney chooses to stay outside, and as I follow Gerry and Jane into the netting, one of their displays flies out.

"We lost a butterfly," I report with concern.

"We lost a butterfly," Gerry agrees, without much concern. After all, we're in the Central American tropics, surrounded by such butterflies in the wild.

"Want to get him back?" I ask.

"No, we can't." Nicaragua is full of butterflies, but that doesn't mean we can just grab the escapee and toss it back in the exhibit. He was flying too fast for us to catch him. "It's not that easy," says Gerry about securing subjects in the wild for the exhibit.

"There's my new favorite," says Jane. "He looks like a Bengal tiger." We're surrounded by about fifty different butterfly species, they tell me, and over three hundred individual native Nicaraguan butterflies caught in nets around the surrounding countryside or in the drunk traps we just observed, and brought to the enclosure for display. "Every week I have a different favorite."

Jane believes the *reserva* is located on the migratory path of some butterflies, a detail she says she's trying to confirm with scientists who study Central American fauna. "Which is why I was so mad at that guy saying all we had wasn't worth studying."

"Who said that?" I ask.

"The North American Butterfly Association president Jeffrey Glassberg, that asshole." I'm quickly learning that Jane peppers her speech with candor and colorful language. Jane tells me she wanted to enter a North American Butterfly Association photography contest, but the organization limited entries to images from Mexico, the States, and Canada. Nicaragua, she knows, expressing disgust with the rules, is part of the North American continent.

Something flutters.

"Is that a butterfly or is that a leaf?" Jane asks. "I don't remember seeing one that little before."

"I think I've seen that one," says Gerry, "but not regularly."

Their enthusiasm is infectious, and their amateur's embrace of their new butterfly-inflected life is intriguing: the two of them are in business, homesteading in the tropics off an isolated dirt road, learning by doing just because they want to and they can. They hope to make enough money renting rooms to travelers, charging admission to the *reserva*, and selling butterflies to offset the costs of their new lifestyle. Meanwhile, Gerry commutes between Granada and his full-time job in Miami, spending as much time as he can with Jane and the butterflies. There is a Wild West, all-American we-can-do-it attitude at work here.

"We didn't know anything," Jane says about their initial foray into the butterfly world. It appealed to them, so they bought the land and learned by doing.

Jane grabs a butterfly and thrusts it at me. "Feel how strong this guy is!"

"Where do you want me to hold him?"

"Here. His body."

I take hold and he does feel strong, his body firm against my fingers.

We leave the enclosure and Gerry points to what he calls the Back Forty of their ten-acre spread where "the nectar-eater butterflies" live, "little ones—*Heliconia*—that really are hard to get. It's easy to trap the *barachos*, the drunks, but not so easy to get the nectar guys. And they're often little," he dismisses the *Heliconia*, "and not as spectacular."

Jane and Gerry are not just offering butterflies for display to passing tourists, although there are notes in their guest book from satisfied visitors. ("Very different," wrote George from Amsterdam. "The butterflies are cute," was the comment by Neal from Boston.) They are also in the butterfly breeding business. Their workers collect the tiny eggs, feed the resulting corraled caterpillars, hook the chrysalises on a board, and then harvest the resulting butterflies for sale to collectors. Examples of local butterflies are on display—pins through them—framed and hung on the walls

"Here's the Bengal tiger one," Jane points.

"And here's the Sandinista," says Gerry about a red and black butterfly sporting the Sandinista flag colors. "Watch for snakes." We're now heading to the main house from the enclosure, crunching through a thick layer of dry leaves. "Rattlesnakes."

"And the reason we're worried is if somebody gets bitten, nobody knows where the antivenom is," Jane adds, decrying the staffs at local hospitals. "That's why we're scared."

"Why does nobody know where the antivenom is?" I ask with some gringo concern.

"Because this is Nicaragua," says Jane, "and they don't know shit." I can't tell if it's her droll humor, her take on reality in her new hometown, or a combination of the two. I suspect it's the latter and watch where I step.

Gerry is rattling off the names of some of the flowers and trees we pass.

"Our biggest problem," says Jane, "is what is all this stuff?" She says she wants to trade accommodations in her cabins to graduate students who will come and inventory the plants and animals on her spread. So far she's failed to find appropriate candidates. "The money in bugs," she complains, "is in killing them."

"Raid," says Gerry. "And ChemLawn."

Jane says that Nicaraguan butterflies are understudied and that there is a dearth of literature about them. With no science background, she and Gerry try to fill in the gaps by learning from locals and with their own observations. "I wrote my tenth grade biology teacher and said that I wished I had studied harder and learned more."

We sit on the porch, Jane in the rocker, smoking one Marlboro after another and washing them down with Coca-Cola. The two of them are eager to help me in the quest Jane assigned me after my flip "butterflies and flowers" remark in Bellingham. They suggest places and people for me to visit. Butterfly World in Florida and the "Dutch guy" who runs it, for one. That would be Ron Boender, I learn later.

"In Miami there's a guy named Dennis Olle," says Gerry. "He's a pompous ass." And a lawyer and president of the Miami Blue chapter of the North American Butterfly Association. The Miami Blue is a butterfly that fluttered toward extinction on the endangered species list, and is making a comeback. "But he knows a lot about butterflies," Gerry continues. "I'm sure he's a warm and engaging human being—although he's always been an aloof, pompous ass to me. I guess I deserved it," Gerry says, his voice thick with sarcasm. Apparently, Olle earned Jane and Gerry's wrath by ignoring them, a manifestation of the antipathy North American Butterfly Association members harbor for commercial breeders. "There's that doctor—what's his name—in Gainesville."

"Emmel," says Jane.

"Emmel," agrees Gerry. "Dr. Emmel. He's an entomologist."

"He's got a lot of dead butterflies," says Jane.

Later, as I began to cast a wide net looking for butterfly experts, the Florida contacts they suggested were spot on, and indeed Dr. Emmel—who explained pupal rape when I caught up with him in Gainesville—has a lot of dead butterflies at his University of Florida facilities. Millions. It's the second largest collection in the world after the British Museum, and closing the gap fast. Just north of all those bugs in Gainesville, they tell me to check out Shady Oak Butterfly Farm, its slogan: "One stop for all your butterfly needs," run by their friend Edith Smith. They call her the Queen of the International Butterfly Breeders Association and tell me she ships thousands of butterflies a week from her farm to collectors. Breeding pupae and butterflies is big business because butterfly houses all over the world must replenish their livestock every month or so. Most butterflies only live for a few weeks.

Another Marlboro. More Coke.

"It seems like the more we're here, the more we don't want to leave the farm." Gerry is relaxed. "It's a lot more *tranquillo* and salubrious here than it is in town," he says about Granada, which certainly is noisy and smelly with traffic compared to the *mariposario*.

We stop talking butterflies for a spell and share stories about our families. A cart pushed by a fellow keeping the sun off with just a baseball cap shows up on the dirt road. Barney barks and Gerry gets up. "Look at this guy. This is a hard-working guy. Imagine pushing this to try to sell fruit. *¡Hola!*" Gerry buys. The pineapple looks perfect.

"One of the reasons I like it here," Jane looks at the fruit, "is I realize how privileged I am. I feel blessed all the time I am here." But she wants more knowledge. "I'm really hoping some retired entomologist will show up." She hopes for one who will stay for a year, study the local natural life cycle, and tutor her and Gerry about their unexpected business venture and new passion. Instead, or at least for now, what she received was me, sitting on her porch, asking questions, and trying to decide if she was correct when she sent the email insisting I should write a book about the dangerous world of butterflies.

"We're normal," she insists about their lifestyle. "I don't mind a pit toilet and cold showers. And when the hose is in the sun, the shower's not cold." She likes the ex-pat lifestyle. "I'm disappointed with our generation. How do you get from sex, drugs, and rock 'n' roll to bombs?"

Gerry takes me back to the paved road in the *reserva*'s classic Land Cruiser, and from there I hail a taxi to my hotel. I liked the two of them and their spirit. So many of us claim we'd like to junk our routines and start anew. So few of us do. But I wanted to spend a less rustic night than the *reserva*'s guest quarters offered; I was headed back to my hotel room. Granada, the Colonial showplace, could use some soap and paint in most places, along with enough gentrification to trickle down through the struggling economy. Ribs show on the horses pulling colorfully painted carriages—a Granada trademark used to haul tourists and ferry locals. Horse manure is left uncollected in the streets. The waterfront on Lake Nicaragua is desolate, the few bars and restaurants I see there are uninviting. Water meter covers are missing from the sidewalks, leaving treacherous holes that are especially daunting at night. The metal covers are stolen, sold for scrap.

The next day I march up a dirt road to the butterfly reserve, walking because no taxi driver I meet knows of Jane's hideaway, and I'm hoping I can remember which turns to take. The shanties I see along the road to the *reserva* have concrete floors and corrugated tin roofs. The walls are rough-hewn unpainted wood. Laundry is drying on fences. Pigs, dogs, chickens, roosters, cows, goats all wander about, as do children of all ages—really dirty-looking children. It's a Sunday and families are hanging out, color TVs are glowing in the huts, Latin pop music is blasting to greet me, a broken high heel lies before me on the dirt track. But all that is left behind as I round the last curve and finally see the *Quinta de Gringa* again.

Jane goes over to the refrigerator and instead of another Coke takes out a well-worn Tupperware container. She pops off the top and inside are stacks of translucent envelopes, each holding a folded-up—and obviously quite dead—butterfly.

"It's a *Caligo memnon,* otherwise called an Owl because he has a big eye as camouflage."

The markings and coloration are disorienting. It really doesn't look, at first glance, like a butterfly. On one folded wing is a distinct and prominent black eye-shaped patch surrounded by a light tan circle. The effect, combined with delicate patterns of adjacent brown and black veins, makes the *Caligo memnon* look much more like the head of a predatory owl than the wings of a tasty and vulnerable butterfly. When alive, and not stacked in cold storage, *Caligo memnon* is crepuscular: the butterflies usually limit their flight to dawn and dusk.

The glassine-enclosed butterflies are all perfect. Their bodies, antennae, and wings are scratch and dent free. That's because Jane and her staff of helpers kill them the moment they spring forth from their caterpillar-to-butterfly metamorphosis.

"As soon as they were born they were put into these glassine papers and put into the freezer. They're newly hatched beautiful butterflies with no flaws. A-1 stock. Beautiful."

These captive-bred specimens provide one of Jane's butterfly revenue streams. She charges admission to the *reserva*, rents rooms for overnight stays, and sells Owls to collectors who "mount them for their collection of dried butterflies in frames."

"But they never got a chance to live out their sweet butterfly life," I protest to her.

She agrees, "They didn't get to live the regular butterfly life of Eden, drink, and be merry."

"You guys are murderers," I suggest. I say it as a joke, but I am shocked to see the stacks of dead butterflies, killed the moment they break out of the chrysalis.

"Well, we don't like to put it that way. To study it you have to be able to see it." Her butterflies go to both collectors and entomologists. "I personally don't like dead butterflies at all. But given no butterflies, I'll take dead ones."

Gerry is without remorse at this aspect of their commercial enterprise. He dismisses my concern. "It's important to point out that they don't live that long."

"They're a lower-order animal," says Jane. "So how much they feel is questionable, too. But look at how far butterflying has come. When it first began with the Brits it was all catch them, kill them, pin them, put them in a museum. Now we're talking about letting butterflies fly in the middle of enclosures and arboretums. Really, we've evolved nicely." Gerry is worried more about habitat depletion, herbicides and pesticides, endangered butterflies, and a shrinking world butterfly population than about more collectors.

"It gives me the creeps to be in a room with pinned butterflies," says Jane about museum collections, and yet she is pragmatic: She supplies collectors as a revenue generator.

"These," Gerry says, pointing to the picture-perfect corpses they are collecting for export, "represent just a few. We're raising them to kill them; these are for art. Some of us," he shrugs, considering life, "are sacrifice." He accepts the fate of his butterflies as leading a life led to satisfy collectors.

"Butterfly art" is the term often used for the display of butterflies encased in clear plastic. As my butterfly odyssey progressed, I would meet artists and a craftsman who use butterfly parts as their medium. There is no call for hanging framed butterflies that died a natural death on walls for decoration because, as Jane, puts it, butterflies that live out their lives are "beat to shit, just like people. Their wings get battered, just like people."

Each Owl brings about $8 on the butterfly market. "It's one of the bigger-ticket ones," says Jane. "It's really strong, too. It's really quite a spectacular butterfly."

The *Caligo memnon* is a common wild butterfly on the *reserva*, one of the drunks that frequents her offerings in the traps. Jane's supply seems limitless for her needs, and Gerry says most of the Owls they produce on the *reserva* go on display in the enclosure, not into the freezer en route to being stuck with a pin for static display far from their Nicaragua homeland. But the ones in the glassine envelopes never get to partake of the fermented fruit.

"He doesn't even get to the drunk tank. Just as he's emerging from the pupa, we get him. He never got to live much of a life."

Freezing butterflies to death is the kind of business that exacerbates the conflicts between breeders selling butterflies to collectors and the people Jane calls "butterfly huggers"—the purists who disapprove of breeding butterflies, especially breeding them for decorative release at events such as weddings and funerals. "We just hate them," Jane says about the huggers and *their* North American Butterfly Association. She calls them "purists who think any breeding is déclassé." She acts offended because the purist huggers reject what she considers is a viable business, butterfly breeding.

Jane puts the Owl back in the envelope. "I'm surprised at how many people are afraid to touch them because they're afraid they'll hurt them."

"I was hesitant when you handed me one yesterday. It felt so delicate."

"When they're dead, when they're brittle, they are. But alive, I'm surprised how strong they are. The female, as soon as she's born her whole job is to mate, so she's flying around looking for a place to lay her eggs. What she's doing is assessing the plants around, looking for exactly the best plant, one that doesn't already have other eggs on it, one that doesn't have disease on it. Most of the ones you see flying around are females. They lay their eggs in a row, kind of like an apartment building. We've got pictures where the eggs are actually being extruded from the female onto the leaf."

Jane is a comfortable proponent of her newfound hobby and business, approachable in a Julia Child–like manner, as she seems to bumble through her explanations and examples. Hers is a satisfied smile, and her earthy acceptance of her role as butterfly freezer, even as she expresses her love for the insects, is in accord with Vladimir Nabokov's memories—induced by ether administered for surgery—of "my one self in a sailor suit mounting a freshly emerged Emperor moth under the guidance of my smiling mother. It was all there, brilliantly reproduced in my dream, while my own vitals were being exposed: the soaking, ice-cold absorbent cotton pressed to the lemurian head of the moth; the subsiding spasms of its body; the satisfying crackly produced by the pin penetrating the hard crust of its thorax; the careful insertion of the point of the pin in the cork-bottomed groove of the spreading board; the symmetrical adjustment of the strong-veined, 'window' wings under neatly affixed strips of semi transparent paper."[3]

"God was having a whimsical day," Gerry says about the creation of Lepidoptera. "We could get along without them, but why would we want to?"

Chapter Two

WITH THE PURISTS WHERE BUTTERFLIES FLY FREE

"SELF-SERVING, GREEDY PEOPLE WHO DON'T CARE ABOUT ANYTHING," Jeffrey Glassberg says about butterfly breeders. "People trying to make money lying to people."

I was smitten enough by butterflies in Nicaragua to continue chasing them, and after Gerry and Jane indicted what they called "butterfly huggers" with such venom, I decided to join them for a spell and check them out myself. Glassberg and I are sitting in the auditorium of the Kernville Elementary School in Kernville, California, headquarters for the North American Butterfly Association national biennial meeting; Glassberg is the president and founder. Butterfly paraphernalia surrounds us, from T-shirts and greeting cards to neckties and books—including Glassberg's *Butterflies through Binoculars* series—and our conversation is interrupted by happy butterfly aficionados seeking his autograph on his *Field Guide to the Butterflies of North America*.

Glassberg appreciates the serendipity of my quest. "Yeah, it's funny how often those throwaway lines you don't mean sort of take on a life of their own." But he's primed to talk butterflies to a journalist, and to hype the association he founded. "To me the big story is that for the first time, really because of this organization, people in this country are looking at butterflies as wildlife." He points to the five thousand or so members his organization has attracted. Like bird watchers, "They go out with binoculars and cameras and look at butterflies. They photograph them and figure out what they are." They decidedly do not catch them in nets, kill them, and stick pins in them. "The importance of that is it just opens up a whole new avenue for conservation. Most of the people here, even though they're all here because they're interested in butterflies, most of them are broad-spectrum naturalists." They like birds; they like flowers; they like an excuse for hiking in the wild.

Kernville is northeast of Bakersfield in the southern Sierra Nevada. From the San Joaquin Valley I had driven up Highway 178 along the spectacular Kern River canyon, past ominous DANGER signs in English and Spanish warning about the river's extraordinarily powerful current as it rapidly descends past its rocky banks. I passed the ambulance, police cars, and rescue helicopter landed alongside the highway, and read the next day in the *Bakersfield Californian* about a presumed drowning. A man had pushed his struggling teenage daughter back to the shore when she went for a dip during a typical riverside picnic outing, but then lost his own ability to fight the current. He was the 244th victim claimed by the Kern since 1968.

As I listened to Whitewater 105 on the car radio ("All the original hits, the best music ever made"), smoke from forest fires faded the view of Lake Isabella at the top of the canyon. This is prime butterfly country; Kern County is home to rare species such as the San Emigdio Blue, a delicate pastel-colored fellow only about an inch across the wingspan. It was also home to "the world's most wanted butterfly smuggler," a butterfly desperado I discovered as I cast my wide research net when I first began to explore butterflies. And I imagined that while the eventually convicted smuggler Yoshi Kojima was doing his time in the federal prison in nearby California City, he was looking out over the desert and watched—helpless to pounce—as one of the little *Plebejus emigdionis* fluttered past his window, taunting him with its elusive value, making a few seductive passes in front of his cell before disappearing.

When I get to the elementary school, I find Glassberg exhausted, but ready to talk butterflies. He's wearing a bright red North American Butterfly Association polo shirt, and his smile comes easily except when I keep asking him about the controversy between his organization and butterfly breeders like the Foulds. In the world of butterfly watching, collecting, and breeding, Glassberg is famous for co-authoring a harangue against commercial breeders and the release for entertainment purposes of butterflies at ceremonies such as funerals and weddings.[4] Such releases, he wrote, represent "the dark side" of the increasing interest in butterflies. "Although this practice is understandable to naïve newlyweds-to-be (what could be more beautiful than adding butterflies to the environment?), it is a particularly long-lasting form of environmental pollution." Among his contentions are the following: Cross-breeding farm-raised butterflies with wild butterflies may confuse the still-unknown process the Monarch uses for its long-distance migration. Commercially bred butterflies may spread diseases and parasites to the wild. Releasing butterflies in regions not native to them may cause "inappropriate genetic mixing." He cited the movie *Jurassic Park* in the essay and wrote, "Don't fool with Mother Nature." He called for a ban on the release of commercially bred butterflies.

The International Butterfly Breeders Association struck back, calling Glassberg's conclusions "unsubstantiated by any scientific data." Glassberg is a scientist himself, with a Ph.D. in molecular genetics from Rice University. They pointed to millions of transactions with no negative results.

To Jeffrey Glassberg that argument reminds him of the early desperate claims of cigarette manufacturers. "They said smoking doesn't cause cancer. All the scientists said it did. There's almost no one who's either a scientist or a field biologist who would think taking farm butterflies and dumping them into the environment is a good idea.

It's only the people who make money at it that claim, 'Oh, it's great and it's wonderful.'"

The breeders claim Glassberg is offended by their entrepreneurship and by the commercialization of butterflies. He doesn't disagree. "Making butterflies into commercial objects is a kind of disgusting idea."

I find disgusting an odd word to choose. But he sticks with it.

"Disgusting to me. Butterflies are beautiful, free-flowing objects and to make them into another object of commerce is to me just repulsive, okay?" He is getting exasperated with me. But I remind him that commerce exists in his world as well. After all, he's selling his *Field Guide to the Butterflies of Western North America* on a table across the auditorium from where we're sitting. And we're talking at the table where he is offering to autograph those $21.50 books.

Of course this is an unbalanced comparison. He ignores it and simply reiterates, "I find it repulsive to sell butterflies. People who like birds don't raise chickadees and then ship them around the country and release them into the environment. It's stupid. It's silly. It's a really silly idea. It only works because they're selling to these gullible people who don't know any better and think, oh, this is a nice thing and it's increasing the number of butterflies. But it doesn't increase the number of butterflies." It doesn't increase the number of butterflies in the wild because those released are not gravid (egg-bearing) and are unlikely to find a mate in foreign territory.

But it must be a spectacular sight, a flock of gorgeous butterflies ascending to the heavens. I realize "flock" sounds awkward. Bevy? Swarm? What is a group of butterflies called? In fact, Glassberg's organization has grappled with this query. They were unable to find a citation for a proper term and as an organization had been using the rather bland "bunch." Suggestions for alternatives adorn the naba.org Web site and include such oddities as a "kiss" of butterflies and a "kaleidoscope" of butterflies, a "flutter" of butterflies and an "eminence" of butterflies, along with a "dance," a "spangle," a "symphony," and a "volley." Whatever we call them, Glassberg rejects the idea that the sight of a staged release is spectacular.

"I've seen it about three times in my life. I was at a wedding. I was at someone's anniversary party. I'm not kidding, all three times the butterflies—they were Painted Ladies—they come in a little box and they go *blunk*." He suggests they are not flying but floundering. "They flop around on the ground."

"It's not some kind of magical up-to-the-heavens flight?" I protest.

"It hasn't been in my experience. If you read stuff that people who see it write, very few have that experience."

I want the description in detail. "Now, they open up the box," I prompt.

"They have these farm butterflies. They imprison them. They talk about releasing them, but they're the ones who imprison them. They imprison them in glassine envelopes. If you think that's good for a butterfly, you don't know anything about butterflies. Then they ship them to somebody and they come half the time dead or dying, but the people don't know this. They open it up, and the butterfly—if it was a 'real' butterfly, it would zip away." I'm thinking wild salmon versus farmed salmon. Pink flesh versus food coloring. "It kind of flops out and after flopping around on the ground, it goes to a flower." Most people know so little about butterflies, he says, they are unaware of the unnatural behavior they're observing. Glassberg's annoyance with me and the subject is clearly growing. "I would say to you, don't talk to me about this. I would say if you want to focus on this, go out and talk to as many scientists as you can. Go to national parks and local state parks and just grab any local ranger or field biologist and say, 'What do you think about this idea of taking farm butterflies and releasing them?' And see what they say. You'll see that 96 percent of them or more will say it's ridiculous."

I push my luck and try one more round. What about the responses to his anti-release essay from the International Butterfly Breeders Association? They claimed, "Dr. Glassberg cannot cite one documented case of a shipment of commercially raised butterflies carrying and transmitting any disease to a wild population. Nor can he document an example of a new disease-causing organism resulting from the activities of commercial butterfly breeders."[5]

"Yeah," Glassberg responds. "That's like saying no one can prove to me that there aren't little green people running around the other side of Pluto. I mean, that's the kind of nonsense . . . ," he stops for a second and changes course from insult to science. Glassberg is strident and expresses no room for a butterfly compromise. "It's documented that farmed plants that get released into the environment decrease genetic fitness. Who's spending a million dollars to study wild butterflies and find out if they've all died off from some disease released by some breeder? Nobody. In the 1880s people wanted to release into the United States all the birds that were mentioned by Shakespeare. One of the birds that Shakespeare mentioned was the starling, European starlings. This group wanted to release starlings, and they did. They released them in Central Park, and the first release failed. They all died off. So they tried again. The second release succeeded. And starlings are now causing billions of dollars of damage in the United States. They decreased populations of native birds, because they're hole nesters and they're very aggressive and they outcompeted the native birds."

"They claim that their butterflies don't have diseases," I remind Glassberg about the breeders' response to his attack essay. "They say that if they had diseases the butterflies would be dead and the breeders would be out of business."

"That's wrong," he insists, "because they carry disease. You know there's a lot of incentive for people not to get serious diseases. How come people keep getting diseases and they spread the disease? What kind of thinking is this? No scientist could possibly ever think like this. It's exactly like the tobacco companies." Glassberg is tired and irritated.

"Okay. That so many people can be so thoughtless and unintelligent and care about nothing other than themselves making a dollar is, to me, yes, annoying." It sounds as if he's talking about the Bush Administration, but he's referring to butterfly breeders.

Butterfly enclosures he accepts.

"I think that's like if you ask a birder, 'What about aviaries?' I think most birders would say they're fine and some of them may even go to them, but it's not our focus." Glassberg seeks butterflies in the wild. "I don't have any problem with these places as long as they're not releasing butterflies into the environment. If they're showing off farmed butterflies, I think that's fine. They're like zoos."

My wife taught me to hate zoos in Heidelberg, Germany. We had visited the elephant enclosure and an elephant kept putting one foot on the concrete edge, which was topped with spikes. He kept putting his foot on the spike, testing it, realizing he was going nowhere, stuck in Germany in a concrete cage, with the two of us gawking at him. That was the end of zoos for me. But a huge butterfly enclosure, packed with nectar-filled flowers: that seems like a different story. Just the ratio of animal to space is a decent argument in favor of accepting butterfly zoos.

Glassberg says that prior to the founding of the North American Butterfly Association there was no such thing as butterflying. Like birding, butterflyers go out with a scope and look at butterflies in the wild with no desire to whisk them into a net, poison them, and stick pins through their thoraxes. He wrote the first field guide for using close-focusing binoculars to observe butterflies close-up in their natural state. He estimates that there are now tens of thousands of butterflyers without nets, and he is their chief cheerleader.

"Butterflies are beautiful. They're interesting. And butterflies are so easy to photograph." Unlike birds, and much other wildlife, butterflies allow us to come close to them as they flutter and sip nectar, making it relatively easy to shoot dramatic pictures.

"They'll sit on a flower very often for a long time." Glassberg smiles at a couple of butterflyers who ask him to autograph books. He's been out in the California heat all day butterflying, and he's tired. "I'm more incoherent than normal, and normally I'm fairly incoherent." But he insists he's lucid when he tells me he's convinced that he's seen almost every butterfly native to the contiguous United States of America. Almost 700 out of some 725, and he says he's seen most of the 1,700 species native to Mexico.

"There are people that don't collect things and then there are people that do. I try to collect things that don't create any terrible downside collecting." He fears depleting butterfly species.

On his list for the day is a Lilac-bordered Copper and a Great Purple Hairstreak. These are not butterflies new to veteran butterflyer Glassberg, but new to many of those he took out touring. He flips open a copy of his field guide to show me a picture of the Great Purple Hairstreak, and it is a wondrous-looking creature: its blue-purple wings edged with an iridescent green, the wings accented with yellow and rose-red flourishes. Glassberg points to the "comments" line in his field guide and suggests I read what he wrote: "The origin of the name 'Great Purple Hairstreak' is hazy. But when this tropically oriented beauty kisses the sky with its brilliant blue topside, you will soar as high as Jimi Hendrix's music." Such corny imagery is common in Glassberg's thorough guidebook. "Warning," he writes in the introduction. "This book is an express vehicle to butterflying. If this destination is not in your plans for this lifetime, you may want to turn back now, before it is too late!"

The idea of butterflying is to spot the critter and record when and where you've seen it. But what matters most to Glassberg is if there is a viable population of species seen. "I'll give you an example. A bird, I forget the name of the bird, some kind of shearwater from the Indian Ocean, normally lives in the Indian Ocean, fell out of the sky in upstate New York in 1884 or something, and this farmer found it as it came down and it was dying, and then it died. He donated it to the local museum, so there's this record for this Indian shearwater in New York. If the guy hadn't found it that day it would make no difference in our understanding of the world whatsoever. A stray does not constitute finding a viable colony; a stray is merely a curious anomaly. If you say, 'Oh, I found this population of butterflies that no one ever knew was here before,' these days, with more and more butterflyers, someone will be there the next day to check up on you. Recording rare butterflies is a fun game people like to play, but it really has very little importance in the real world in my view."

But it would be important and satisfying to find a new species.

"Yeah, if it really was a new species, and certainly you can find a new species of butterfly not that rarely seen in South America. I don't think there's been a really new species of butterfly found in North America since 1950 or so. I may be forgetting one." What is found with relative frequency is a slightly different characteristic in a species already listed, and such a find may result in a new name for the deviant from the preexisting norm. The real thrill would be to find something entirely new.

I ask Glassberg to explain the lure of butterflies throughout history and across cultures. He uses words like beauty and transformation, ephemeral and ethereal. And he uses the term "non-working," which brings up the butterfly's role in nature. Is it just to bask in its beauty? Is it a consequential pollinator? Opinions vary.

Glassberg's opinion is, "You can come right up to them and kids love them and they don't bite and they don't sting and they don't carry diseases that people can get. There's really no downside to them. If you ask people what kind of wildlife they most want near the house, in surveys they say butterflies."

After suffering my Lieutenant Columbo–like grilling for an hour or so, Jeffrey Glassberg pleads exhaustion and I let him go to his hotel to freshen up before the dinner meeting at which he will preside, but only after extracting a promise that I can join the group he leads the next day to Cedar Creek, high in the Greenhorn Mountains above us at six thousand feet, where we'll chase butterflies. He guarantees me it will be therapeutic. "It really engages all your senses. It engages your mind, it engages your body, but in a way that's not stressful. Tiring maybe, but not stressful. Problems that you might have kind of go away. It is a release."

Ah, the Zen of butterflying, I think.

Dinner is in a rented church social hall a few miles around the lake in Wofford Heights, just past Pirate Ink Tattoos and the Hideaway (the sign reads POOL SHUFFLEBOARD COCKTAILS OPEN 6 AM) and Kern Valley Auto Body, advertised with a dead 1950s Packard out front, the shop's phone number painted on the door.

"Do not take lasagna unless you signed up for our vegetarian option," yells Bob Barnes into the microphone. "If you signed up for chicken or beef, do not take the lasagna. I thought that was clear last night." He is annoyed, but not as annoyed as Jeffrey Glassberg was earlier. "Excuse me for raising my voice." Barnes is the local North American Butterfly Association chapter leader. "It was an amazing day today," he told me as he prepared a poster listing the butterfly sightings made by the couple of hundred conference attendees. The tally was 111 different species spotted. "This means people are going to go away happy, with none of them seeing all 111, but all of them seeing a lot."

The butterflyers—a pretty even mix of men and women—are lined up for chicken and beef (and the rare lasagna) wearing T-shirts adorned with butterflies, blouses made from butterfly prints, butterfly pins (me, too—I'm wearing my pin), and they hail from all over the country: Texas and Illinois, Florida and New Jersey. A distinguished gentleman is pointed out to me as coming from the United Kingdom. The British were some of the most enthusiastic butterfly collectors in the halcyon Victorian days of sticking pins in dead bugs, but many have now embraced nonviolent butterflying. Jim, the owner of a local grocery, oversees the chow line and looks dapper in his red apron, showing off his nametag. He's the caterer for butterflyers hungry after a day in the mountains and the hundred-degree temperatures.

Jeffrey Glassberg looks refreshed, and he takes me aside to point out butterflyers he thinks worth my while to talk with and one he thinks I should avoid. "He's got a net," he says pointing out the heretic. "He's off on the wrong foot, it's the wrong approach."

But Dennis Olle is a Glassberg-like butterflyer. Olle is the president of the Miami Blue chapter of the North American Butterfly Association (and the fellow Gerry Foulds called "a pompous ass"). I find him Florida-tanned, relaxed, joking, and ready to talk. He tells me he started birding when he was five years old, fifty years ago, and he was looking for a new excuse to be outside. "Butterflying is like baseball and birding is like football. It's better for birding when the weather's bad and it's raining and gloomy. Butterflying is more civilized. We only go out when it's good weather and the sun is shining. We don't start too early, we end early. It's like playing in Wrigley Field back when there were no lights—when the sun goes down, butterflying is over. You go home and relax. Birding is like football, out in the mud and the rain—the poorer the weather, the better the birding."

Olle is not surprised so many birders become butterflyers. "Birding is a young man's sport. Up at four in the morning and out.

Butterflying offers the challenge of learning something new, and it's a much more intimate sport with your subject than birding is. With birding, the bird's a thousand feet away and you're trying to identify some gull. With butterflies, you're three feet away trying to study the intricacies of some wing pattern." For him the appeal of the butterflies is obvious. "There's this sort of embedded memory that it started as a worm or a caterpillar and now it's something beautiful. That's not really the case with anything else you look at. It can't harm you at all; it's the one thing in nature that you can approach and touch and not worry about any negative reaction."

There are no butterflies poisonous to human beings, and no stinging butterflies. He likes their spectacular colors. He likes it that butterflies counter what he calls the "icky factor" of bugs. He likes the huge populations. "Insects exist in huge numbers. It's not about the individual, it's the sheer ability to reproduce over a wide territory with lots of eggs. It's not ones and twos. It's thousands and ten-thousands." He talks about the complicated life cycle from egg to caterpillar, chrysalis, and then what he calls "the end product," a butterfly with a relatively short life. "They just exist to mate and reproduce, it's so ephemeral." There's that word again to describe them. "And to think that they've been around for millions of years, and in certain places for tens of thousands of years the same species has flown in this certain valley—forever, for all of human history." He stops for a second, perhaps remembering the fight in his own backyard to save the Miami Blue. Lepidoptera fossils estimated to be 190 million years old have been found in England, and most butterflies were flying by 40 million years ago. Losing a species whose predecessors have been brightening Earth with their harmless and magical life cycle since the dinosaurs depresses him. "We're doing our best to get rid of them, it seems. It's just tragic."

After chatting with Olle long enough to appreciate his work with the Miami Blue, I next catch up with Ahmet Baytas, the author of *A*

Field Guide to the Butterflies of Turkey, the first butterfly field guide for his native country. Butterflying without nets, poison, and pins is new enough that there is plenty for the ambitious aficionado to add to the pastime-sport-business—whatever you decide to make of it. Baytas, a university economics professor who is new to butterflying, returned from his New Jersey home to his birthplace in Turkey, a village in Artvin province. There, he writes, he was astounded by the number and types of butterflies he found, "particularly on damp ground near streams, the density of blues and whites reached several hundred per square meter." There he "watched dozens of ringlets and whites gracefully dance among the alpine vegetation, noted over a dozen species of brilliantly colored coppers, and observed a remarkable variety of fritillaries fly in the flowery grasslands."

Artvin province is the northeast corner of Turkey, up against the Georgia border, land of Islamic fundamentalists opposed to the sectarian Turkish state. Eastern Turkey has been a battleground for years between Kurdish guerillas and Turkey's army. The southeast corner of the country borders Iraq, and the Turkish army has crossed that frontier, chasing after Kurdish fighters who seek refuge in the Kurdish-controlled north of Iraq. Such volatile current affairs seem at odds with genteel butterflying.

Baytas is sanguine, insisting, "Most of Turkey is very safe." He dismisses concerns about eastern Turkey. "A couple of times I had problems. A few places the military would not allow me to go in for butterflies. The Turkish people are really hospitable, and in the remote mountains villagers always say, 'Come have some drink, some food.'"

Turkey is outstanding butterfly country, says Baytas, because of its location spanning Europe and Asia. There are some five hundred butterfly species in Europe, and four hundred of them are found in Turkey, making it the richest European country in terms of butterfly diversity. Factor in the enormous number of butterflies that can be seen at one time, and it is understandable why Turkey is a butter-flyer's mecca.

Bucolic butterflies amidst the chaos of the Middle East. "It's always in your mind," Baytas says of the fighting and unrest. "But butterflying, you just go out and you enjoy nature. In a way you run away from the world's problems." He considers. "But, the Iraq problem or any other problem is always in your mind, of course. It's just weird. Life has to go on, but it is hard."

Maybe there is a lesson I can learn from the butterflies regarding fighting and wars and civil unrest.

"I wish we all could be as peaceful as butterflies. When I was in southeast Turkey last and I come back in the evening from butterflying and people are talking about the war, the fighting, the Kurdish issue. Then I say to myself, 'Wow, what am I doing here looking at butterflies? But then that's what I am here for and I'm doing that.' It's a strange feeling, but what can we do?"

I don't have a ready answer. Here I am in Kernville with a bunch of butterfly huggers because I suggested I needed a break from reporting war stories and sought refuge with butterflies and flowers. I suggest to Ahmet Baytas that it would be nice to take the peaceful feelings he gets from butterflies and somehow influence those making war.

"I don't know," he says. He's skeptical and suggests a butterflyer may be a different type of person than a fighter. "People who are normally into nature—wildflowers or birds or butterflies—tend to be more peace-loving people, anti-violence in every aspect of life." But then he considers the idea of somehow introducing warriors to his world, and smiles at the thought. "Yeah," he muses about a soldier with changed thinking, "you are in nature. You look and you say, 'Wow, why are we fighting?' You look at butterflies in a mountain meadow, and that's enough. That should be enough. I mean what is there to fight for?" Henry David Thoreau addresses the question in

Walden when he muses, "No humane being, past the thoughtless age of boyhood, will wantonly murder any creature which holds its life by the same tenure as he does."[6]

It was time for a drink, but there in the Family Life Church social hall the strongest choices were lemonade and iced tea.

The next morning I meet Jeffrey Glassberg and the dozen or so butterflyers assigned to his field trip. We're en route to Cedar Creek, a forty-five-minute drive up into the Greenhorns. It is blessedly cool when we arrive, and we're in crystal-clear air, high above the smoke from the forest fires. The creek runs fast past towering conifers; it is a peaceful paradise. We march about a hundred yards along the creek bank to a clearing where a local butterflyer told Glassberg we'd find Kern County butterflies of note, particularly Gold-hunters or Golden Hairstreaks, both of which are native to these mountains. Hairstreaks, according to Glassberg's field guide, get their name from lines on their hind wings or from their tail points that can look like pieces of hair. Almost forty species live in the West. The mood is jovial and relaxed; cameras and binoculars are in hand.

"Keep your eyes open. Look at these oaks," Glassberg instructs us. "Golden Hairstreaks like to hang out on these oaks, fairly high up." Somebody spots a flutter and points at it. Cameras click. There's a yell from a spotter, "I got it!" That means he sees it, not that he squashed it or netted it. "Right here, folks," he points it out.

"Oh, yeah," says Glassberg. "I see it. Definitely a California Sister. That's new for the day." That means it counts for the count, and it is a gorgeous bug. On its top side, the forewing tips are a soft burnt orange and two rows of white spots flow across the wings toward the tail, almost converging in a V with tiny crescents of a matching orange facing the center. The wings are trimmed with white edging.

On the underside of the Sister's wings peach and gray are added to its palette. It flies off, up through the oak.

"There's a Mylitta Crescent," calls out Glassberg, spotting another butterfly.

"Nice specimen," hollers a spotter.

"Individual," Glassberg corrects him firmly. "Specimen is if it's dead. Nice individual. It's like if you see a good-looking woman, you don't want to say, 'Nice specimen,' just individual." He might want to choose still another word for the woman; "nice individual" isn't much of a pick-up line but certainly less offensive than most standard variations.

"That was a good look at a Mylitta Crescent," says Glassberg. It was a stained glass window–like burst of orange and black.

Suddenly one of the butterflyers starts throwing rocks into an oak tree. My initial thought is that these butterfly huggers are crazy. But Glassberg explains. "If you've got some big trees, a big bush, and you think something might be up there, you can sometimes disturb it a little. If it's low, you might shake the bush. If it's high, you throw a rock. You throw a rock and the butterfly says, 'Oh!' and it moves five feet and you see it."

More rocks are thrown. Somehow it seems contrary to the passive butterfly hugging tales of the last two days. I'm taking notes and photographs, and Glassberg reconsiders, calling out, "Honestly, to tell you the truth, I don't think you really need to throw rocks. I think if they're here, we're going to see them moving around. I think random throwing of rocks . . . " He's interrupted by one of the rock-throwing contingent calling out, "We just saw a butterfly fly out of there!"

"You did?" Glassberg quits calling for an end to the rocks and adds with enthusiasm, "Let's look at this tree carefully." The search party laughs as he says, "I'm getting a boulder! Where did you see it?"

"He threw the rock and it flew out."

"You saw it after he threw the rock?"

"Yeah!" And then a dragonfly passes by to a cry of disappointment. This crowd is unimpressed. It wants butterflies and butterflies only, and we tramp farther down the creek side in search of the so-far elusive Golden Hairstreak.

"Right here!" calls out another spotter.

"I see it," answers Glassberg running up to her side. "There it is!"

"That's not a Golden," dismisses a naysayer.

The entire party is looking: binoculars poised, fingers pointed with anticipation, cameras ready. They look like eyewitnesses at a disaster site to my jaundiced journalist's eyes, all of them staring up at the burning building, the crashing airplane, or the man on the ledge threatening suicide.

"It's gone behind the leaf," announces Glassberg. "There it goes! There it is!"

"There's more than one," says the woman who first saw whatever we're looking at or for. "Just keep your eyes peeled."

"I got one," says another spotter. And we all focus on the butterfly, amidst audible signs of relief and satisfaction.

"It's a Golden," Glassberg confirms. "You see it when it opens up? Most Hairstreaks don't open up, and this is one that does." He is excited, his voice is rising in pitch and getting louder. "There's one low!" He points to it. "See the one open over here?" he asks me. And I do see it. I'm looking at this tree with new eyes, seeking sights I previously was not aware I would find in an oak. Prior to this moment, butterflies in the wild were happenstance for me as in, "Look! There's a butterfly." I'd never sought them. I'm reminded of a training clinic I participated in in the English countryside, survival training for journalists working in conflict zones taught by retired British Marines. I was taken out into the vast grounds of a Kent manor and taught to look for threats in places my eyes would otherwise not be focused, seeing the landscape from a new perspective.

"It's a tiny little guy," I report to Glassberg.

"Yeah, tiny," he agrees with my minimal description. All I see is its orangey and brown mass.

Glassberg switches into professorial mode. "There are about a thousand species of Hairstreaks in the New World. Of those thousand or so, all but two of them are closely related. Two species of the thousand are Old World Hairstreaks. This is one of the two."

"Oh! Really?" says a spotter.

"Yeah," Glassberg tell us. "The other is the Colorado Hairstreak. Most Hairstreaks don't open up. Some do. But not many. This one does, as does Colorado."

Ah, it's an Old World thing. "Open up" meaning they spread their wings when they alight.

Wow. We've seen something special, I guess.

"Yeah," Glassberg confirms. "It's a butterfly of fairly limited distribution and limited flight times. Who has seen a Golden Hairstreak before in this group?"

"I've never seen it yet," complains a dejected failed spotter to sympathetic laughter. Only two raise their hands.

Another California Sister flies by us. "Nothing special about seeing it today?" I ask Glassberg when he tells me it's common, and he sets me straight.

"They're beautiful butterflies. Each time you see it it's a beautiful butterfly. I'll see something and I'll see it a thousand times, and it's still beautiful. If a beautiful woman comes into a room you notice, even though you've seen a few of them before."

Heading down the mountain I realize I've gone native to a certain extent. It was exactly what Glassberg suggested it would be: a Zen-like moment in the now. Nothing else was going on for me while I was searching for the Golden Hairstreak and spotting the California Sister. There was something pure about not chasing them with a net, just searching and observing. It reminded me of the license plate game my sister and I played while driving with my family across

America. Look! There's one from North Dakota! Rare is valuable, but not vital. If you're in North Dakota, there's another and another. But the sightings still can amuse those of us lucky enough to be in touch with the childlike parts of our minds.

The excitement was real. It was impossible not to be seduced by the focus of the moment, the pristine beauty of the rushing Cedar Creek with its towering pines and the burly oaks. The satisfaction of seeing the fluttering rare Golden Hairstreak and the glamorous common California Sister was real. I was an observer in this odd subculture but at the same time an active player delighting in the moment, not just observing as a news reporter.

I feel a bizarre sense of accomplishment: my first two officially sanctioned spotted butterflies. Silly. But fun. And I know something new about two animals which, had I seen them a day before, would have only been pretty butterflies to me.

These butterfly huggers may be a little nuts. But their act sure is more appealing to me than chasing the butterflies with nets, putting them in the killing jar, and sticking pins in them because they're pretty to look at and we're bigger than they are so we can grab them and play God with them.

Driving down the west side of the Greenhorns on Highway 155 into the smoke-filled San Joaquin Valley toward Delano, I realize the morning spotting experience has permanently changed me. My eyes and attitude are now attuned to see butterflies. As I slow for the hairpin curves on 155, I see butterflies. I know where and how to look now: around plants, focusing on movement. I see butterflies I would have overlooked before, like 1952 Studebakers. I enjoyed my time with the huggers; now it was time to check out their nemesis, the breeders.

Chapter Three

My Successful Commercial
Butterfly Release

Edith Smith is charming—smiling, with bright blue eyes, and enthusiastic—one of those types who can make you feel at home immediately. In fact, she made me feel at home even before I met her and listened to her butterfly farming stories, stories told with the soft lilt of her country Florida accent adding an innocent-sounding charm to her love affair with the insects. She responded positively to my request for an interview, inviting me not only to tour her Shady Oak Butterfly Farm, but also to skip the anonymity of another road-trip night at a hotel.

"We'd be delighted to have you as our guest at the farm," she wrote. "Just let me know when you'd like to visit. If you need a place to stay in this area, we can recommend a bed-and-breakfast nearby, or you could stay with us. Now that our children are married with their own houses, we have a spare room or two. Thank you, and we look forward to meeting you!"

Gracious hospitality seems the norm in the butterfly world. Jane and Gerry Foulds had offered me a room at their *reserva*; Jeffrey Glassberg and his butterfly huggers made me welcome in Kernville and fed me dinner along with butterfly chasing stories. Now Edith Smith offers me a bed in remote Brooker, Florida. I head for Shady Oak along Bradford County Route 231, a two-lane blacktop absent of all traffic. The wide sky is a deep tropical blue, punctuated with huge, cottony clouds. The temperature readout on the dashboard of the rented Chrysler is well into the nineties, and the humidity feels the same to my California sensitivities. The air conditioner is cranked up, and I remember the Egyptian I encountered in my Cairo hotel elevator on a scorcher of a day who cautioned me in his heavily accented English, "It's not the heat, it's the humidity." Wise words, even if by accident. I drive past stands of pines and moss-dripping oaks. Here and there I catch a sixty-miles-per-hour glimpse of the bright flutter of a wild (or escaped from Shady Oak?) butterfly.

Greenhouses and a WELCOME TO THE SHADY OAK BUTTERFLY FARM sign greet me at the end of her driveway. Right off Edith tells me what I've already learned in Nicaragua: "Most of us who raise butterflies, we enjoy talking about them." While Florida was preoccupied deciding the 2000 presidential election (flawed, remember, by the infamous "butterfly ballots"), she and her husband stumbled into butterfly breeding at their homestead, which she (correctly) identifies as being "in the middle of nowhere." The two were growing herbs, and trying to market them—without much success. Looking at her unsold fennel, Edith saw a butterfly laying eggs. "After she left I checked, and there were seventeen beautiful yellowish, creamy eggs." The eggs were destroyed by hungry parasitizing wasps, so the next time she found eggs on her fennel, Edith took the plant into her house and watched the eggs hatch into larvae and eventually become butterflies.

What started as a rescue mission morphed into a business when an existing butterfly farm offered to buy the results of Edith's care and feeding. Eight years later the growing family business is raising and selling as many as five thousand butterflies a week, and as many as twenty different species. The Smiths are self-taught entomologists. Edith, now a grandmother, studied horticulture in school, and her husband, Stephen, is a retired pharmacist.

Their labor-intensive business is hands-on manual labor for the couple. The caterpillars are voracious, and their specific food plant must be cut and brought fresh every day to the containers where they live. Shady Oak is as much a caterpillar food plant nursery as it is a butterfly farm, growing the food the larvae need. The correct food and enough of it, along with pristine hygiene, keep the farm in business. "It's hard to be careful, and it's even harder for an employee who isn't as worried about tomorrow and the business," Edith says she quickly learned. Disease can wipe out their stock in trade. Although the larvae can recover from some diseases, other diseases require destroying all the caterpillars in order to ensure a clean environment for future generations. "Once you step outside the laboratory door, you're in nature and that's where disease comes from. The problems come when you start washing your hands less between the breeding containers, and you're not following disease prevention precautions. At the end of the day you're too tired and you don't wipe everything down with bleach water so if there are any pathogens in the air they'll land and be trapped and killed. Just little things like that." Parasites are a continuing worry. "These are the rascals that lay their eggs in a pupa or a caterpillar, and then you're not raising butterflies, you're raising tiny, tiny bugs. They're waiting right there for us to leave the door open so they can come in." Lizards are another problem, sliding in through those open doors and other cracks in security to feast on the stock in trade.

The exhaustive work of raising butterflies makes teaching others the business an attractive alternative, and Edith runs classes at Shady Oak for entrepreneurs considering a career in the butterfly business. Rather than build the breeding business further, she hopes to increase her teaching load. United States Department of Agriculture regulations forbid commercial breeders from raising exotics—butterflies not indigenous to the state where the farm operates—unless they have a USDA-approved facility licensed for breeding non-native species. Exotics cannot be used for ceremonial butterfly releases—an important market for Shady Oak—so Edith sticks with the locals, and local butterflies in Florida, as I had already noticed on the drive to her farm, are brilliant and colorful enough to satisfy her customers, both those who want butterflies for a celebratory release and those who seek them as live display stock for butterfly enclosures.

Throughout human history, the butterfly has been a symbol for transition and transformation. It is a natural choice, of course, because of the magic that is its metamorphosis from caterpillar to a delicate-looking, fluttering flower-like creature. Cultures around the world have employed the caterpillar-to-butterfly miracle in their myths and legends in an effort to explain death and what comes next. Butterflies appear in stories worldwide as messengers, and as representatives of love and luck—both good and bad.

Breeders promote butterfly releases for all sorts of parties: bridal showers, school graduations, wedding anniversaries. But they are most popular at weddings and funerals, and the most popular butterfly for releases is the Monarch, followed by the Painted Lady, a pretty companion to the more familiar Monarch. The Painted Lady sports vibrant orange and brown wings decorated in black on the edges, the black accented with white spots. Its wingspan is just under three inches, large enough to enjoy during a staged release as it flies off into what for it is a strange new land. Again the USDA governs what can go where. Farms are not permitted to ship butterflies for release to states in which the species shipped is not part of the natural habitat. The butterflies are shipped chilled to a dormant sleep, and packed into individual glassine envelopes for protection against wing damage. They are boxed with the type of cold packs that keep beer cold during tailgate parties, and they stay dormant; once they're exposed to warmth—removed from their envelopes and placed in a container for release—they are supposed to wake up and fly. For a most dramatic flight, Edith recommends accordion release boxes in which the butterflies are pressed between folded and connected paper pages. These are pulled open in a rush and if all goes as expected, the butterflies—en masse—whoosh skyward.

Breeders give credit to Rick Mikula for founding the release industry. Mikula calls himself The Butterfly Guy, and he travels the countryside from his Hole-in-Hand Butterfly Farm in Pennsylvania, performing shows and teaching classes about butterflies for audiences from kindergartners to prison inmates. I asked him how he came up with the idea of staging butterfly releases. "I had been rearing butterflies and moths for some time. I was always impressed with how beautiful they looked swarming around inside my flight house. I am also fascinated by Native Americans and their legends. One of those legends is from the Papago tribe concerning the creation of butterflies. It states that butterflies were created to serve as messengers who would deliver wish requests to the Great Spirit on behalf of his human children. The beauty of a flight of butterflies combined with the beauty of the legend made it seem like a natural fit. I introduced the idea, and it just took off." Mikula considers the study of butterflies especially appropriate for prisoners. From it, he says, they develop an appreciation for "the interdependency and fragility of all living things. I feel they learn that with nurturing and education things can reach a positive level with a productive outcome. Hopefully it will help them from becoming incarcerated in the future."

"Monarchs are the best all-purpose release butterflies," the Shady Oak promotional material tells customers. "They are large, strong, and majestic gliders. Monarchs are perfect for accordion release boxes." But Shady Oak does not recommend them for release from boxes with see-through sides. "The reason is that they simply do not see the glass or plastic sides and try to walk. This gives the impression of them being stressed, which is not so. It can, however, stress your guests to see them act in a way that appears as if they are trying to escape!" That image of the struggling Monarch is reminiscent of

Jeffrey Glassberg's impassioned complaints about commercial butterfly breeding and releases.

Edith Smith knows his point of view well. "Mr. Glassberg believes that there should not be butterfly releases, that it's detrimental to butterflies." She dismisses his concerns with a terse, "There have been butterfly releases for twelve years, and there's never been a documented case of it causing a problem."

I tell her he characterized her industry to me as "disgusting" and that he called commercial butterfly breeders self-serving, greedy people who don't care about anything.

"Oh, yes," she says with the air of someone who's been called that—and maybe worse—before. She advises me to reread his indictment of the breeding business and "notice how many time he uses 'could, might, maybe'—all noncommittal words. He's appealing to the emotional side of people. There's no science in what he says."

But he's a scientist, I remind her.

She nods. "He has a passion for butterflies that I admire greatly. I am not sure why he really believes it is detrimental. I don't see any scientific basis for what he's saying." She rejects Glassberg's concerns about disease spread and genetic mixing because in all her years of breeding she says there's been no evidence of such problems, and she wonders why he worries only about butterflies and ignores ladybugs and other insects shipped nationwide without regard to where they are native. "It boils down to emotion," she theorizes.

Edith says the food plants she grows are controlled for disease, and she tests her butterfly populations regularly to ensure their health. She is convinced she ships healthy animals and that when she does detect contamination, disease at her farm is quickly eradicated. Were it not, she points out with some logic, she could not stay in business because if her product were faulty it would not sell. The market provides the ultimate regulation and control, and Edith smiles wide as she reports that her business is thriving. I notice the diamond pendant she wears around her neck, shaped like a butterfly. "Sometimes at the end of the day we're dragging, but it's good."

But what about complaints from the Glassberg crowd that it is viscerally offensive to be breeding God's creatures for sale? Edith Smith worries that emotion-fueled legislation could be passed that will shut down her livelihood just because some take offense at what she does with such success. "It just feels wrong, it seems wrong" is a complaint about breeding that she says she frequently hears. I ask her to try to explain their point of view. "We're making something that's very precious to their hearts a commercial venture, and butterflies should be above that." She shakes her head with some frustration. "I don't understand it." She again takes the offensive. "One of the things Mr. Glassberg says is, 'Why release butterflies? They're already free.' Two percent of eggs laid live to be an adult. So nature is not doing a very good job as far as raising butterflies."

"Or nature is doing a fine job," I offer, "and the other 98 percent have other functions, such as being food for parasites."

She agrees, "If Mother Nature raised them all we'd be scraping them off of windshields; we couldn't even breathe outside there would be so many of them. So Mother Nature is doing a good job as far as keeping a balance. But if you want to take what he is saying literally, they're already free, but they're free to die—98 percent of them." Her butterflies, she points out, are raised in a protected environment and many of them—released at festivities—fly free. Others fly in enclosures, and some are dissected for study or are stuck with pins for collections. And only 5 to 15 percent of her charges are casualties prior to emerging as adult butterflies.

"Butterflies mean a lot to people, and people connect with butterflies," Edith knows. She grew up, south of her butterfly farm near Ocala, pulling weeds on her father's peanut farm and killing what she thought were just worms on the weeds, not knowing they were caterpillars en route to becoming butterflies. Her interest wasn't piqued until she realized a parasite was killing the butterfly eggs found on her fennel. "I got mad. That was it." The beauty of the wings intrigued her. "Now I raise all of them, whether they're pretty or not. I like to do the life cycle of all of them. I really enjoy butterflies."

The magic of that life cycle cannot help but be compelling: a tiny egg hatches into what passes as just a worm that wraps itself up in a self-made container, and out pops the finished product. It's a tale well told in one of my favorite children's books, *Hubert the Caterpillar Who Thought He Was a Mustache*. The story, by Wendy Stang and Susan Richards, is about a "very mixed-up caterpillar." Hubert is ostracized by the other caterpillars because he fancies himself a mustache, and he seeks faces on which to act as such. One day, tired and unhappy, he goes to sleep and wakes up a butterfly. The final lines of the book never fail to make me smile. "When he looked at his wings, Hubert no longer thought he was a mustache. Now Hubert thinks he is an eagle! And he is very happy." The illustration by Richard L. Anderson on the last page shows Hubert striking a proud pose at the top of a flagpole flying Old Glory.[7]

"If I find a caterpillar, I raise it," Edith Smith says, laughing. Including moths. "I love the metamorphosis." What we like can be inexplicable. "I don't find myself drawn to dragonflies, even though dragonflies are absolutely gorgeous." But for some reason they aren't as compelling for her as butterflies and moths. "Emotion is what creates our business, and emotion is against our business." She rejects as propaganda Jeffrey Glassberg's claim that releases often fail, with butterflies climbing out of boxes and fluttering a moment, only to collapse in death.

"Let me ask you a question." Edith is intense and paces her words carefully, looking directly into my eyes. "If we release them and they flutter out, crawl, and die, would our business be growing? And second, if they flutter out, crawl, and die, how can they be spreading disease? Either they live and spread disease, or they die and they don't. He's contradicting himself. But people don't stop to look at that."

What makes it all worth it for her are faces of people at butterfly releases. She considers the happy-looking faces the most magical part of a release. The experience is fleeting; the butterflies fly and disappear. As pretty a picture as the flying collection of colorful wings may be, as satisfying as it may be to watch the faces of happy customers, it is the sounds she hears that she finds most dramatic. "The whole crowd will just gasp all at once, and there will be laughter, just peals of laughter, from throughout the whole group."

Edith worries Jeffrey Glassberg may eventually close down her industry, and she says the main reason she works to keep butterfly releases legal is the joy and comfort she witnesses in audiences, especially at funerals where the butterflies can symbolize renewal and resurrection, peace and hope. "My favorites of all are funeral releases," Edith crosses her arms, rubs her bare shoulders and smiles. "I get chill bumps every time I talk about it. We had one funeral director who called us after the release and said, 'It was the first funeral I attended where everyone turned away from the casket with a smile on their face.'" She fears Glassberg will use his political influence to lobby for legislation outlawing commercial releases, and she rejects his argument that since we have no proof that releases of bred butterflies do not harm wild butterflies, we should take no chances. Such logic, she says, applied across society would severely hinder progress.

At the University of California at Davis some weeks later I ask evolution and ecology professor Dr. Arthur Shapiro, who has been studying butterflies since he started chasing them as a child, to weigh in on the controversy over butterflies bred for festive releases and butterflies bred for grammar school projects. Students who raise butterflies from eggs to larvae, watch the pupae develop and witness their eclosion (emergence from pupa) usually release the butterflies at the end of the exercise. "Various arguments have been brought forward," he says, framing his response to the commercial business of butterflies with appropriate balance. "It all depends on the species that they're releasing and where the stocks come from that they're releasing." He sees no problem shipping and releasing Painted Ladies around America, because they were living throughout the country before the breed-and-release business launched in the early 1990s. They migrate south for the winter, and commingle in their overwintering southern territories. "It's essentially one panmictic population, that is to say there is no geographic differentiation of population. One from New York can mate with one from Kansas, and then mate three weeks later with one from Riverside in southern California. So in that case, no harm done genetically."

But species that do not migrate, he's convinced, develop individualized genetic traits and mixing them could create unexpected hybrids. "The Gulf Fritallary is one that's released at events. It's easy to breed. If you had stock that you ordered by mail from Florida and released it in the San Francisco Bay Area, you could really foul things up because the West Coast and the East Coast populations are almost certainly genetically quite different." I ask him if he's worried that things must be getting "fouled up" since 100 percent oversight on releases is impossible. Shapiro is sanguine about damaging cross-pollination. "The Feds have a list of what can be shipped interstate and what can't," he points out.

"But a list doesn't mean buyers are obeying the rules," I argue. "Even if a breeder follows the regulations, a buyer could trans-ship the butterflies to a state where they are forbidden."

"Well, of course," he allows. "But at least nominally we have controls. The argument is that if the species is already present in the destination, it can be shipped there."

In addition to genetic contamination concerns, I ask Dr. Shapiro to address the question of disease. Do the commercially bred butterflies hold the potential of introducing pathogens into native wild butterfly populations? "That is potentially a problem," he asserts, "especially since animals in rearing facilities are in a very artificial environment and may become contaminated with pathogens that don't occur in the wild." But in the next breath, Professor Shapiro makes Edith Smith's argument. "They're in the business of providing healthy, vigorous animals. If their animals are feeble and can't fly, nobody wants them. So it's in their interest to maintain quality control and good sanitation in the rearing facilities."

"Do you buy the argument?" I ask him. Is he okay with this relatively new business, butterflies as a commodity for sale?

"To some extent I buy it." He identifies the Monarch as a species where potentially dangerous pathogens from commercial breeders could infect wild populations. "But it's a hypothetical problem, it hasn't been demonstrated it's real, and to what extent do we want to take precautions against a hypothetical problem?"

Were he in charge of policing the business, would he err on the safe side, worried about wild populations?

"I think I would not close down the breeders, but I would restrict them to about three or four species that I thought were harmless."

The more I hear about and talk about the releases, the more intriguing they seem. An eruption of sudden color! A flurry of wings! The group flight heavenward! That's what I imagine. Arthur Shapiro, an expert who may well have seen more butterflies in the wild during his career than any other human being, was himself impressed by such a show. He stifles a laugh when I ask him about it. "It is kind of fun. The particular one I saw was at a wedding in Capitol Park in Sacramento. What was interesting is that it was Monarchs and they hung around for at least a week, they didn't go anywhere. They stayed in the park." After the flourish of the release, at least some of them made the grounds their home for the few days of life left in them. "They had everything they wanted there." He smiles, "It was kind of fun. Of course it's fun."

What about the comparison Jeffrey Glassberg makes: We don't breed farm animals and release them into the environment. We don't raise cattle and set them free.

Shapiro laughs. "We don't release them into the wild, but we buy them and we keep them in feed lots."

"We make them into hamburger," I add.

"We make them into hamburger, that's right. I think releasing them into the wild might be a lot better for them than making them into hamburger."

"Some people are afraid of butterflies," Edith Smith says, and she understands why. "When you get right down to it, they are just bugs. When you take the wings off, no one is interested." So many people are afraid of butterflies, in fact, that there is a support group for those suffering from what could be called lepidopterophobia. The ihate butterflies.com community was established for what its organizers identify as "people that fear, are disgusted by, and generally dislike butterflies (and moths)." The category on the Web site marked "Horror Stories" is a strange counterpoint for those of us who delight in spotting a butterfly or being surrounded by them in flight.

Lauren writes, "I've had this phobia for as long as I can remember. I seriously can't remember a time when I haven't been scared of the pesky fluttery horrid things. What I don't get is, why do people think butterflies are beautiful and lovely? Spiders are on the ground where they can't chase you. How is that more scary than a fluttery thing flying around your head?" Magic was one of the many who answered her with support. "I get the same thing, 'They're harmless!'

and 'They don't bite!' blah blah blah. They fly erratically, their proboscis is like this creepy flexible needle, their coloring is like a bad acid trip, and they always aim for your face!"

Perhaps these lepidopterophobes are recalling the serial killer in the film *The Silence of the Lambs* and how he left his calling card—the Death's-head Hawkmoth—lodged deep in the throats of his victims.

Coasie checks in with this lament. "I was sitting outside having coffee with my neighbor this past Sunday, and I spotted a blackish blue butterfly outside the gazebo. I tried not to pay attention in hopes it would flutter away, but wouldn't you know, it decided to play havoc with my psyche. It came into the gazebo where I did the old duck-and-cover as it fluttered back out. Trying to explain to my neighbor that I have a legitimate fear of the winged creatures, it decided to flutter back into the gazebo and head right toward my head. I immediately sprang out of my chair, put my hands before my face, and screamed, 'Get away from me, get away from me!' as I did the old shake-and-quiver. My neighbor looked at me as if I were a nut case and all I could do was feel embarrassed for making a scene. My motto is: The only good butterfly is a dead butterfly."

Traumatized Coasie seems to be unaware of the fact that Aristotle named butterflies *psyche*, ancient Greek for soul. Butterflies flourish across cultures as symbols for rebirth of the soul leaving the body.

Glitch Baby blamed butterflies for an injury. "I was outside at my boyfriend's house in the country. It was mid-spring and the butterflies were awful. I was sitting in the back of my truck when a swarm of yellow and black Monarch butterflies came flying straight toward me. I was totally freaked out. I was lying in the bed of the truck kicking and screaming for them to go away. My boyfriend and a couple of our friends were laughing at me, but my boyfriend told me they were gone and I got up. Not a minute had passed when they came straight back at me. The kicking and screaming started again along with some crying because I was scared. That's when I jumped out of the bed of the truck and sprained my ankle. It was awful. It's like they know I'm scared and come straight for me."

ihatebutterflies.com is filled with pages and pages of such horror stories. When I last checked in at the site, over 125 correspondents were swapping tales of butterfly phobias.

Edith Smith takes me on a tour of the farm, showing me the stacks of Styrofoam shipping boxes and ice packs in her office, the end point of her production line, from where the chilled butterflies are placed in the glassine envelopes or accordion release books for shipment. Chilled, the cold-blooded butterflies just wait until the air around them warms, at which point they spring to life, revived. On the office wall, an office packed with butterfly paraphernalia such as butterfly postcards and butterfly carrying bags and butterfly coffee cups and butterfly coloring books, a reminder calls out to the staff: "When we hear the word 'metamorphosis' we think of caterpillars changing into butterflies. The wonder is not of chance or the working of nature but the genius of the Creator—God."

Being chilled in the envelopes or accordion books doesn't seem to bother the butterflies, Edith asserts. But the timing of the release is somewhat critical. "You will need to make sure it is not raining to do the release," the Shady Oak directions instruct. "Remember that butterflies survive through thunderstorms and hurricanes, the rain will not kill or harm the butterflies. The reason you do not release when it is raining is that they will not fly in the rain." Rain and cold weather can ruin a release party. "You will need to make sure it is not below 63 degrees during the release. Butterflies will not fly if it is too cold." Oh, and a warning that may seem obvious, but it wouldn't shout from the instructions were there not a history of mistakes. "Insect spray will kill your butterflies. Do not store them in an area that has been recently treated for insects. Do not use insect spray near your butterflies!" As Edith reminds me, butterflies may be pretty insects, but they are insects nonetheless.

There are indications in the office that the business is not stress free. I've already heard stories about disease, parasites, and predation. Now I see on an office door a sign marked with a big black X and the instructions: BANG HEAD HERE.

We head into the greenhouses and the hatcheries. There are rooms with breeding stock butterflies laying eggs on leaves, eggs bleached to kill disease and collected into containers in which the eggs hatch into larvae. More rooms are filled with voracious larvae growing in their little plastic containers busy eating more foliage than the on-site nursery can provide (Shady Oak buys supplemental feed from other nurseries). Other rooms contain chrysalises carefully glued to the lids of large Rubbermaid tubs—tubs lined with soft paper towels so the butterflies do not damage themselves when they eclose. The last stage of the operation is the rooms alive with adult butterflies. Each of these is dated to keep track of when the butterflies emerged to ensure the wings of those shipped were open long enough to harden prior to being chilled for their journey forth to customers.

In an extraordinarily perishable business, the short life span of the adult butterflies means that Shady Oak must sell and ship the beauties before they die; they can only survive chilled and dormant for a few days, and their life span once released is not much longer. Just a chipped wing means no sale. Damaged product is moved to the on-site enclosure where Shady Oak flies Monarchs and Painted Ladies to show off to visitors. "I call it our bent and dent room," says Edith.

"Boop, boop!" Edith and I are now in a caterpillar room, and she is boop-booping at the little worms. "They dance," she tells me.

"Have you seen them dance?" Indeed their tiny heads bounce toward her voice.

"You like the caterpillars as much as the butterflies?" I ask. She seems so happy as she repeats, "Boop, boop! Boop, boop!"

"Oh, I like them better." She continues to sing to them and they keep bobbing their heads. "It's just amazing," she's smiling and laughing. "They have personality!"

"Personality?" I'm looking at a plastic tub full of green worms with black and tan spots, unconvinced. "Personality expressed how? By their appearance?" They all look the same to me.

"Partly by their appearance." She is serious about her emotional response to them. "But a lot about the way they eat, the way they move. Different ones have different ways they do things; it's kind of fun." She points out some Swallowtail larvae and insists, "They're hilarious."

"Hilarious?" They just look like generic caterpillars to my untrained eye, pretty colors, maybe even cute if I stretch my definitions, but I'm challenged trying to distinguish personalities.

"When you get a lot of them on a tree, they are hilarious, these little guys. One of them will crawl on a leaf where there is another one, and put its head under the other one and flip it off the plant onto the ground. It's just a little bulldozer. They are so funny. I don't know what it is, but they are so funny."

Survival of the fittest.

Frolicking in the mountains with Jeffrey Glassberg and his spotters was great entertainment; witnessing the entrepreneurial delight of Edith Smith was inspirational. I'm stuck on the question of who's right, the huggers or the breeders, the Glassbergs or the Smiths. Do the bred butterflies fall out dead when released, a depressing sight?

Or do they soar to the heavens, inspiring their audience? When I returned to California from my visit to Shady Oak, I decided to check it out for myself and ordered a stack of Painted Ladies from Edith Smith. While I waited for UPS to haul my chilled *Vanessa cardui* from Florida out to California, I checked in with integrative biologist Robert Dudley at the University of California at Berkeley, one of the very few researchers working worldwide studying butterfly flight. In his Animal Flight Laboratory and in the field, he and his colleagues study butterfly flight dynamics, and I wanted to learn about the mechanics of what I would be watching when I yanked open the accordion case packed with Painted Ladies.

Either butterfly research attracts good-natured scientists, or spending a career around butterflies makes researchers good-natured. Or a combination of the two may be at work. I've yet to run into a curmudgeonly butterfly expert—except for Jeffrey Glassberg the afternoon when I first met him, but to be fair, he was exhausted and I was acting the part of the in-your-face journalist. Perhaps I've just been lucky. But Professor Dudley quickly proves to be another charming interlocutor, putting aside his work to patiently answer my questions. He is surprised to hear of the growing popularity of butterfly releases at Easter services and funerals as symbols of rebirth and ascent to heaven. "How weird," he says. "You're analogizing yourself to an insect for a start. That's wild."

I start by asking Professor Dudley the rather innocent question of how butterflies fly. He smiles, and with a great deal of patience explains, "They fly by flapping their wings." There's no question from his smile that he's used that line before, and he proceeds to fill in details. Butterflies have bodies and they have wings. They are equipped with two wing pairs: fore wings and hind wings. The two pairs are not connected, but they overlap. On the down stroke they work as a unit, on the up stroke the wings separate slightly—the fore wings moving faster. The wings are large relative to the body, adding to the flashy appearance of butterflies: the color and the design dominate the insect body. Most of what we see when we spot a butterfly are the wings.

"You made it down to Nicaragua, and you saw how the Morphos do this," and he uses his hands, thumbs locked, to imitate the slow flapping of Morpho wings.

"You mean how they lumber through the air, almost looking clumsy and graceful at the same time?"

Graceful yes, but he wouldn't call them clumsy because they're hard to catch, which suggests the flight is controlled. "The Morpho is pushing air down, and in the up stroke it feathers the wing—like when you're paddling a boat, you have a drag stroke and then you feather. They're almost paddling through the air." This paddling is what makes butterflies appear to be almost bouncing along in flight. Once the Morphos gather speed, aircraft-like wing lift plays an increasingly important flight role. For the most part, bigger animals fly faster than smaller animals, and Dudley's crew has clocked some tropical butterflies loping along at almost twenty-five miles per hour. That's fast. They weigh much less than a gram. "For small things," says the professor, "they're cranking."

Butterfly diversity means there are different strokes for different types of butterflies. Some can hover; for others, lift is used more than drag. There's plenty still about butterfly flight dynamics yet to be understood. The potential exists to adapt some of what can be learned from butterfly flight to what are known as micro air vehicles, flapping devices designed for surveillance. No surprise: the funding for this sort of research is primarily targeted for military applications, which are of no interest to Dudley. "The whole technological side of it has really exploded in the last ten years, but it's all very militaristic in nature. I would rather work against the U.S. military than with the U.S. military these days. So I have nothing to do with those guys. The level of venality I've seen on this campus, it's really quite disturbing, the willingness to collaborate with imperialists for personal benefit. It's impressive; you've got to hand it to them. I've just totally shied away from all that kind of stuff. That whole technological side has been completely corrupted by the military in my opinion."

No matter how hard butterflies flap their wings, no matter how efficient their flight systems may be, the feather-light insects are at the mercy of wind. "Wind is a huge factor," Dudley confirms. I can't help but be distracted while he talks by a hummingbird that keeps coming into his office from the wilds of the Berkeley campus. He's installed a Plexiglas box in the window open on one side. The birds can fly in the open window, into the box, which puts the humming-birds on view well inside the office, confined by the five closed sides. "You have these relatively large wings," he says about butterflies, "and once they start flying, small-scale turbulence can easily impose asymmetrical forces."

The erratic-looking flight of the common Cabbage White butterfly can be attributed in part to buffeting from the wind. However, Professor Dudley says when researchers fly Cabbage Whites in still air, the erratic patterns do not disappear and are used for defense. "If you swing a net at them and miss, they'll start doing it faster. That's an intriguing feature that distinguishes butterflies essentially from all other flying insects, the high degree of erratic, seemingly unpredictable flight."

That lack of predictable pattern adds to their aesthetic appeal to us, he and I agree, and inspired Robert Graves when he wrote his ode to the Cabbage White, the poem "Flying Crooked." "The butterfly, a cabbage white," observes Graves, will never "master the art of flying straight." The poet then expresses appreciation for what he considers is a gift he and the Cabbage White share: the ability to fly "crooked," which we may interpret as non-conformity.[8]

Butterflies do fly to specific destinations. Some, like the Monarch, migrate to specific grounds. They seek mates, look for nectar, and find places to lay their eggs. Their flight is purpose driven. The erratic-seeming short flights of other butterflies serve them as they search for mates, nourishment, and locales for their eggs—all while trying to evade predators.

Professor Dudley divides flight styles of butterflies into two groups. In the first he places slow-flying toxic butterflies that birds could catch but don't because eating them makes birds ill—Monarchs are a prime example. The second group is made up of palatable erratic-flying butterflies. Morphos are delicious treats for birds, and what appears to be a lumbering, graceful flight is deceptive. "I would call it semi-erratic. It looks regular, but it's hard to predict. If you swing a net, you get one shot and one shot only."

An erratic flight path is eye-catching—as are colorful and big butterfly wings—and the attention the Cabbage White and other erratic-flying butterflies draw to themselves is another defense mechanism. Dudley offers an intriguing theory for it. "It's an advertisement of 'unprofitability of capture.'" It's a warning that the butterfly "would be difficult and a lot of energy for a bird to chase and catch, and it might not be successful." The erratic flight paths may discourage predators, but not without cost to the butterflies, which end up expending extra energy getting wherever they're heading if they reject a straight line from Point A to Point B. The slow-flying toxic butterflies—and those that mimic their appearance—use wing color to scare off predators. The reds and yellows and blacks announce, "We taste foul and make you sick, remember?" The toxicity and message are not without their own costs, the professor points out, since extensive evolutionary changes were required before Monarchs became color-coded and nauseating. Vast meals of Monarchs were enjoyed by predators before the species managed to develop the traits that allow it to flourish today.

Going every which way requires a sophisticated navigation system so the butterflies can keep track not only of where they're going, but also which way is up. Their keen eyesight is part of the process as are their antennae, which perform gyroscope duties to help sense rotational acceleration. From his studies Dudley has concluded that wing beat by wing beat, the insects make adjustments to their strokes in order to get where they're going as efficiently as possible. "I call it controlled instability because it's unpredictable but it's controlled," he says, adding an intriguing human comparison. "It's sort of like Tourette's Syndrome. This is the closest analogy I can come up with. People can still function with Tourette's, but it's not predictable."

I leave the Berkeley Life Sciences building, walking through the lobby past a replica skeleton of a *Tyrannosaurus rex*, with a comforting thought from Robert Dudley in mind. "My best definition of science is 'advancing the frontiers of ignorance.' We're generating more questions than we're answering. That means we're successful."

Butterfly huggers versus butterfly breeders. Who are the good guys and who are the bad guys? No question, it was fun thrashing around Cedar Creek with Jeffrey Glassberg and his band of merry butterfly spotters, intent on seeking butterflies only in the wild. But no question, I also appreciated Edith Smith's passionate defense of her industry during my grand tour of her Shady Oak Butterfly Farm. I ordered a stack of Painted Ladies from her in hopes I'd be better able to judge the merits of butterfly releases after witnessing one.

A stack they were when they arrived. The package came in a corrugated cardboard box. Inside the box were Styrofoam liners for insulation and the ice packs, those faux ice cubes you can refreeze to keep stuff cold. And in a box padded with wads of tissue paper for padding was a stack of glassine envelopes, each envelope holding a Painted Lady, her wings folded and her body chilled to dormancy.

The box arrived a day before I wanted to release the butterflies, so I followed the instructions that came with my girls, carefully refreezing the three ice packs in sequence in order to keep the Painted Ladies' resting place cold enough that they would not rouse, but not so cold that the temperature would kill them.

I had ordered thirty Painted Ladies. (Journalistic transparency requires me to announce here that I wrote to Edith Smith asking to purchase the butterflies, and she did send an invoice with the shipment, an invoice she graciously decided to discount substantively for my test flight. They retail for five dollars each if you buy at least a dozen.) There were three delivery systems in the carton: a standard white box in which the butterflies would be held in a holding pattern until the lid was flipped open and they (theoretically) flew free, a bright red heart-shaped box with a clear lid through which the butterflies could be observed prior to release, and an elegant white accordion box with organza see-through sides and a satin bow on the top.

As per the enclosed instructions, I removed the ice pack more than an hour before the scheduled event "so they can warm up prior to the release." Weather at my Marin County, California, place was a perfect eighty degrees and sunny. After about a half an hour an eerie sound filled my office. The butterflies were waking up, becoming active. Their little legs were squirming against the glassine envelopes, scratching . . . scratching. There was something creepy about their entrapment, but at the same time something magical about them revitalizing while we watched. The butterflies in the organza box were not in glassine envelopes. Inside that box was a strip of paper folded accordion-style, and nestled between each fold was one of my Painted Ladies; they too were coming out of their stupor and scratching . . . scratching. The other boxes needed to be loaded, and my wife Sheila and I followed the enclosed instructions to do it in "a small room with a low ceiling (a bathroom is perfect) and shut the door while you are making the transfer." The low ceiling is insurance against an escapee, making it easier to catch the runaway.

I sat on the floor of the stall shower. Sheila was in charge of the box lids. I opened the glassine envelopes and learned immediately that Jeffrey Glassberg was wrong: These butterflies were not dead! They were anxious to fly, fluttering now that they were warmed up. One by one we shuttled them into the heart box and the white box. Two or three escaped, but the shower proved a pragmatic choice; they were easy to grab and stuff into the boxes. "No problem," the instructions advised. "Despite what you've always been told, handling a butterfly gently will not harm it." We just cupped them into our hands and then coaxed them into the boxes. Then we set the boxes on a shelf in the kitchen to wait out their warm-up time, and we left them alone so we would not be witness to their scratching . . . scratching, and the even more unsettling sound of the butterflies now free in the boxes beating their wings as they tried to fly in captivity.

We invited the neighbors to come over for the show, and they brought their children, three little girls and a little boy. The small yard where we chose to release them was sun-dappled and surrounded by trees. We hoped the foliage would keep them from flying off immediately so that we could watch their post-release antics.

"They're really excited," said Sheila, as we carried them outside. "They want out." She decided to offer them a few words of guidance. "May you be happy and peaceful. May you be healthy and strong. May you be safe and protected from harm. May you be at ease in your lives."

Our friend Carol took the heart-shaped box for the first release. The butterflies inside were brilliant, flapping their bright black, white, and orange wings for us to see through the window in the lid. She opened the box, and a few of the Painted Ladies fluttered forth, heading for the nearby tree leaves. A couple of others were more lackadaisical. They got up, looked around, and took their time before they took off. One chose to hang out for pictures on Carol's extended index finger, preening for the camera.

"Wow," offered the assembled neighbors in unison as the last butterfly left the box. Everyone was smiling, laughing. And the butterflies stuck around, some staying in the trees, others fluttering around the yard. Next little Zoe and Ava opened the little white box together. The butterflies didn't leap out. They leisurely looked about, and took their time joining their compatriots in the trees and wandering the yard.

"Wow!" was the crowd's response again, along with encouragement, "Fly away! Fly, little butterflies." One decided to stay with Ava for a while, sitting on her hand. "Does it tickle?" she was asked. Not enough to bother her; she was smiling as her butterfly beat her wings slowly, showing off her colors, exploring Ava's fingers. "Bye, bye, butterfly," she said as it finally flew off.

It was my turn. I took hold of the accordion box and, following Sheila's advice, pulled the box open slowly.

"All right!" yelled the crowd. There were other cheers of delight as the Painted Ladies took off en masse, scattering over the yard in glorious flight, disappearing around the neighborhood. All except for one. It lit on Sheila's white blouse and stayed put on her shoulder. As the audience dispersed, she and I returned to my office. The butterfly remained on her blouse. We talked, and toasted the butterflies with a glass of Chardonnay. The butterfly remained on her blouse. It walked around, it primped its wings, it looked relaxed, and it spread its wings to look like a brooch. But it stayed on her blouse. And stayed. Finally, almost three hours after our official release, as it was getting dark, Sheila walked back outside and it took off, flying toward the trees, leaving a stain of bright yellow frass on her stark white blouse.

Chapter Four

DIAPAUSE

THE MORE I IMMERSED MYSELF IN BUTTERFLIES AND THEIR WORLD, the more captivated I became. To this day, I carry around a yellowed newspaper clipping for inspiration, a story written from Hay-on-Wye, Wales, by Larry Bleiberg of the *Dallas Morning News*. Hay-on-Wye is a village jammed with bookstores overflowing with used books. I've been there on one of my road trips across Britain, and it's a fun place to prowl around. Within its few quaint medieval-looking blocks are over two dozen stores. But as Bleiberg points out, a journey there can be superficial—bookstore browsing ad nauseam. "When I visited recently," Bleiberg wrote, "I walked purposefully into town because I had remembered to pack the most crucial part of any trip—a mission." He was looking for three specific rare books. This gave him the opportunity to peel back the veneer of the tourist-oriented burg, meet storeowners, and consult local experts. Bleiberg experienced the real Hay-on-Wye, not the Disney version. Bleiberg's experience is universal. Working on a news story creates such mission-oriented travel for me wherever I am, wherever I go. That's one of the reasons I thrive on being a journalist. I love the license that role gives me to gain access to the closed doors of society, and I lust after the excuse for mission I get out of a project developing in my notebooks. Since my first trip down to the Nicaraguan butterfly reserve, I grabbed just about every opportunity possible to look for butterflies.

On a business trip to Chicago, I take advantage of a few free hours to wander over to Grant Park and check out the butterflies in the Field Museum. The primary exhibit is on the wall of a basement hallway. Two huge East Indies Birdwings are in the case: the larger, the female; the more colorful, the male. I gaze at the spectacle of these enormous specimens, trying to transcend the fact that they're dead in the case. Perhaps that's why butterfly collecting had never much interested me—by definition, butterfly collections are dead things in a box. But now, as my butterfly quest continued, I was searching all aspects of the butterfly subculture, pinned dead bugs included.

Hanging adjacent to the Birdwings is another prized butterfly: a translucent Morpho from Colombia, its soft pastel blue still radiant despite the fact that this specimen too is long dead. The butterfly guidebook I bought in the Field Museum store explains that those rich blue wings serve a purpose: the butterfly I'm admiring is a male, and his coloring appeals to the ladies. Next to the Blue Morpho is a tiny Clearwing from Brazil, looking like a delicate line drawing. The wings appear as if they are windows with distinct dark coloring outlining them—a frame defining their shape, while fine filigree-like detail comes from the thin dark lines etched by the wing veins. Gorgeous. Well-preserved. Dead in a glass case.

In that same showcase a butterfly net is displayed alongside a scattering of old black-and-white photographs of little girls. I date these pictures to be from the late fifties or early sixties, based on the girls' short white socks and what look like saddle shoes, their shorts and sleeveless blouses. No logo T-shirts and Nikes like those of the little girls running around the museum the day I visit. The label in the case describing the pictures reads, "Collecting butterflies. Sunshine. Open fields. The fun of the chase."

I leave the Field Museum and head north along Lake Michigan to Lincoln Park and the Notebaert Nature Museum. There most of the butterflies are not stuck dead in a case. On the roof of the museum is a butterfly enclosure, a humid room filled with flowering plants for dozens of different butterfly species from around the world to frolic. The rules are simple for joining this live display, and they are a clear indicator of human nature: "Do not touch or grab the butterflies. They're quite fragile and their wings are easily damaged. Overcome the urge to pet the butterflies."

I go into what the museum calls its "butterfly haven" and sit down on a bench. I'm not there a minute before a pair of bright blue, black, and white butterflies land on my leg.

"Pretty spectacular," I say to a guard watching nearby. I want to share this wonder.

She smiles, but she's been working her beat for years and says, "I'm not as impressed as I once was," just as I'm thinking she must love her work, that hers is a dream job for a guard.

Next an orange, yellow, and black butterfly lands on a red flower. Out rolls its proboscis, and the butterfly sticks it deep into the flower. The wings pump as it feeds itself; they move slowly, purposefully, rhythmically—not the seemingly erratic flutter it had been using in flight—as the proboscis moves in and out, in and out. This is my first close-up experience alone watching the butterfly-flower relationship since I started researching this book. I'm enthralled and I'm transported to another world: the butterflies' world. My pending business meetings move out of my mind, replaced with watching the magic occurring just a few inches from my face.

A third blue, black, and white butterfly lands on me. "That's unusual," says the guard about their decision to light on me. I realize that I feel honored by the little insects' visits, and then my cynical news reporter self scoffs at such thoughts—that the butterflies would be making some sort of sentient decision to choose me.

There is a chart available with pictures of the butterflies in the haven, but I can't seem to match the ones I'm watching with the pictures. Are the ones that like my leg Blue-and-white Longwings? At that moment I don't much care. My job this day is to hang out with the butterflies, not identify them. I feel tranquil with them darting and gliding around, drinking from the flowers, resting on my leg.

Some of their wings show wear and tear even in such a controlled environment free of predators. These damaged specimens are no good for collectors. That's why Jane Foulds takes her Nicaraguan beauties directly to her freezer after they come out of the pupal casing and unfold their wings.

Two more butterflies land on me. Their delicate beauty captivates me, and I do, in fact, feel privileged that they choose me. I allow myself for a moment to think they are showing off to me or acknowledging my interest in them. Their looks combined with their antics—the erratic fluttering and the placid feeding—are all calming to me as I watch them.

I discover that butterflies permeate the culture as metaphors, and I start making lists. In billiards, a butterfly shot drops six balls assembled in a butterfly shape into all six pockets with one stroke of the cue stick. The Butterfly Effect: a butterfly bats its wings in Asia and influences weather in America, and thinking about that butterfly influences the development of Chaos Theory. Of course, butterflies in the stomach. The infamous Palm Beach County, Florida, butterfly ballot, so poorly designed that thousands of confused voters are presumed to have voted mistakenly for Patrick J. Buchanan instead of Al Gore in the 2000 presidential election, enough to swing the final election results to favor George W. Bush—resulting in the Iraq War. Butterfly chairs, making a comeback as retro-chic. The butterfly bandage. Bow-tie pasta is called *farfalle* in Italian, the word for butterfly. The butterfly kiss, eyelash to eyelash. And splitting food: butterflied prawns. Swimming: the butterfly stroke. Making love: the butterfly position.

My traveling routine is changed. I now seek butterflies wherever I land. In Yorkshire, England, I stop at Roundhay Park in Leeds to check out the butterfly house. Outside is a huge floral display, multicolored flowers planted in the shape of a giant butterfly. Inside the greenhouse, the blustery English weather is replaced with heat and humidity to comfort the lush tropical plants and fluttering butterflies.

"Do you see the butterflies?" a woman coos to her little boy. How could he not? They're everywhere. "Do you see all the lovely butterflies? Do you see all the colors of the butterflies? Look at all these butterflies!"

And look at them we all do, enthralled by their magic. It's impossible not to look as they flutter and light, closing their wings and muting their colors.

Calming magic, they are.

Another mother to child: "Look! Look!"

"Six!" exclaims the child, pointing. Then, "Seven, eight, nine!"

Orange and white and black. Spotted and striped. Sucking nectar. Feeding on rotting fruit.

One lights on a woman's wrist, and she shows it off to her date. He teases her, "Looks like he's taking a big bite." He snaps a photograph and suggests she check for damage. She laughs. The butterfly lifts off, and then comes back around toward her. "You smell good," the man says.

Smiles, laughter. Butterflies, magic.

A wing of the Hall of Flowers in San Francisco's Golden Gate Park is converted into an ad hoc butterfly house. A little girl holds out her hand.

"Come here," she says in a soft voice. "Come here, butterfly." She looks at it fluttering around her. "Oh! He touched me!"

The gold filigree glistens on a Monarch chrysalis, crown-like. I watch another chrysalis crack and a Zebra Longwing come out with its wilted-looking wings not yet dry and ready for flight, but moments later it is ready to lift off.

Biologist Rachel Diaz-Bastin is busy here with the chrysalises, escorting the eclosing butterflies from their display box into the wilds of the display.

"That's where Monarch butterflies get their name," she says, "because of the beautiful jade-green chrysalis. I think they're the most beautiful chrysalises I've ever seen, and with the thin gold iridescent band it looks like they're wearing a crown." That gold is not just decoration, although we agree it makes the chrysalis pretty enough to consider using it as an earring. "When it refracts light, it's really hard to see hanging in a tree or on a plant because the green color blends in and the iridescence makes it look like a drop of water. It looks like a dewdrop, and a lot of times predators don't even see it."

Diaz-Bastin enjoys watching the delight the butterflies foment. "You don't have to teach people to love butterflies. That's what I love about butterflies so much. They are insects, and a lot of people forget that. They just see the beautiful colors and are entranced by them. Butterflies are not afraid of people. They will fly around your head, and some even will land on you if you're wearing their favorite colors like red and green and orange. That's really special because visitors can have a really personal, intimate experience with the butterflies."

It wasn't always thus for her. "I was terribly afraid of insects." Not good news for a biologist. She immersed herself in insect study and insect handling, and learned to love even what she calls the "creepy-crawlies," like huge hissing cockroaches. "When you pick them up they make this really loud hiss," she says with some awe, if not new-found appreciation.

Talking with her is a primer of basic butterfly facts. She's quick to differentiate benign adult butterflies from their crop-destroying lar-val form. "Butterflies are not pests as adults. When you see an adult Cabbage White or an adult Swallowtail, they're not doing any of the munching on your food. What's happening is the caterpillars of those butterflies are doing all of the damage. The caterpillar is designed to eat, that's their whole purpose in life. They can increase their body size about twenty-seven thousand times. That's like a nine-pound baby becoming two hundred and forty-three thousand pounds."

The weight is stored to fuel metamorphosis.

"Metamorphosis is energy-draining for them, and they need to carry that energy into the adult stage, which is when they look for mates and they lay eggs. That's pretty much all adult butterflies do." That and make us happy, apparently. "And they pollinate as adults. There's a trade-off. As caterpillars they can do some damage, but s adults they pollinate."

Metamorphosis is the ultimate butterfly magic. The worm becomes a god or goddess.

Rachel Diaz-Bastin is a scientist. She accepts my use of magic as an explanation for metamorphosis, but prefers something closer to her discipline. "It's so science fiction. The caterpillar increases its size twenty-seven thousand times and then decides that it's time to harden its skin and make a chrysalis. It has a little bit of silk that it can spin, almost like a spider silk. The silk is very strong and the larva attaches itself to the underside of a leaf or a twig and hangs upside-down." Lucky for me, since Diaz-Bastin often tours children through the butterfly house, she's perfected a simple and straight-forward explanation of the incredible transformation. "The skin on the outside of the caterpillar hardens. This is the final molt. Caterpillars have a hard, tough exoskeleton. They must shed their skin just like a snake in order to grow. This is the final shed of their skin. As adult butterflies they don't grow anymore." Inside the hard chrysalis the transformation is in progress. "All of their body parts, every cell, liquefies." It is, as she said before, science fiction. "This is weird stuff. All of their cells differentiate and begin forming the adult butterfly. It's basically this big butterfly soup inside."

Were you to cut the chrysalis at this stage, you would find nothing resembling a caterpillar and nothing resembling a butterfly: only liquid.

"It is amazing." Diaz-Bastin's personal delight in the process is contagious. "This process usually only takes about two weeks—to go from a liquid into an adult beautiful, gorgeous butterfly. And it only takes them about a minute, sometimes under a minute, to come out of the chrysalis, to emerge."

What exactly goes on in the soup to make the change remains an unknown to scientists despite some research being done in this area, but Diaz-Bastin is in no hurry for the question to be solved. "We don't need to know this mystery of nature to appreciate it," she points out with characteristic enthusiasm. There is something captivating about our inability—so far—to map the magic. One of her favorite magic shows is the eclosing Monarch "because the outside of their pupa, which is the chrysalis skin, turns translucent. You can actually see the butterfly through the skin, these beautiful orange and black markings of the Monarch butterfly about to emerge." Next the chrysalis itself will start to shake. The butterfly comes out headfirst at the bottom of the chrysalis. "They climb up on the shell of the chrysalis and just hold on for dear life. They definitely don't want to fall because that would hurt their wings. This is a really delicate stage in their life. They're using a lot of energy at this point to pump the blood from their wings." This unfurling, drying, and hardening of their wings lasts a couple of hours, after which "their wings are incredibly light and aerodynamically efficient." My guide encourages visitors to come to the Hall of Flowers early in the morning, the time of day the Monarchs and other pupa in her care tend to eclose.

Pretty as butterflies are, Rachel Diaz-Bastin tells me she may prefer moths. The general differentiation—although some species break the rules—is that moths fly at night, butterflies in the day. She rejects my further suggestion that butterflies are beautiful and moths are ugly. Moths are not delicate. They look like the sumo wrestlers of Lepidoptera; they've got massive bodies. Blame this on their night life; since they cannot rely on the sun to heat their bodies, they must equip themselves with more fat than the svelter butterflies. Their massive bodies keep them warm, and are covered with a much thicker fur than butterfly bodies. Diaz-Bastin insists, "They are actually kind of cute, if you get to know them, fuzzy and cute. There's a moth from Madagascar called the Madagascar Sunset Moth. It's just completely iridescent. Every color you can possibly think of. It looks like it's from the eighties, all these bright neons." They're not just cute. My father told me intriguing stories about raising silk moths, the valued *Bombyx mori*, when he was a child. The Luna moth, which I observed close up at the Los Angeles Natural History Museum, is quite beautiful. But as she rhapsodized about moths, I tried to stay focused. I was not seeking dragonflies or even moths. My target was butterflies.

Nonetheless, the butterfly's Lepidoptera neighbor, the moth, is hard to ignore when studying butterflies. They are closely related and the dangerous world of butterflies (and moths) hits home when I go out to my driveway in the summer of 2008 and pick up the morning Sonoma County *Press Democrat*. "Third Apple Moth Found in

County," screams the headline under a photograph of the dainty lepidopteran. The moth illustrated looks as if it is dancing on its caption. Its antennae are held high, like arms outstretched, and there is a jaunty twist to its abdomen, almost as if it's swinging its hips. The caption is direct: "A light brown apple moth was found southeast of Sonoma." The Australian native is considered a pest by some grape growers and California state agriculture officials.

This is a potentially dangerous situation for the world-famous Sonoma County grape crop harvest, which fuels not just great wine but our local economy. It's dangerous for those of us who live in Sonoma County and have been fighting—successfully so far—the state's efforts to continue to combat the LBAM (as the light brown apple moth has come to be known locally) with aerial pesticide spraying. And, of course, it is dangerous for the LBAM, because this Australian native is not going to stand a chance in a battle with the wine industry. Alternatives to the county-wide spraying include targeting only rural regions and using ground-deployed pesticides. Some opponents of the spraying question the state's conclusion that the LBAM presents a consequential danger and they suggest a wait-and-see approach to the exotic invader.

The year before, Santa Cruz and Monterey Counties were sprayed. Hundreds of residents reported health problems they blamed on the chemicals—itchy eyes and trouble breathing—but state health officials claimed the complaints could not be conclusively linked to the spraying. Those with the itchy eyes and shortness of breath pointed out that the state couldn't prove the spraying was not responsible.

After my initial butterfly trip to Nicaragua, whenever I encountered anything to do with butterflies, I secured the reference in my growing butterfly files. Piles of newspaper and magazine clippings littered my office. I collected DVDs and CDs with butterfly references in their content. I found advertisements, drawings, photographs, toys—in the most unexpected places (plastic surgery!) I found butterflies.

Item: In autumn 2008, murder charges were dismissed against Mario Rocha, and his conviction was overturned after he served ten years in prison. "I feel like a butterfly coming out of its cocoon," was his smiling reaction to the news.[9]

Item: The children's supply catalog hearthsong.com sells toy butterfly wings. "Hours of imaginative make-believe play are guaranteed when young children slip on these gauzy nylon wings and transform themselves into lovely butterflies—choose classic Monarch, glitter adorned Karner Blue, boldly dotted Red Fantasy, or ethereal green/violet Luna Moth," $12.98 each.

Item: "Take the Lunesta 7-Night Challenge," offers an advertisement for a sleeping pill. A floating butterfly illustrates the ad.

Item: Endangered Species brand chocolate sells a 70 percent cocoa organic dark chocolate in a package adorned with the image of a Karner Blue. Inside the wrapper is the story of the endangered Karner Blue, along with the message, "Astoundingly, 19 of the 38 insects listed under the Endangered Species Act in 2004 were butterflies."

Item: A hanging chrysalis and a nectaring Monarch make the case in an advertisement for a Buenos Aires, Argentina, plastic surgery clinic, offering a metamorphosis-like *transformación.*

Butterflies are ubiquitous, and they attract intriguing devotees. Allow me to introduce you to Elliot Malkin, Web designer and innovator in "interspecies communications," as he calls it. I was introduced to his work at his Web site, which advocates what he calls graffiti for butterflies.[10] Malkin lives in Brooklyn. He worries that migrating Monarch butterflies, in search of their plant food milkweed, will find a dearth of the needed vegetation in the urban reaches of New York City. Intent to do what he can to help, he placed potted milkweed plants on the balcony of his apartment. Concerned that it might be difficult for the butterflies to locate his few plants in the asphalt jungle, two ideas came to him: paint giant pictures of milkweed adjacent to the real plants to alert the flying Monarchs, and then paint them with sunblock.

His logic is unique. "Milkweed flowers," says Malkin, "have natural ultraviolet patterns that are recognizable to Monarch butterflies. These patterns are invisible to us because we can't see light in the ultraviolet spectrum. So graffiti for butterflies uses sunblock to paint the graffiti in a way that mimics these natural ultraviolet properties." Sunblock is a perfect medium, he says, because it reflects ultraviolet light. Malkin considers his work "the equivalent of a fast-food sign on a highway, advertising rest stops to Monarchs."

When Elliot Malkin first began experimenting with graffiti for butterflies, he was not concerned with feeding the Monarchs. "I was going to just try to entertain them and give them some art," he told me. He made his graffiti with both sunblock and a paint visible to humans because he wanted to engage in what he calls "broadcasting bi-directionally to both humans and butterflies. My first idea was just to make art that the butterflies could see. I was trying to go for some interspecies communication, to bridge a couple of species and bring us together. Then it occurred to me to make it more functional, to help them and advertise their food sources as they're migrating over or through urban areas."

I asked him if he's detected any results, if he can ascertain that he is communicating with the butterflies and drawing them toward his milkweed. "I hope so," is his optimistic response before a more realistic, "but I can't scientifically prove that. I mainly wanted to introduce this concept to the world, to instigate thinking about beneficial interspecies communication, to think about other audiences besides humans." His efforts sound like a performance art piece, with the intriguing added value of investigative purpose.

Malkin may not be able to scientifically prove his artwork attracts Monarchs, but the anecdotal evidence intrigues him. "There was a Monarch on my balcony, and it was flying to the milkweed that was flowering, and it spent time there. It was drinking from the milkweed flowers, and it laid some eggs. I raised those caterpillars." He adds, wistfully, "There was graffiti that I made near the plant."

I realize I've started a collection, I'm gathering a growing list of intriguing characters with a single common denominator: they all thrive on a specific interspecies relationship that brings together humans and butterflies.

Chapter Five

THE FLIGHT AND PLIGHT OF
THE MONARCH

INDEPENDENCE DAY IN MEXICO—SEPTEMBER, 2008—GRENADES
were lobbed into the celebrating crowd in Morelia's downtown, capital of Michoacán, hometown of Mexican president Felipe Calderón.
"On this national holiday, there are cowards hidden in the crowds of
patriotic people that have converted joy into sadness and the happiness of Mexican families into sorrow," Calderón said after the attack,
explosions that killed, maimed, and emptied Morelia of its tourists. It
was a shattering blow to Morelia, a city that celebrates the Monarch
because it is a staging ground for butterfly tours into the mountains
a few hours distance.

The next month, I'm in Morelia, en route to the nearby Monarch
overwintering grounds high in the Michoacán mountains. Taxi drivers and restaurant waiters, hotel desk clerks and passersby I encounter in the streets all express despair about the attacks. The shock to
the city's economy is secondary; the targeting of innocents in their
usually peaceful city has them dumbfounded. Across the street
from my hotel in the charming Spanish Colonial downtown is the
eighteenth-century cathedral with its wedding cake steeples and the
park where two of the grenades exploded. It's a perfect autumn day,
the sky clear and blue, accented with puffy white clouds kissing the
nearby mountains. Bloody tragedy seems far distant.

An ad hoc memorial and scars on the sidewalks are the only
physical reminders of the blasts, otherwise life goes on: families

stroll, lovers embrace, the shoeshine men wait for customers. The memorial is a circle of dried stalks, along with flowers, arranged on the paving stones, along with two wreaths of flowers on easels. Candles and a card showing an image of Jesus with Mary are set amid the flowers. A handwritten note is amongst the offerings. It is weathered and torn, covered with candle wax, but a few words are still legible. *"Viviremos siempre en los corazónes de la gente que nos amó en vida."* We will live forever in the hearts of the people who loved us when they were alive.

Passersby slow as they walk past the memorial, and say a few hushed words to each other before continuing on. Periodic army patrols pass the square: an armored personnel carrier equipped with a machine gun, and a pickup truck—the bed of the truck filled with heavily armed soldiers and a machine gun mounted on the roof of the cab, manned by a gunner.

There is a war going on in Mexico under the still placid façade of Morelia's sidewalk cafés and their guacamole and *huchepos*, hot chocolate and *cerveza*. The attack on the *zócalo*, the massacres in border cities of police, prosecutors, and soldiers—along with alleged drug traffickers—are manifestations of the illegal drug business. But the same type of terror plagues the Monarch grounds, where the currency is valuable trees illegally logged instead of marijuana and cocaine, methamphetamine and heroin.

Before heading into the mountains, I stop at the Palacio del Gobierno for a meeting at which the Michoacán governor, Leonel Godoy, gives the introductory remarks. There is a cup of coffee on the dais in front of him; it's traditional local pottery adorned with a delicate, painted butterfly. It's official state tableware. After the meeting I walk out of the building and think for a moment I see an early Monarch, only it's late October and their scheduled arrival date is *El Día de los Muertes*, November 1. It is lively, fluttering around the governor's grounds, but it is yellow, not Monarch orange, and the only Monarchs I see in Morelia are pictures: decorating the state's license plates, and illustrating the sign in my hotel that suggests I save water by sleeping in yesterday's sheets and drying myself with this morning's wet towel.

$$\rightleftharpoons$$

The strange-but-true story of the Monarch lures and mystifies butterfly aficionados from grammar school children to wizened entomological specialists. The North American Monarch living east of the Continental Divide doesn't only magically change from a clown-colored caterpillar to a majestic butterfly, it defies logic with a multigenerational, ultra-long-distance commute that transits Canada, the United States, and Mexico. The navigational details remain a mystery—no one knows for sure how they plan their route from the northeast of North America to the few specific mountaintops where they winter in one central Mexico neighborhood. Tropical Monarchs live their summers as far north as Canada. As winter approaches they migrate south to Mexico where they hibernate en masse—millions jammed per acre—in Michoacán and the state of Mexico in an isolated range of the Sierra Madre, the mountains made famous in the 1948 film *The Treasure of the Sierra Madre* starring Humphrey Bogart.[11] It was Bogart who asked a Mexican bandit posing as a *Federale* for his badge, eliciting the classic line, "Badges? We ain't got no badges. We don't need no badges. I don't have to show you any stinkin' badges." That lawlessness is a reality that unfortunately plagues the Monarch overwintering grounds to this day.

In spring the warming weather rouses the Monarchs. They mate as they head back north, an activity that quickly kills off the male. But unlike the direct trip south, the journey north takes a few generations. The Monarchs that made the long trip south and spent the winter in Mexico only make it as far as Texas and Louisiana. The gravid (egg-bearing) females stay alive long enough to find a suitable locale for their eggs, whatever milkweed they can find—this being the plant food that both nourishes their larvae, and fills the caterpillars and the butterflies they eventually become with the poison that makes them unpalatable for most potential predators. This next generation ecloses in short order and continues the trek north toward the Great Lakes where they lay their eggs. Soon their offspring head toward the East Coast, and it is their progeny who make the long haul—as far as three thousand miles—back to Mexico. This is an annual event: it takes four or five short-lived generations for the broods to make it north, and then, before winter sets in, the Mexico-bound generation—which lives several months—makes the epic journey south.

How do these butterflies—great-grandchildren of the Monarchs who flew to Mexico the year before—know where to go and how to get there? That is still a fascinating and delightful mystery; theories include a role played by the position of the sun and another by the Earth's magnetic force. The excellent eyesight of the Monarch is a navigation factor, the visual cues interpreted by the butterfly's pinhead-sized brain. Favorable winds and air currents help make for a successful trip, along with plenty of luck. Those are theories of how they fix their route. How they know—generations separated from the ancestors who last were in Mexico—where their destinations are located remains a phenomenal mystery.

There are Monarchs elsewhere making similar but not quite so epic journeys. Those west of the North American Continental Divide, for example, head down the California coast, and find a comfortable staging place for the winter. Some of them cluster near my home in Sonoma County, hanging together on imported Australian eucalyptus and local Monterey cypress trees in the Bodega Dunes park. Others go farther south. Pacific Grove calls itself Butterfly Town, U.S.A., and threatens fines of up to $1,000 for harassing any of the thousands of Monarchs that overwinter in the Monterey Bay city.

Wandering around in the midst of the millions of Mexican Monarchs is a thrill that attracts a growing crowd of tourists to the remote few mountaintops favored by the butterflies for their winter grounds. Tour guide Carlos Juarez ferries me from Morelia to the former gold mining village of Angangueo, nine thousand feet up in the Sierra Madre, where I have scheduled an appointment with a couple of desperados working to save the Monarchs' Mexican habitat from marauding timber poachers and from local villagers struggling to survive.

As we careen through hairpin turns on Highway 15, his Chrysler hauling us past cornfields and through pine forests, Juarez regales me with what compels him about being in the midst of the Monarchs.

"The first thing you see is the trees and what looks like dead leaves. You see these bunches of 'leaves' and you don't realize that it's Monarchs. As the day gets warm, they go from brown to orange because the wings open." The undersides of the wings are brown, so when the butterflies are roosting, their color is hidden. Once they fly, the brilliant orange topside of their wings—accented with black—is on display. If the day warms up gradually, they leave the trees slowly, and he tells me it is a spectacular sight: their massive movement and the change from brown to orange. But if the day warms up quickly, the show is an even more startling display. "If the day starts cloudy and then the sun comes out, they break formation and suddenly cascade. You can even hear them—they sound like falling leaves. Incredible: gray sky to blue sky to orange sky. It's like flying confetti. They are gracious," he is smiling at his many Monarch memories, "very, very gracious." Juarez uses the Spanish, *graciosas,* which is more than graceful—the word connotes a sense of the charming. "*Graciosas.* They don't flutter much," he says with admiration, "they glide gently. They let the wind take them."

It was a sight witnessed by Dr. Fred Urquhart, a Canadian zoologist and the granddaddy of Monarch-specializing scientists, when—using tagged Monarchs—he and his researchers were able to trace the migrating butterflies to their overwintering grounds for the first time in the mid-1970s. He reported that they "filled the air with their sunshot wings, shimmering against the blue mountain sky and drifting across our vision in blizzard flakes of orange and black." At the time Urquhart mused about the unknowns, acknowledging that he could not be sure the oyamel fir forests of central Mexico were the Monarch's only overwintering grounds, even though "I feel certain they are all situated within a restricted range on the same general area."[12] The continued belief that the migrating Monarchs require the specific environment—climate, altitude, tree type—located only in the handful of specific places where Urquhart found them fuels the worldwide effort to preserve what is left of forests in the reserves the Mexican government set aside for the butterflies beginning in the decade after Urquhart announced his discoveries.

The sun is setting as Carlos Juarez and I wind out of a valley that is reminiscent of Switzerland, verdant and sprinkled with dairy cows. We climb the last steep few kilometers into Angangueo, past mine tailings and the defunct mills where the gold was extracted from the rich ore. A carnival is setting up in the plaza between the two churches ("one for the rich, one for the poor," says my guide before he heads back to Morelia). Monarch images are ubiquitous: on the street signs, decorating the taxis, for sale as key chains and napkin holders, as hotel names. The old mining camp ekes out a living as a jumping-off point for Monarch tourists. I'm here to meet José Luis Alvarez Alcalá and Ed Rashin (the desperados), and to learn about their reforestation work. The two of them operate the nonprofit La Cruz Habitat Protection Project—a seemingly quixotic effort to preserve the Monarch's winter homeland by providing alternative sources of wood to the local population, people who depend on the forest for heating, cooking, and revenue.

As I walk down the main street—the only commercial street—
toward my hotel, a tired-looking Ford Explorer with a cracked wind-
shield pulls up next to me and stops. "Peter?" asks the guy riding
shotgun. It's Ed and José Luis. I get in the back seat and the Explorer
crawls back up the hill toward the plaza. Angangueo reminds me of
Nevada mining camps where I've lived—places like Silver City and
Dayton—where the glory of the rich old days is faded, leaving a legacy enjoyed at a slow pace by those who inherit the mined-out towns.
And Ed and José Luis remind me of a couple of grizzled Nevada desert rats. As soon as I am in the car, the conversation between them
resumes, banter about their passports (both are dual U.S. and Mexican citizens) and escapades they've experienced at the border when
they've neglected to keep their documents up to date. I feel as if I've
walked into a buddy road movie.

"You've got cow shit on your boots," Ed complains to José Luis
when we get out of the Explorer, "and now you've got it in my
truck."

"I did not step in cow shit," José Luis objects.

"You did. Look at your boots."

José Luis shows off the bottom of his left boot. It's clean. "See?
Nothing," he says.

"Look at the other," Ed instructs him.

José Luis turns up the sole of his other boot and, indeed, there's
manure pressed into its treads. He looks slightly sheepish, shrugs,
and doesn't apologize. Ed doesn't care about the lack of an apology;
he's just satisfied to be vindicated. For a dozen years these two have
been prowling the back roads of Michoacán together; their bickering
is so natural it sounds scripted.

We adjourn to Simon's restaurant in the plaza, a cantina where
the exquisite fresh grilled trout with garlic can be had for about five
bucks, and dessert is a butterfly-shaped tart. José Luis tells me about
the old Spanish hacienda where he lives, down near Morelia—a place
with enough land around it to nurture the close to one million tree

saplings he's now raising each year, most of them destined to be given away to landowners living just below the Monarch sanctuaries.

"I used to grow three million trees," he tells me, "and sell them to the Mexican government." But he quit that business because he felt the government mistreated the trees when they transported them, and they transplanted them to the wrong new homes. "They would take the wrong species to the wrong elevation. I decided to stop selling to them." The endemic corruption that plagues business and government in Mexico was another factor. "To get paid, I had to spread it out before I could get my money." Spread it out means the *mordida*, the "bite" that he was forced to pay to officials all along the chain of command, right up to the top. "The big guys had to have their cut before they would sign the checks. I got fed up with it."

In the mid-1990s Ed and José Luis met by coincidence. Ed trained as a forester and was looking for an opportunity to ply his profession in the Third World, and to do some good. José Luis wanted a partner to help him reforest the nearby mountainsides that he watched fast losing their tree cover. The two formed a nonprofit and began raising money in order to grow and give away trees. Under their model, they choose landowners they are convinced will nourish the trees and value them; they give these landowners the saplings at no cost, along with specific training and instruction in the care and feeding of the growing trees. The concept is disarmingly simple: When local landowners can be taught to appreciate and maintain sustainable forests at elevations below the butterfly sanctuaries, they will not encroach on the Monarch reserves for their firewood and other timber needs. Yet even if the two pioneers are wildly successful with their efforts to reforest the lowlands, the Monarchs' forests still face devastation from the organized gangs of loggers illegally felling and removing commercial-grade timber from protected zones.

Neither Ed nor José Luis entered the reforesting business motivated by their concern for the Monarchs; they were worried about disappearing forests. They saw forests being cleared for marginal farming operations and sought to convince policy makers and landowners that the return on the farmers' investments would be better with wood than corn and oats—with the added value of denuded landscapes refilling with towering conifers and a consequently refreshed water table. It was only later that they developed the focused strategy of conserving Monarch habitat by reforesting the neighborhoods surrounding the monarch grounds.

It appears to be such a Sisyphean struggle, literally pushing trees up hills to plant them in the face of perpetual illegal harvests, but José Luis is sanguine. "I think in these twelve years I've put a pretty good dent in it," he says, and he and Ed are not alone. The Mexican government continues to plant trees, as do other groups of reforesters. "I've got forests where they're thinning now, extracting wood. They're making money." Why go up to the overwintering grounds of the Monarchs, he repeats the strategy, if you can get the wood you need in your backyard? "I'm a very practical guy. These people need a practical solution, and an easy solution. It's been very successful. We've transformed thousands of acres of farmlands back into forests." In addition, he's convinced the reforesting is changing a local culture that was set on a wrong course by modernity. "These people are forest people, they have the forests running in their blood. They've lived here for thousands of years in harmony with the forests. All of a sudden they're bombarded by all these new concepts of dressing and eating." He blames television. "Something happened to their minds. They started consuming this shit, and they started polluting the rivers, they started throwing trash. I remember when I was going to high school in Mexico," José Luis is from the border city Juárez, "all the towns were clean. There was no plastic. You could get a soda pop, but basically everybody had fruit drinks. There was none of this crap in the stores, which is just all junk food." He says once the local inhabitants plant trees, they start to fall back in love with the forests and their lives change. "It's awakening people."

"You must feel awfully good about this," I suggest.

His eyes literally twinkle, and he smiles and agrees, "Well, yes. Yes!"

The trees Ed and José Luis give away cost about 50 U.S. cents apiece to raise and transport; in addition to the donations that keep the nonprofit able to give trees to impoverished property owners, José Luis Alvarez Alcalá helps keep himself going by selling other trees he raises on the hacienda nursery to those able to afford to invest in their land. It's money that helps him to support a hobby he and I share: he likes old cars. Parked at the hacienda is an old Citroën 2CV, just like the one I bounced around in Paris when I lived along the Seine. I tell him about the London black cab—an Austin FX4— that I brought back from England, and he tells me if I ever want to sell my taxi, he'll buy it. I reminisce about my dream car, a Citroën Traction, and about how I missed out on securing one I found for sale in Bonn. "You want to buy one? I can find one for you," he says authoritatively. José Luis combines his do-gooder instincts with the business sense of a seasoned horse trader.

"I've never been a butterfly aficionado," says Ed. He's eating his second butterfly cake of the evening as we talk at Simon's. "What appealed to me was the rare forest." The oyamel fir trees that the Monarchs prefer for their winter perch are Ice Age relicts, he tells me between bites of the sweet butterfly. During the ice ages, the boreal forests in North America extended down to Michoacán. The glaciers pushed the climate south. The oyamel firs were not just at the tops of the mountains, at thirteen thousand feet. They extended down into the valleys, to places like where we were eating, at nine thousand feet. As the glaciers receded, the boreal forests too receded, up to the highest elevations, where they continue to thrive today—except where they are devastated by clear-cutting poachers.

A more tropical ecosystem, the one that exists today, formed at the lower elevations.

"To think that we can re-create what God created—that forest ecosystem—by planting a few trees here and there, is absurd." He states the philosophy behind the La Cruz Habitat Protection Project. "We know that people use wood." Absent the illegal commercial logging, the per capita firewood consumption is about two cubic meters of firewood a year. That's equivalent to one full-grown pine tree for every person per year, and there are one hundred thousand people living within reach of the Monarch reserves. "Even if you could stop the illegal logging, the demand for wood is not going to go away. Our strategy is to get these people to reforest their own parcels of land down here, down below where the butterflies spend the winter, to create alternative sites for food harvesting." That, he is convinced, will take the pressure off the natural forests. "Leave the natural forests alone, but give them an alternative. Don't just say, 'We're going to build a wall around it. You can't cut wood anymore.'" No one was converting farmland back into forests before the two of them started their project, Ed and José Luis tell me. Wood, they insist, is a better crop than corn and oats for the steep terrain, the cold, and type of soil in the region, and planting trees helps stem erosion, improving the adjacent land not reforested for use growing food crops.

Initially, even though the two were giving away the trees, there was resistance from the farmers. "Their whole mentality," says Ed, "was grow corn and mill it to make tortillas, and grow oats so the animals have something to eat." Ed feigns the dumbfounded response of a farmer: "Use my land to plant pine trees?" The first to take a chance on trees were really brave, he says; their neighbors thought they were crazy. Most of the landowners are not subsistence farmers, they have day jobs or their children send them money. They do not need the land to grow their food in order to survive, and if they wait a dozen years or more, thinned trees provide substantive cash: as much as $4,000 a hectare. "They all want to leave something for their children," says José Luis. "They know that the corn is no good, they know that oats are no good. The trees are a savings account."

The commercial timber poaching is a distinctly different problem from the ma-and-pa wood harvesters. "They're organized," says José Luis in a sad voice. "They have cell phones and guns. They just go in and they outgun or they frighten these people, and they load up the trucks."

The Mexican government claims to be in hot pursuit of the timber poachers. In late 2007 President Calderón, his army already extended across the country, fighting drug traffickers and corruption (and some of those soldiers undoubtedly are engaged in drug trafficking and corruption, so rife is the corruption in Mexico), announced a new multimillion-dollar campaign to protect the Monarchs' forests. "It is possible to take care of the environment and at the same time promote development," he told reporters.[13] But a few months later, geographer Daniel Slayback published photographs taken by the Ikonos satellite that he says showed "wholesale clear-cutting," illegal logging deep inside the government-protected Monarch grounds.[14] Nonetheless, just a few months after the photographs were distributed, the Mexican government announced success against the thieves. Environment Secretary Juan Elvira Quesada insisted illegal logging diminished 80 percent in the year ending April 2008, because his department was enforcing a "zero tolerance" policy against poachers.[15]

"They've been saying that forever," complains José Luis. "It's still going on."

"How many trucks did we see coming down today?" asks Ed.

"We saw trucks," confirms José Luis, "but I don't know if they were illegal or legal. But illegal logging is still going on. There are people doing it on horses, too. They'll come down every day with two trees. That's bad, too. It's not the huge trucks, but it's an easy way to make a living."

The illegal trees dragged behind horses are worth about five U.S. dollars each, in a country where five dollars a day is a typical minimal wage.

"The organized guys are selling the timber to big lumber mills that are protected," says José Luis, his voice resigned to the facts of contemporary Mexican life. "They bought off the police and whoever may be the other officials. They slice them up into boards and beams. They load the big lorries. The next day they're in Mexico City; it's disappeared with illegal papers." He puts supply and demand into perspective. "Think of this. You have the biggest city in the world, that has a huge appetite for natural resources, and it's only a three-hour drive from here." He says the government has lost control of the forests to *La Familia* and *Zeta*, crime syndicates operating throughout Michoacán, fighting for control of drug trafficking, people smuggling, timber poaching—whatever sector of the economy they can garner control of, and hence revenue.

Now that the Monarch grounds are a UNESCO World Heritage site, publicity may force the government to increase security in the forests. If the security forces are not corrupted, and that in Mexico is a big if, illegal commercial logging may wane. Meanwhile, some local residents are operating vigilante groups, arming themselves and confronting the pirates. Logging trucks have been burned and loggers run off into the woods after exchanges of gunfire.

But as is always the case with news events, the deforestation story has many sides. The lands in question were distributed following the Mexican revolution and they are held in common by the local communities, known in Mexico as *ejidos*. When the Mexican government decreed that the Monarch nesting grounds were untouchable, some of the *ejidos*—with long traditions of making their livings from wood—responded by clear-cutting their own forests and pocketing the revenue earned. Their attitude was: if you say we can't use it, no one can use it. This is short-sighted and selfish, but perhaps understandable, especially in a region oppressed with poverty. Other communities were aware of the ongoing value of their wooded lands. Today the contrast is stark and easy to see on the mountainsides. Some *ejido* property lines coexist with tree lines, on one side a lush forest, on the other side scrub where trees formerly stood. The land is so fertile, reforestation can occur relatively quickly, and some *ejidos* who clear-cut their land are now aware of their error and are busy planting trees.

The damage is devastating; swaths of forests have been clear-cut, the valuable wood harvested. At lower elevations more woods have been cleared for farmland. Yet at the rate Ed and José Luis are planting, they are convinced enough of the trees they send out to be planted will survive to eventually satisfy the legal wood needs of the communities surrounding the Monarchs.

The church bells peal in the plaza, Ed finishes his second butterfly cake, and we leave Simon's cantina for La Margarita, where we're staying, and an early call the next morning for a trip up to the highlands.

Before we go to our rooms, José Luis wants me to know that the dangers in his philanthropic business are real. Informants tell him that he's on a kidnap list compiled by the illegal loggers. "If they get some of their people taken to jail, they could get one of us, and then swap us for one of their people." He shrugs. "They know who I am. I've never had any problems with them." He knows who they are, too. And he's encountered them in the woods. "But I've been with people that know them. I've been protected by people that know of their activities, and that are friends with them." It is a small, tight-knit community living adjacent to the Monarch grounds. "Everybody knows each other here. I've been very lucky and protected the times that I've encountered them." The next morning I would see evidence of the divergent elements of the community cooperating.

"Am I concerned about it?" José Luis mulls over my question when I ask him if he is worried about the kidnapping threats. "I don't think about it too much. I just try to do my job." That job includes not just raising and delivering the saplings, but teaching farmers how to care for the trees and monitoring the success of the operation for reports that the project's donors require. "I don't feel I'm a problem for them," he says about the poachers. He smiles. "*Au contraire.* I'm basically their future." He laughs and explains that he's planting trees for their sons to poach.

Despite his jocular attitude, attacks occur. A credible Michoacán source intimately involved in habitat preservation told me, for example, of a visiting environmentalist who shot video of passing trucks hauling illegal logs. The truck driver saw the camera, stopped, and waited. Later he grabbed a forester who was working with the environmentalist, as the forester was coming off the mountain. He beat him severely, and stole his mobile telephone, his money, and his truck. After the beating and the theft, he told the forester, "We're going back and I want that fucking film." Remember, the forester did not make the video. But he was a handy target to grab and use as a tool to extract the pictures from the hands of the environmentalist. The attack worked; the video was surrendered to the logger. A sense of the fear lurking in the Monarch grounds can be measured by the fact that the source who told me the story only did so with the stipulation that I not reveal his or her identity. As for the forester who was beaten, "He was scared shitless." For months he avoided the reserve because the illegal logger who beat him threatened worse if the forester returned to his job site.

The story doesn't surprise José Luis. He sees the illegal loggers often enjoying impunity for their actions. "They've bought protection. They have guns, they have cell phones, and they have good trucks. They know where they are going to cut, and they know where they are going to sell. Everything is organized." He is convinced the few authorities assigned to protect the trees are desperately afraid of the illegal loggers. "They've been taken hostage and had the shit beat out of them. They're making very little money. They don't carry guns. What would you do in their place?"

The next morning dawns October cold at nine thousand feet, but not cold enough for La Margarita to stock wood for the fireplaces in our rooms. Of course La Margarita is adorned with the obligatory Monarch painted on its façade, this one lighting on a flower. Birds sing, cocks crow, as the old mining town wakes up. José Luis is already en route back to his hacienda to tend to his trees. Ed Rashin and I eat beans and tortillas, tropical fruit and fresh orange juice, fuel to get us through a day in the highlands checking the status of trees planted a month ago and a year ago. We climb into the old Explorer and head for the San Cristobal indigenous community, where we're going to pick up the elected political leader—essentially the mayor—and check on trees in San Cristobal's common lands below the butterfly reserves. But just before we get to Andrian Garcia Angeles's house, we come upon a signpost announcing, "*Puesto de control militar*," and we're pulled over by a soldier waving a red flag at us at an army checkpoint. We're ushered out of the Explorer, and forced to wait while soldiers search it thoroughly. They say they're looking for weapons and chain saws.

We're late when we get to Mayor Garcia's place, but he understands, he's accustomed to the checkpoints. A smiling young man, wearing a red pullover, slacks, and flashy white shoes that look too dressy for a hike, he climbs into the Explorer and he gives me his business card. *Los Hijos de Chava*, it reads, *Grupo Banda*. He's not just the mayor, he plays electric bass and saxophone in a San Cristobal dance band. We pass sawmills as we drive up the steep track toward the Monarch reserves and the San Cristobal forest-in-progress.

We turn off the paved road and Ed worries over the Explorer as he slips the automatic into low gear. "I hope this truck doesn't overheat. It's been giving me some trouble." The road gets steeper, and it gets muddy. The automatic is slipping. Ed pushes it along and we get to a rise where he stops to let it cool. We're near the border of lands belonging to the *ejido* El Paso and San Cristobal. El Paso resisted slash-and-burn logging, and its lands are lush with mature trees. The community is famous for managing its forest in a sustainable manner: the woods thrive and the *ejido* members share consequential revenue from commercial sales of timber. San Cristobal was thoroughly logged; its lands are scrub covered, with only a few tall conifers rising from the brush.

Ed puts the Explorer into drive and we proceed. Ahead the track is not just muddy, it's rutted, and the ruts are water filled from a recent rain. The ruts are deep, and when we hit them the Explorer gives up the fight. It's not just mired in the mud; the overheated transmission quits, refusing to even spin the wheels. We are at about ten thousand feet, and far from help.

We get out of the stuck truck and look at our impossible plight. The Explorer needs a tow truck. The mayor, his fancy white loafers now slopped with mud, takes out his mobile phone. Amazing: he grabs a cell signal and calls the El Paso *ejido*. El Paso fields a patrol to protect its forest. Perhaps they can send help.

While we wait for an answer, there is movement on the rise above us. Two horses. Two horses hauling loads of timber, about ten poles hanging off the backs of each horse and dragging in the mud, each pole a good thirty feet in length. Poachers? No question, according to my guides, but the mayor is in no position to question them. We're stuck. They join us surveying our mess, one of them casually hanging onto a long-handled axe slung over his shoulder, a subtle smile on his weathered lips. While we talk over the possibilities—could their horses pull us out?—footsteps approach from below. Three more men with axes are hiking up the mountain, obviously in search of wood. They stop and join the inspection. Few words are exchanged. The ironic scene speaks for itself. The hunter has become if not the hunted, then at least seeking help from his prey.

Before long a rope appears. It is secured to the front of the Explorer, and the mayor, along with five poachers trespassing on his community's land, grab a hold of it and pull. Ed pushes the gas pedal down. They yank and dig their feet into the mud. Slowly the mud yields the tires, and the Explorer eases out of the goo and onto dry road. The thieves/rescuers unhook the rope. We all shake hands. The horses drag the freshly harvested logs down toward the saw-mills near the mayor's house. The three axe-wielders in search of their day's wood continue their trudge on up the mountain. And the mayor asks no questions, requests no permits for inspection. It is a pragmatic trade-off.

"I am angry," Mayor Garcia says about the poaching, "when I think about all the work we've done to reforest." Because the five we encountered help us, he ignores their activities. But generally, when he finds individual trespassers felling San Cristobal's timber, "I take their axes away." When he comes upon commercial poachers, he calls the authorities. The risk is too great for him to confront them alone. "If they come up in trucks, they're armed."

The road and the Ford cooperate, and we manage to get the few kilometers farther along which brings us to San Cristobal's hopes for a renewed forest. Ed takes out his notebook and the three of us walk along through the scrub, finding and noting yearlings, tiny sprouts of pine, an inch or two high, struggling to survive and grow into trees.

Ed points to the sprouts with pride. But to my eyes his work is hard to fathom: tiny sprouts amid vast acreage, and even if the sprouts mature, it's acreage crawling with insatiable poachers such as those who just rescued us. "Keep in mind," Ed says, his Texas drawl still noticeable, sounding both confident and calm, "we're just adding to legal harvesting, which is about one hundred thousand commercially mature trees a year." It takes fifteen to twenty years for a pine to mature around the butterfly reserves. "Last year we planted seven hundred and fifty thousand trees." He figures about a third of them will survive. "That's two hundred and fifty thousand trees!" He's buoyant. If La Cruz Habitat Protection Project can keep such a ratio going year after year in the communities surrounding the Monarch grounds, their work will result in more than enough trees to meet the legal requirements of the populace living adjacent to the forests protected for the Monarchs. "If you think about the numbers, it's positive. I don't think that's overly optimistic. We are creating an alternative source for future wood harvesting." In addition, he says, in just a few years, the massive tree planting restores water balance in the soil. Already plots Ed and José Luis planted in the mid-1990s are thick with maturing trees ready for harvest.

Despite his optimism, as we head back to the Explorer, Ed spots a fresh cut. It is a severe loss. "This is the stump of about a fifteen-year-old tree," Ed says, counting the rings. "It was cut very recently, I would say within the last week by illegal wood cutters. They were stealing wood. Wood rustling, motivated by greed or necessity. Ignorance is not a factor."

The reforesting efforts in the Monarch overwintering grounds are worthy even absent the needs of the butterflies. Creating a sustainable supply of firewood and commercial-grade timber for those living in marginal conditions around the Monarchs is both good for their meager pocketbooks and beneficial for a healthy environment. A vibrant forest means biodiversity and a sustainable water table. But—despite the beliefs of the late Dr. Urquhart and the entomologists who continue his work since he tagged and followed Monarchs from Canada to Mexico—the migrating Monarchs may not need the oyamel forests for their survival. Such a suggestion is blasphemy to believers in the Urquhart-based theories, but one that Dr. David Bray, professor of environmental studies at Florida International University, considers. Bray specializes in researching community forest management, and Mexico is one of his beats. In the late 1990s he wrote that "it is not entirely clear that the butterflies will pass winter only at this altitude, in this kind of forest," referring to the reserves in the Sierra Madre. He noted that the eucalyptus trees favored by Monarchs in California suggest "if the oyamel fir forest were to be extinguished, there appears to be some evidence that the Monarchs could adapt to some other altitude, on some other trees even, as one daring biologist ventured to me privately, on artificial tree limbs!"[16] Not that Bray condones denuding the Sierra Madre: on the contrary.

I found Dr. Bray in his office on the crowded campus of Florida International University, on the far east side of Miami, almost in the Everglades. He is quick to share his contacts and ready to talk Monarchs and forests. "Lincoln Brower will say that what's in danger here is the migratory phenomenon." Dr. Lincoln Brower is a zoology professor at Sweet Briar College in Virginia, a scholar whose long career has been spent studying butterflies, and chasing Monarchs to learn about their migratory behavior and overwintering habits. He is the scientific heir to Fred Urquhart, following up on Dr. Urquhart's studies for half a century and working to protect what he calls on his Web site "the Monarchs' fragile and disappearing habitat." But Dr. Bray, with an easy smile, isn't ready to accept that the Monarch habitat is all that fragile and disappearing, and it is a habitat that he's prowled thoroughly.

"His argument," anthropologist Bray says about zoologist Brower, "is that there is a unique, co-evolutionary, synergistic relationship between the butterflies and this particular place." He's speaking of the Sierra Madre oyamel fir forests. Bray isn't convinced. "There may well be other overwintering grounds that have not been discovered yet." And if the forests are cut down, he says, the butterflies may go somewhere else and thrive. "The monarchs I saw in Santa Cruz," he says, giving a California example of adaptation, "were overwintering on eucalyptus trees, which is an exotic. Nature is pretty resilient and pretty adaptive."

"You mean," I ask him, "we can cut down all those trees and the monarchs will simply winter happily somewhere else on a different type of tree?"

He hesitates. "I'm not an ecologist, so I have to be careful about saying things like that, but I think that can be one extreme conclusion." He certainly does not advocate destroying the forests or forcing the Monarchs from the Sierra Madre. "There are lots of good reasons for trying to preserve the butterflies where they are. They have been coming there for a very long time. It's a source of income for the community. It's a nice thing." He just questions the theory that the oyamel-Monarch relationship is unique to the survival of a migrating Monarch. But he's happy that the oyamel forests benefit from worldwide concern for the butterflies.

Lincoln Brower has searched the terrain around the Michoacán butterflies in low-flying, slow-moving aircraft, hunting for other Monarch colonies. "We looked and looked and looked, and the only sites we found were ones that have been known about for years. Lots of other people have looked in other regions and haven't found them. That really surprised me because it seems like there is a lot of habitat that ought to be able to support the butterflies." Brower told me that the fact that he's been able to locate no other colonies reinforces his conviction that the migrating butterflies need the specific conditions of the forests where they overwinter. "I think that it's a combination of altitude, the oyamel forest, and cool moisture-laden air." The moisture in the air prevents the Monarchs from desiccating, and the temperature is high enough that the butterflies don't freeze to death, but it's low enough so that they can essentially hibernate in order to preserve their energy for the spring when they mate and fly north.

The Monarch is an adaptive and thriving butterfly. None of the experts studying it that I encountered suggest it is in danger of becoming extinct. What is threatened by deforestation in Michoacán is the specific migration of the cohort of butterflies that makes the multi-generational trip from northeast North America to Mexico. Deforestation of the overwintering grounds is not the only challenge facing the Monarchs. They need milkweed for their larvae to feed on, and nectar-filled flowers to fuel their long flights, and the milkweed supplies the poison Monarchs employ to defend themselves. Cityscapes void of green space, suburbs plagued with lawns treated with chemicals that kill insects and all the plants but grass, factory farms that wipe out weeds with herbicides—these are North American dangers that plague the Monarch migration.

"At some point, the fabric starts to unravel." Dr. Brower sees the Monarch story not just as biology but as an element benefiting our quality of life. "People ask me, 'What's the difference whether we have a Monarch migration or not?' I say, 'Why do we care about the *Mona Lisa* or classical music?' We care because it is a cultural treasure. We have to start viewing the natural world as a cultural treasure."[17]

Mexico-based economics professor David Barkin, at the Universidad Autonoma Metropolitana–Xochilmilco in Mexico City, agrees with David Bray that the oyamel forests may not be a crucial destination for the migrating Monarchs' survival, just a convenient one, and a replaceable one. His more immediate concern is the economic well-being of the marginal peasant communities surrounding the Monarch overwintering grounds.

"Natural creatures will do everything that's necessary to keep themselves alive," economist Barkin points out when we talk, and it's clear he includes humans in that category. "One of the peculiar things that I know about the Monarchs that people in Mexico don't want to believe is that about forty, fifty years ago—for reasons that I don't know and I haven't found anyone who does know—a colony of the Monarchs actually set up living quarters in the Sierra Maestra of Cuba. People can't explain to me how they got there."

In fact, Lincoln Brower has an explanation. He and his researchers cite winds that at times blow Mexico-bound migrating Monarchs off course, and he says his studies show the Cuba-destined Monarchs go native: they mate with indigenous Cuban Monarchs and stay on the island. They do not head north to procreate.[18]

Although he is an economist, Dr. Barkin takes the liberty of suggesting that the Cuban colony raises questions about the importance of the Mexican oyamel forests to the survival of the migrating Monarchs. He believes the Monarchs are extraordinarily adaptable to the changing conditions and find new nesting places to replace those lost to loggers. Not that he dismisses the magic of the Monarchs' return to Mexico. "I think that's a very exciting and a very charismatic characteristic of the Monarch butterflies. But I don't think that means that they must stay there, that they don't have any adaptability to other kinds of areas."

David Barkin disputes the goal pursued by Lincoln Brower and others—especially the World Wildlife Fund—to set aside vast acreage in favor of the Monarchs at the expense of *campesinos* who cohabitated with the Monarchs since long before Fred Urquhart tracked them from Canada to their southern terminus. "I think it was a romantic notion," Barkin says about Brower's belief that Monarchs can only overwinter in the remaining oyamels, "and he wanted to make sure the forest on the mountaintops was protected and saved."

"That's not necessarily bad," I offer, "if the result is a saved forest."

"It depends on who you are." Economist Barkin is ready with a hierarchical answer: People trump insects. "Should we be in the business of making a decision about a particular species in favor of a human colony?"

"That argument is a false argument," Brower counters. "The argument is that if they don't cut down those forests, the local people are all going to starve to death. The fact is that they are all going to be much worse off if they do cut down that forest than if they don't. If you do what José and Ed are doing and develop a pine forest at lower altitude, you can have your cake and eat it, too. They're so damned disorganized in Mexico, they can't seem to get a sustainable forestry industry going in that area."

"My solution would be to put a great deal more emphasis on self-management of the reserves by the communities themselves," is economist Barkin's answer. His vision includes resorts and other tourist accommodations owned and operated by the local com- munities rather than international interests cordoning off the land from those who have used it for generations. Not that he expects the peasants and indigenous people of the region to regain control of their lands. "I'm not optimistic. I think the World Wildlife Fund is one of the greatest enemies of the Monarch butterfly, and contin- ues to be so." The WWF, along with other international conservation groups, pressured the Mexican government to expand the off-limits mountaintops, in return for relatively token cash payments to the nearby residents who owned the land and used the wood on it for fuel and as a cash-generating resource. "The notion that if you give the peasant communities small amounts of money—what are called payments for environmental services—then the people will behave responsibly, is just absurd, a travesty," says Barkin. "The amounts of money involved are so small that they are not a viable alternative to develop a meaningful economy. As long as you have that problem, it doesn't seem to me that you can expect these people to behave differently than people elsewhere."

In other words, poverty transcends concern about butterflies, and the forests will suffer from pragmatic need.

"There's the rub, as Shakespeare would have said," concludes David Barkin.

"They're not paying them enough," agrees Brower, while insisting the butterfly grounds must be protected. "David Barkin pits the environment against people's well-being, which is a really good excuse to do nothing about protecting the environment. The forests," he tells me, "need a steady, savvy management hand," which he imagines is impossible to find among the peasants and indigenous communities that surround the Monarchs' dwindling Mexican turf. Instead the status quo is a patchwork of poor forest management, inadequate policing, criminal clear-cutting, subsistence wood poaching, and a collection of Monarch advocates working, if not at cross-purposes, then clearly with a distinct lack of adequate coordination of their varied strategies.

"It pisses me off," Dr. Brower's voice is rising, he's no longer thinking only about his Monarchs and their forest. "I think humanity is a disaster for this planet."

While traveling back to California from my trip to the Monarch grounds, I stopped off in Tlaquepaque, on the outskirts of Guadalajara. My wife and I decided a couple of days' vacation would be appropriate, and we relaxed at a resort hotel. After we packed for the flight home, I sat poolside for a few lingering minutes before the rush of taxis and airplanes. *Señoritas* were singing on the juke-box about *corazón* and *alma* and *quizas mañana*. Trumpets were lamenting between choruses. I spotted a Monarch fluttering from flower to flower in the garden—an early scout, I imagine, a fellow traveler—stopping off in Jalisco en route to Michoacán, its bright orange enclosed in its black borders reminding me of Ed and José Luis, and the endangered forests at its destination.

Chapter Six

IN PURSUIT OF THE WORLD'S MOST WANTED BUTTERFLY SMUGGLER

MY MOBILE PHONE RANG WHILE I WAS WASHING MY FACE. "UNKNOWN caller" flashed on the screen, and by the time I picked it up the recording already was in progress. "This is a prepaid call," the voice announced. "To accept this call, press five."

"Telemarketers!" I cursed, hung up the phone, and rinsed off the suds.

The next day, at about the same time, the phone rang again. Once more it was an "unknown caller," but this time I punched it on as the message started. "This is a call from a federal prison," the voice told me. And then again the instruction, "This is a prepaid call. To accept this call, press five." I quickly pressed five.

"Hello," I said.

An accented "Hello" came back at me, and then, "I receive your letter." The clumsy English and thick Japanese accent matched the voice on the Skype Internet wiretaps I'd listened to just days before. A call from a federal prison? I knew immediately that on the line with me from the Metropolitan Detention Center in Los Angeles was Hisayoshi Kojima, the self-proclaimed "world's most wanted butterfly smuggler."

It was U.S. Fish and Wildlife Special Agent Ed Newcomer who first introduced me to Yoshi by intriguing me with the cloak-and-dagger story that had finally put the smuggler out of business (at least for two years). Newcomer works from an office that belies the romantic sound of his agency—Fish and Wildlife. It's in a nondescript Los Angeles sprawl strip mall ("Turn left at the oil refinery," he tells me), and it's marked only with a small generic-looking sign reading OFFICE OF LAW ENFORCEMENT ("We don't want to call attention to ourselves").

Agent Newcomer ("Call me Ed") does not look the part of a mean cop. He's a charming fellow, quick to smile. I noticed his bright eyes first as he came to greet me in the lobby, a lobby protected from the rest of the Fish and Wildlife offices by a wide bulletproof window. Newcomer's eyes caught and engaged mine as soon as we met, and he stayed focused on me as we talked in his office. His desk was covered with stacks of papers, and every available open space was filled with memorabilia: stuffed birds and award plaques and family photographs.

I ask Newcomer to start at the beginning and tell me how he managed to land the "world's most wanted butterfly smuggler," and as he begins he punctuates his story with the long and complicated scientific names of butterflies and the acronyms of international treaties. I make it clear to him that this is all new territory to me, that I am no butterfly expert. He nods. "When I first got this case, like you, my butterfly experience probably ended at about thirteen years old and it was whatever I caught last in my net. My idea of insects was," he is smiling now, this federal agent sworn to protect fish and wildlife, "I'd as soon step on them as anything else and it wasn't a huge priority for me as a special agent. I was fairly new to the service at that time. I wasn't real anxious to jump off onto a butterfly smuggling case." He thought the drama and heroism were elsewhere. "I wanted something like tigers or elephant ivory, right? So I was very reluctant to get into it and I wasn't very excited about it."

But then Newcomer started cramming for the assignment, studying the butterflies known as CITES Appendix I and Appendix II animals. CITES stands for the Convention on International Trade in Endangered Species of Wild Fauna and Flora. The idea of the agreement is for the international community to work together preventing international trade in animals and plants if such trade threatens the survival of the species being bought and sold. CITES regulates more than thirty thousand species, including butterflies, and each of the 171 nations signatory to the agreement passes its own enforcement laws, a complex bureaucracy that results in a Byzantine pile of rules, regulations, and laws, along with the penalties for violating them. Yoshi Kojima was caught trading in CITES Appendix I and Appendix II insects. Appendix I lists the most endangered animals and plants in the world. These are species on the verge of extinction, and almost all trade in Appendix I species is prohibited. Appendix II species are not quite as vulnerable, but trade is monitored, and a permit is mandatory for legal exportation and importation of a collected Appendix II animal or plant out of or into the United States and the other countries that agreed to the terms of the treaty.

After getting to know the endangered and threatened butterflies on the lists, Ed Newcomer stopped stepping on bugs. "I really started to think if we're at this point in our history as human beings where insects, one of the most common living organisms aside from the microscopic, are becoming extinct and endangered, what does that say about our conservation ethic and our conservation efforts?" His gaze remains steady, and his enthusiasm and dedication are convincing as he explains his epiphany. "I started to get a little more motivated from that perspective and I also thought most likely the real culprit here is habitat loss as opposed to individual poachers." The butterflies are endangered and threatened not just because Yoshi and gangs of his ilk are catching them and killing them to sell to collectors, but because we all are destroying the places they live. "What's going on with the mammals and the bigger animals that rely on that same habitat?" Newcomer asks. "Certainly they're in more trouble. So I got more motivated about really going at butterflies a hundred percent."

Butterflies grabbed Ed Newcomer and me from different perspectives: for him, as a cop; for me, following the scene at the Bellingham bookstore, as a reporter. Protecting animals is a dream job for Newcomer, and when he talks about how he chose his career he smiles through the entire story. "As a kid I got bullied a lot. I just was obsessed with the idea of being a good guy, and I found out you could be a cop who protected wildlife. Wildlife can't call 911. They really can't defend themselves when you can shoot them from three hundred yards away with a high-powered rifle. What more noble profession could a person have? I didn't articulate it that way when I was a kid, but that's how I felt." Growing up, little Ed would sit in the family's 1965 Plymouth station wagon, put a lantern with a flashing red light his mother gave him on the car's roof, and pretend he was a policeman. He went to law school and bided his time as a prosecutor, waiting for a chance to compete for a job as an agent. It's a rare opportunity; there are only a couple of hundred Fish and Wildlife special agents nationwide. Once he finally earned his badge and gun, he became almost too happy with his work. "You go home at night and there's no question about it, you're the white hat. I actually have to be very careful, watch my time and not overwork. Because, you know, to stay married I have to make sure that I'm not at the office all the time or out doing undercover work or creeping around at night in the bushes, because I'd just as soon be doing that."

Yoshi Kojima, the butterfly smuggler, first caught the attention of the Fish and Wildlife Service in 1999 when Special Agent John Mendoza, Newcomer's predecessor, started a file on him after he received several complaints that Yoshi was illegally grabbing protected Swallowtail butterflies from federal lands in Texas and selling them in Japan. Swallowtails are especially favored by collectors because of their dramatic hind wings, wings that taper off into twin tail-like points.

Mendoza alerted fellow agents in the Los Angeles office because Yoshi kept an apartment in L.A. But the trail went cold until springtime in 2003. When butterflies break out of their cocoons in the southern California spring, the Los Angeles Natural History Museum stages its annual Bug Fair. Collectors come to Exposition Park and exhibit their finds; vendors take advantage of the captive audience to trade in bugs. It's a good-time party, attracting thousands of visitors. The Bug Fair is not just for collectors and traders; chefs come and cook insect specialties while spotlighted tarantula feedings enthrall and terrify the crowd. Signs at the Bug Fair mandate that vendors comply with federal laws regarding bug trade, and the museum requires that anyone selling at the fair agree to such rules in writing.

To coincide with the Bug Fair, each year the museum stocks California's largest collection of butterflies in an outdoor pavilion and provides butterfly observers an opportunity to mingle with rare species. It is a perfect spring southern California day when I sit down on a bench in the tennis court–sized enclosure and watch the butterflies fluttering around the flowers—and the children running around trying to catch them. The shadows of their wings cross over my notebook.

These are all farmed butterflies—hatched at the museum from pupae bought from commercial breeders. A couple of butterflies buzz me, dancing in front of my eyes. Others are gliding with grace and ease. Still others look hyperactive as they flap their wings and seem erratic in their journeys—haphazard with no particular goal that I can ascertain—eventually lighting on flowers. One little girl in a red and white sundress and a head full of blonde curls—maybe three or four years old—kneels at a flower and holds out her hand. For an instant and to her delight, a butterfly chooses her. "That's my favorite butterfly over there," announces a little boy in a red T-shirt. It's actually a Luna moth, and with its long tapered hind wings it looks a taste ominous, almost like the Stealth bomber. A monarch lands in a woman's hair and stays long enough for her to pose for pictures.

"Sir, you've got one on your back," a fellow pointing a camera equipped with an extraordinarily long lens calls out to me. I look over my shoulder and there it is, relaxing—its black wings just easing up and down, their tips striped with yellow. "It's a Mourning Cloak," he calls out to me with appreciation, so named, I learn later, because it's dressed in what looks like mostly black. On closer inspection, its wings are more deep burgundy-brown than black, edged with yellow and light blue.

~~~

Just before the 2003 Bug Fair opened, Ed Newcomer was tipped off that Yoshi Kojima would be selling there. Yoshi was living as a legal resident alien in Los Angeles, and it's pretty difficult to live in L.A. without a car. Ed checked in with the Department of Motor Vehicles, obtained a copy of Yoshi's driver's license picture, and went fishing. "I just went to the fair and mingled around and soaked it all in because this was my first real exposure to this trade. There are little kids running around and families that are buying toys and buying fifty-cent beetles that you could probably pick up right outside your back door. And then there are these guys walking around with very sophisticated collection boxes. They're kind of slinking around from table to table and very particular about which tables they go to, and there's a lot of money changing hands not only for butterflies, but for beetles and other types of insects."

Money, butterflies in fancy boxes, a tip that a smuggler might be in the midst of families introducing their children to the insect world—it's not quite James Bond, but close. Special Agent Newcomer went to work looking for Yoshi. Newcomer was working undercover, of course, dressed down in L.A. casual: jeans, a work shirt, and a worn baseball cap. With his young-looking face adorned by a Fu-Manchu mustache and his endearing smile, Newcomer—calling himself Ted Nelson—did not look like a bug cop. He found his prey fast.

"I immediately saw that Yoshi had a table—he was a vendor at the fair, and people were crowding his table." Plenty in that crowd were carrying the fancy wooden boxes that marked them as serious collectors. "I just started loitering at his table and ended up asking some naïve questions. For whatever reason we seemed to hit it off, and at that point I realized that I was going to be the primary undercover contact with Yoshi."

At the 2003 Bug Fair "Ted Nelson" saw no illegal butterflies in Yoshi's display, but Yoshi did show off a live *Dynasties* beetle—illegal to import from its Central America home without a permit—and told Newcomer he could sell it for thousands of dollars in Japan. "Ted Nelson" continued to stroll about the museum grounds and when the weekend fair ended, Yoshi sought him out and gave him a box of mounted legal and common butterflies, adorned with his email address. "This will start your collection," Yoshi told the agent as he presented the colorful array of dead butterflies. Later, as their business relationship developed, Yoshi provided Newcomer with a CD-ROM, marked with a Sharpie, "To Ted Nelson." On the disk were hundred of pictures of protected butterflies.

Newcomer waited a credible few days' interval and then started an email correspondence with Yoshi. The messages were increasingly friendly, and soon Yoshi sent a note suggesting the two discuss a "business arrangement." Newcomer looks gleeful as he remembers the evolving correspondence.

"Isn't that nice when it just falls into your lap," I suggest.

He nods. "It just came out of nowhere," he says about the business offer. Yoshi had already introduced Ed to his Japan-based Web site, where the first butterfly displayed is an *Ornithoptera alexandreae*— the Queen Alexandra's Birdwing, which is on the CITES Appendix I list—so Newcomer figured Yoshi was well worth chasing. It didn't directly offer the *Ornithoptera alexandreae* for sale, but right above the image of the endangered butterfly was a banner announcing that the site accepts PayPal and various credit cards. The message was clear and obvious: this stuff is for sale. Prominently displayed along with the *Ornithoptera alexandreae* was a *Teinopalpus*, which is on the Appendix II list. Newcomer perused the site and concluded, "This was someone who could supply me, or was supplying people, with protected insects."

Long after Yoshi was locked up in federal prison, his bilingual Japanese and fractured English Web site, www.worldinsectnet.com, remained up and active on the Internet. "Quality insect specimens from around the world—livestock and dried," its homepage head-line advertised. Click on "announcements," and Yoshi beckoned with pictures of butterflies and the awkward, "If you interesting flow. Over $100 all shipping free. We are back Los Angeles now." Caterpillars and pupae were displayed alongside the perfectly formed butterflies. And what did he mean by "if interesting flow"? Flow messages to him, or was it a mistake and he meant show?

Ed Newcomer met Yoshi for coffee at a Los Angeles Starbucks, and Yoshi proposed an illegal business deal a few weeks later. But not before he made a passing attempt at engaging in some due diligence regarding "Ted Nelson's" bona fides. He queried Newcomer about his telephone availability: why was he impossible to reach in the eve-nings and on weekends? The real reason was because the agent was using an untraceable phone line installed at the Fish and Wildlife office; when he went home to his wife he was not available. Ed told

Yoshi he enjoyed an elaborate love life with lots of dates and hence was never at home. When the two went out to the Starbucks parking lot, Yoshi looked hard at the license plates on Newcomer's car (expecting to see government numbers?), looked inside the passenger compartment (for a shotgun or a police radio?), and inspected the grill. "There's only one reason to look in the grill," the agent tells me, "and that's for hidden emergency lights."

Satisfied, Yoshi proposed the two start trading insects on eBay. He wanted Newcomer to set up the account and handle the eBay trade. Yoshi would supply the product. Apparently he was intimidated by the technical aspects of eBay procedures and felt he needed a partner. Yoshi offered to supply the insects in return for Ed taking care of the retail sales. They would split the profits. At this point in the negotiations, Yoshi decided to tutor his new partner regarding the risks and how to avoid them, specifically how to avoid U.S. Fish and Wildlife special agents.

"He called us 'fish and wild guys,'" Newcomer tells me, and the smile is broad, "which I loved. Or just fish and wild. That cracked me up. He said, 'You have to watch out for the fish and wild guys.' That's what he always told me. I, of course, feigned ignorance."

Newcomer asked Yoshi who the fish and wild guys were; he said he had never heard of them. He questioned Yoshi about why the cops would be chasing them. How serious could it be? he asked Yoshi, saying after all we're only dealing with butterflies. That's when Yoshi convinced Newcomer that the agent was going to do whatever he could to get the smuggler off the street. Yoshi told him about Special Agent John Mendoza coming to his house in 1999, looking for signs of illegal activity. "He loved to say that Mendoza had a gun and handcuffs. Then he went on to brag that Mendoza was unable to catch him because Yoshi never kept his illegal material at his apartment. Once I heard that Yoshi thought he'd outsmarted a Fish and Wildlife agent, I knew I was never going to let go of him."

The eBay scam was conjured up by Yoshi to ensure that if it were busted, Newcomer, as the front man, would be the fall guy. Nonetheless, Yoshi was incredibly quick to take into his confidence a man he barely knew.

"Why?" I ask Newcomer.

"I don't know, I don't know."

"You've got that smiling face that looks innocent and naïve," I suggest.

"I guess. I don't know. I never was able to figure that out. I mean there were quite a few phone calls between us before we had that first meeting, but yeah, as far as I know he didn't make any real effort to figure out who I was. I played it as I'm new to this. I'm naïve. I don't know anything about it. Which seemed to fit what he was looking for." Newcomer smiles, and then tells me, "There is another possibility." Yoshi may have already been seeing more than a business partner in Newcomer; his romantic fantasies may have clouded his judgment. But that's getting ahead of the tale.

Yoshi instructed Ed Newcomer to start the eBay business with legal butterflies, build up a clientele, and then start offering CITES-protected species. The agent followed the instructions and soon suggested to Yoshi that it was time to start making the big money that they had been talking about—it was time to start offering the illegal butterflies. That's when Yoshi provided the CD-ROM filled with images of rare and expensive species, but still no actual products.

"I kept bugging him," Ed tells me. "So to speak."

In an attempt to speed up the process and build a case against Yoshi, Newcomer began to pollinate the Internet butterfly chat world with suggestions that collectors check out his eBay offerings. On

Insectnet.com, a crossroads for collectors, "Ted Nelson" announced that he was about to go in business on eBay, selling insects. He posted a notice claiming that he was working with a reputable insect supplier in Japan. "If you're interested," Newcomer wrote in his Insectnet.com posting, "please send me an email so I can let you know when our first auction jumps off." The emails expressing interest came in from all over the U.S., and Newcomer took the list of prospective customers to Yoshi.

"I said, 'Hey look, I've already generated some interest. We need to get going on this!' Unfortunately that backfired, and Yoshi was furious. He said, 'What are you doing? You're going to get us caught. You don't know these people. Who knows who they are? You're crazy. I don't want to do this arrangement anymore.' So I thought oh, crap. Here goes my case, right? I just tanked it."

Newcomer left Yoshi alone for a few months, but in early 2004 he began implementing a plan designed to stir the smuggler's competitive spirit, to lure him back into a working relationship. He set up decoy auctions on eBay illustrated with pictures of a box of CITES Appendix II butterflies from another Fish and Wildlife case along with photographs from the CD-ROM Yoshi had given Newcomer as a gift. Fellow agents around the country worked with him, making outrageous bids to ensure that they won the auctions. The result: the illegal butterflies were not distributed into the marketplace, but from the outside it appeared as if business was booming. Newcomer conducted over three dozen of these auctions in his quest for Yoshi, a new twist on the company's famous slogan, "Whatever it is . . . you can get it on eBay." He advertised his eBay auction on Insectnet.com, knowing Yoshi was visiting the site because Yoshi was busy selling beetles via Insect net.com classifieds. "I'm pleased to announce my association with a reputable butterfly collector," said Newcomer's Insectnet.com notices. "Items will be regularly auctioned on eBay. Introductory auctions will start at ridiculously low bids. I know you'll like the product...."

Newcomer snagged Yoshi with the ruse, but it was not the response he anticipated. Yoshi was angry and he sent "Ted Nelson" a note demanding that he stop using his photographs. Meanwhile Yoshi started matching the auctions. Whatever Newcomer offered for sale on eBay, Yoshi posted for sale on his site for a lower price. Newcomer tried another lure. "I wrote to him and said, 'Hey, Yoshi, I don't know why you're so mad at me. I'd much rather be working with you. My supplier's charging me so much money, it's driving me crazy.' And he just didn't bite."

Not only did Yoshi not bite, but in mid-2004 he turned "Ted Nelson" in to a California Fish and Game warden, alleging that "Ted" was trading in CITES butterflies. He sent one last email to "Ted" threatening him with "big trouble," and signed it, "Not your friend, Yoshi."

It was time to secure enough evidence for a conviction. Newcomer assigned a fellow agent in the San Diego office to order a protected butterfly from Yoshi via Insectnet.com. That agent sent Yoshi $137 and received three *Bhutanitis lidderdalei*, Appendix II butterflies native to China—butterflies that require an export permit. The beauties arrived, wings folded neatly, in glassine envelopes, via international Express Mail. Inside the package along with the butterflies was a CN23, a U.S. customs declaration form. Despite the $137 he received, Yoshi identified the butterflies as a gift of zero value. Folded up with the false declaration was an expired and photocopied CITES permit, expired by several years. "Now we had him," Newcomer tells me, "on smuggling, failure to declare, false customs declarations, false labeling, violating the Endangered Species Act. But the problem is you can't indict somebody on a $137 smuggling charge."

The U.S. Attorney is not going to waste the government's time and money for such a minimal offense, and after three years of work, Newcomer wanted Yoshi locked up—not just because of all the time and effort invested in the case, but because he was convinced that Yoshi was a consequential player in the butterfly smuggling business. "He's a bad dude," he says, insisting traffickers like Yoshi need to be forced out of business. But after the three *Bhutanitis lidderdalei* arrived, the trail went dead again for two years. Newcomer was about to close the case—all that effort for nothing—when he received another anonymous tip: Yoshi would be at the 2006 Bug Fair.

"I showed up at the fair, and saw Yoshi. He was running around talking to different dealers. People were flocking to him." Ed bumped into him. "To my surprise he immediately started talking to me, and it was as if we had never had a problem. He asked, 'Are you still selling butterflies?' And I said, 'Oh, yeah, I'm doing great.'"

Now all the gumshoe detective work was about to pay off. Newcomer took Yoshi aside and confided in him. "'Yoshi,' I whispered, 'Some asshole turned me into California Fish and Game a few years ago, but thanks to you, I took your advice on how you dealt with the Fish and Wildlife agent and I didn't keep anything at my house. They came to my house. They checked it out. Didn't find a thing. So I owe it all to you.' He loved it."

Newcomer's undercover identity could not have been more secure. Yoshi thought he had been an anonymous tipster to the state Fish and Game warden, but when that warden played the recording of the phone call to him, Newcomer recognized Yoshi's voice immediately. Now Newcomer was telling Yoshi he had been reported, but managed to avoid arrest. From Yoshi's perspective "Ted Nelson" was one of the gang; and here "Ted" was, thanking Yoshi for teaching him the tricks of the illicit trade and how to avoid arrest.

"It stroked his ego and it let him know that I didn't think he turned me in." Yoshi suggested lunch, and while they ate, they talked butterflies. "I told him the types of species I was selling and that I had

a very unpredictable supplier and that I didn't like him very much, he charged me too much. Of course Yoshi started to bite." Newcomer told Yoshi he had developed a select customer base, that he only sold to customers he knew. Yoshi told him to make a list: whatever he needed, Yoshi said he could procure. He told Newcomer he could secure all the endangered species. Newcomer ticks them off as we sit in his office: *Alexandreae, chikae, Papilo homerus,* and he shakes his head, "These names light up all kinds of lights with me because you just don't see them around, they're not around." The *alexandreae* and *chikae* are indigenous to Papua New Guinea. The *Papilio homerus* is found only in Jamaica.

At this point, Yoshi dropped another gift in Ed's lap. He suggested that once he returned to Japan the two of them keep in touch via Skype, a system that allows for real-time conversations over the Internet, complete with moving pictures of the callers while they talk and document transfers of anything they wish to exchange during their talks, such as photo files. From a police perspective, Skype is a valuable tool because it keeps a record of when and whom you call, and it allows for storage of any electronic files shared during the calls. Agent Newcomer poised a second camera in his office, focused on his computer screen, and he recorded the sound and pictures of the calls that began as soon as Yoshi was back at his Kyoto home. As we talk about the case, he clicks on a PowerPoint presentation in his desktop computer and plays Skype conversations showing Yoshi holding up illegal butterflies that he's offering for sale and describing how he evades international law.

"You can change anything you want to," Yoshi tells "Ted" during one call as he explains how to forge dates and documentation.

"Make it look like before CITES?" asks "Ted." Butterflies documented as collected before the agreement went into effect can be bought and sold.

"Yeah, before CITES," the smuggler confirms to the agent.

On another call "Ted" asks Yoshi if he sells CITES butterflies without permits.

"Yeah," Yoshi tells him, as the call is recorded for evidence, adding the clear explanation "with rare butterflies more making money."

For several months the two of them did business facilitated by Skype calls. The original $137 sale turned into thousands and thousands of dollars worth of merchandise—and by the time of his arrest, Yoshi had offered to sell "Ted" $294,000 worth of endangered and threatened butterflies.

Ed Newcomer is gleeful as he describes collecting the evidence; we are talking just a couple of days after Yoshi agreed to the plea bargain that put him in federal prison for almost two years. "It doesn't get any better than this," he says, "because you've got the audio and the video. He's showing you a butterfly in Japan that's CITES Appendix II. He's telling you he has no permit for it, that it will cost you whatever—$300—and then five days later it arrives in Los Angeles." On the recordings Yoshi incriminates himself repeatedly, confirming that he traffics illegally in protected butterflies and advising "Ted" on business tactics to fool the authorities. Yoshi's voice is recorded not just consummating the sales, but also explaining more tricks of the trade.

On one particular recording, Yoshi's voice comes through the static of Skype, with his heavy Japanese accent saying, "You must be careful there is no evidence. Use cash." Both his voice and his face are recorded as evidence.

"Everyone knows you're the number one smuggler," says "Ted," feeding Yoshi's ego.

"That's true," confirms Yoshi, nodding his head and smiling on the webcam.

I can feel the thrill of the successful hunt as Newcomer shows off his success. "You must have been just jumping up and down in your office, right? You must have been just jumping up and down."

"Yeah," he agrees. "When someone tells you you better get cash so there's no paper trail, that's pretty good." But not good enough. Newcomer wanted Yoshi to return to the U.S. for arrest and conviction. He wanted him locked up in an American prison. He suggested Yoshi come back so that "Ted" could pay him in cash, avoiding bank transfer fees and a paper trail. Meanwhile the butterflies kept coming. "By the time it was all over, we had this huge volume. He had sold me *Papilio hospiton*—endangered, *Papilio alexandrae*—endangered, and *Papilio chikae*—endangered, and promised me *Papilio homerus*, which he never sent. Really beautiful stuff." The dichotomy was not lost on the agent: Yoshi was a criminal, but he did really outstanding work, work of scientific value. Newcomer doubts Yoshi captured the butterflies himself. He figures Yoshi hired poachers to do the deed for him. As pleased as he was to put Yoshi behind bars, Newcomer regrets failing to discover who supplied the precious butterfly product to Yoshi. The Fish and Wildlife Service donated the evidence to the University of California at Riverside after the case was closed. Scientists there were astounded at the rare specimens Ed brought to them, anxious to place them on campus display.

Another smile crosses Ed Newcomer's face as we talk, and he tells me something that initially seems to come out of the blue. "I'm a completely tolerant person. I'm not homophobic. I'm not threatened by that in any way." I'd asked him how he managed to lure Yoshi back to California. "Yoshi had a huge crush on me, it became very obvious during our last meetings in 2006. And he constantly asked me to show him my body on the webcam. It was a very bizarre situation." He worried that if Yoshi returned to L.A. before he secured an indictment and he rejected a date, Yoshi might disappear again. "I knew if I rebuffed a pass, he'd cut me off." He laughs. "But there's only so far I'm willing to go for the service." Nonetheless over Skype, "Ted" suggested there might be a romantic future for the two of them if Yoshi returned to the States.

"Can you do me a favor?" Yoshi pleads to "Ted" on one of the recordings. "One second. Can I see your beautiful thing? Then I can sleep tonight."

"Not until you come to L.A.," responds the coy agent. Meanwhile he secured an indictment from the U.S. Attorney's office.

In July 2006, convinced Yoshi would not give up the names of his other U.S. customers, Ed Newcomer made his move. "On July 31 he arrived in LAX and we were waiting for him and arrested him without incident, as they say."

The two didn't talk until the next day when Newcomer went down to the jail to pick up Yoshi and transport him to court. "It was great. I'll never forget it. I had shaved off the mustache and I was wearing my wedding ring, which I hadn't worn any other time. When he first saw me his expression was relief and pleasure. I had the feeling he thought I was there to bail him out. He was very excited." Yoshi quickly figured out the truth. The two of them sat down at a metal table in the U.S. Marshal's jail, Yoshi handcuffed to the table. Yoshi broke the silence.

"Have you been a fish and wild since the first day we met?"

"I told him yes. He didn't respond, looked a little disappointed, like he was thinking over all the things he'd said to me." And then Yoshi asked his only other question.

"Have you been married the whole time?"

Those were the only words the two exchanged.

"But now you know why he referred to agents as 'fish and wild guys,'" I offer. "It was his wishful thinking."

"That's right. He was hoping to hook up with one."

Ed Newcomer exhibits no sympathy for Yoshi, a criminal he groups with others who make their money breaking laws written to protect animals. "They're not in it because it's their hobby, which a lot of people think is the case—that they're insect collectors and it's their hobby. In reality they're crooks and it's a great way to make money, and the penalties are generally much lower than for other felonies. The only reason they're very interested and they have a lot of knowledge is because it's their profession." He rejects the idea that Yoshi may appreciate the beauty of the butterflies he peddles. "It's not fuzzy, touchy-feely people who love wildlife that are involved in wildlife crime. When we execute search warrants we've run into people with felony warrants, felony histories. We've run into assault weapons underneath Mickey Mouse sheets. Drugs, you name it. It's the same people that are involved in the drug and gun crime who are involved in wildlife crime."

As big a fish as Yoshi Kojima may be in the butterfly trade, he's still just a middleman. Ed Newcomer wanted to know who supplied Yoshi. After Yoshi's conviction, he tried without success to convince Japanese authorities to gain access to Yoshi's computer files in Kyoto. He wanted to find other customers of Yoshi in the U.S. Buying those butterflies Yoshi offered for sale is as illegal as selling them. "He claimed to have sold three other *Ornithoptera alexandreae* to customers in the United States. That's the largest butterfly in the world. It's endangered. It sells for $8,000 a pair. And I'd love to know who bought those."

The news of Yoshi's arrest made headlines back home in Japan. "World's Most Wanted Butterfly Smuggler Arrested at Los Angeles Airport," screamed the English-language *Japan Today*, accepting Yoshi's description of himself. His was a case that evoked both skepticism and ridicule among readers who posted an opinion on the newspaper's Web site. "It's going to be a bit difficult to get other prisoners to take this guy seriously, eh?" wrote a correspondent named Mo. Another, Kasumi, offered, "Wasn't it Kafka that had the idea of pins being stuck in someone as a punishment? Sounds about right for this guy."

But Fish and Wildlife agents obviously don't consider butterfly smuggling a joke. Threatened and endangered species are a priority for their investigations, no matter the animal. "We don't say insects are more or less valuable than a grizzly bear," is how Ed Newcomer explains it, which sounds incongruous until he points out that securing habitat from poachers and other abuses serves all wildlife. "You protect one, you're protecting more." And Yoshi was a big fish. "It's very unusual to find dealers that can get you all of the Ornithoptera or a majority of the Appendix IIs. The thing that really jumped out about Yoshi was that global reach and the species he had available, which really is unmatched. At all the insect fairs I went to and with all the people I spoke to, it was well known that Yoshi was the guy to go to if you wanted something, but it was going to be illegal."

As soon as Yoshi was convicted and sentenced, I contacted the Bureau of Prisons, seeking approval for a jailhouse interview. Authorized visits by journalists to federal prisons require specific paperwork outlining why a reporter wants to meet with the prisoner, detailing what types of questions will be posed to the inmate, and specifying the nature of the story being pursued. While Yoshi was still at the Los Angeles Metropolitan Detention Center, I drafted my request to the warden. I tried to cover the criteria in a non-threatening manner for both the institution and Yoshi, since I figured the prison might well show it to him in order to determine if he wanted to meet with me.

"Please consider this letter my formal request to come to your facility to interview Hisayoshi Kojima, the Japanese national convicted and sentenced last month for illicit trade in butterflies," I wrote. "I would like to conduct a face-to-face interview with Mr. Kojima; however, if you and your facility prefer an interview during which some sort of barrier separates me from the inmate, that too will serve my needs. To facilitate note taking, I would like to make an audio recording of the interview with a compact audio recorder; however, if you prefer no such equipment at the meeting I can document the interview with simply pen and paper. My questions to the inmate will be about the case, about butterfly collecting, and about the international trade in butterflies for sale. I estimate an hour would be adequate for the interview, but if your institution requires a time limit, I can accommodate it. I will be the only one conducting the interview." And I added a couple of lines that I thought might increase the warden's comfort level regarding a visit from me: "It may interest you to know, and perhaps be germane to this request, that I have experience conducting interviews in jails and prisons. My book *Nightmare Abroad* investigates the status of Americans incarcerated overseas, and for it I traveled to twenty-one countries interviewing Americans in prisons."

A few days later, I received the telephone calls from Yoshi indicating that he was willing to tell me his side of the story. But the bureaucracy often moves at a caterpillar's pace. Before I heard back from the MDC warden, Yoshi had been transferred to a prison in the high-desert desolation of California City in Kern County, east of Bakersfield—quite a contrast to Yoshi's lush Kyoto cosmopolitan hometown. Correctional Institution California City—as it is known in prison parlance—is one of the federal prisons the government has outsourced to a private company, what the Bureau of Prisons calls "contract facilities." These private jails, according to the official explanation, "help the Bureau manage its population and are especially useful for meeting the needs of low-security, specialized populations like sentenced criminal aliens." This outsourcing, as practical as it may be for the Bureau, presented new challenges for my visit. Not only did I need to start fresh with a new request to the California City warden, but his assistant informed me that it wasn't enough for me to meet Bureau of Prisons criteria for the interview; she would have to "send my request up to corporate." A private company, holding prisoners, is in charge of screening independent oversight of its operations. The potential for abuse is sobering.

There was no need to send my request to corporate. From California City, Yoshi scrawled on the back side of the letter I sent to him as a follow-up to our phone conversation that there was nothing else he wanted to say. "Dear Mr. Laufer," he wrote. "Sorry this time and I think no more info my story. I don't care about America. If need information ask Ted Nelson and his friend Ed Newcomer. They know everything story about me. And I advise you, I am not Big Dealer." It was a signed a friendly, "Yoshi."

Talking for a few hours with Brent Karner, who calls himself the Bug Guy, is like taking a graduate seminar in bug appreciation. This entomologist (and classically trained bassoonist) with spiked hair, two studs in one ear, and cut-off cargo pants, earned his degrees at the University of Alberta and now presides over the Los Angeles Natural History Museum's live insect collection and the Bug Fair. "Although you might think so," he tells me about the Karner Blue, "the butterfly and I are not related. I've always seen it as an interesting coincidence." I asked him to help explain the lure of butterflies, and why, when I was trying to come up with a symbol contrary to war during my speech about the Iraq debacle, I conjured butterflies as an image. And he knew Yoshi, too. I wanted to hear his take on the prisoner.

"People like butterflies; they're the pretty insects." He pauses, smiles, and then adds, "There are a lot of people who don't even see butterflies as bugs. They're really just a pretty-colored cockroach." We are talking in the museum's insectary, surrounded by nasty-looking beetles and hairy tarantulas and patient pupae. But because butterflies are pretty, they provide Brent an opening as he tries to educate the public about the value of insects. "When I want to talk with people about why cockroaches are necessary, people will tune out fairly quickly. But if I build them a room they can walk into where there are all these butterflies flying around, culturally they associate butterflies with everything good and pretty."

"Why?" I ask.

"It's just something that is imbedded in our culture—butterflies are viewed as being very pleasant things, they are angelic. Think about what butterflies represent when you see them. A butterfly is in tune with a nice sunny day. Butterflies need the nice sun out; they need flowers blooming. These are things we find serene, calming. Picture it in your head, close your eyes: you have that beautiful mid-morning, the temperature is right, the sun is out, you're sitting on your deck, the flowers are blooming, you hear the birds chirping, and then the butterfly goes flying by."

Butterfly movements are benign, he points out, they just flutter around, and not too fast. Butterflies don't make sudden movements or offensive noises. They don't sting or bite. The butterfly is never the villain—at least not in American culture. But Yoshi and his ilk are villains and criminals. I suggest to Brent Karner that greed must be the motivating factor. "It's so hard to understand the psyche of a poacher," he says, not ready to blame greed completely. Karner calls Yoshi's business—both the legal and the illicit—the dead bug industry. He met Yoshi when the poacher set up his wares with other dead bug vendors at the museum's Bug Fair. "I am not in the dead bug business anymore," Karner tells me. "I don't collect or trade with any of these people. But I know a great many of them because of what I do, because of this event that I run." He takes a quick breath and reflects.

"Yoshi Kojima was a very cordial fellow, as is typical with people like that that I have met in the past. There's almost a . . . ," he pauses, "how do I describe it? There's a sense of attention, that he actually enjoyed being able to get you that specimen that nobody else has been able to get you. He was that important person. That's part of what drove him, even more than the money that came in. However, I'm sure that the money wasn't a problem," Karner laughs, "because he did very well."

"He was driven by ego?"

"I think ego plays a big role. He was always one of the most self-important guys, and he was a fun guy to talk to." He would tell Karner stories of what he'd been doing, where he'd been in his pursuit of butterflies. "He was a very friendly man. But he dealt with some pretty illegal stuff—taking them out of national parks, taking them out of countries he shouldn't have been taking them out of, not having the permits for this, that, and the other thing. And taking far more than he was meant to take." Karner was talking philosophically about the quantity captured by Yoshi, not about the law. "He had no internal regulation."

That Yoshi was a poacher and smuggler was no secret to Brent Karner. He saw violations when he first met Yoshi at the Bug Fair and he asked Yoshi if he had CITES permits for specimens he was selling. Yoshi always had an excuse—telling Brent he had permits, but not with him. "I would tell him politely to remove these things, but there's no saying he couldn't sell it from under the table. And that's what he was doing. Even when he wasn't bringing things that were illegal, you come to his table, he says, 'I've got one of those. We'll talk next week. Here's my number.' This is how a lot of those transactions occur." Yoshi used the Bug Fair to build his illicit business.

Karner was gratified when Ed Newcomer arrested Yoshi and took him out of circulation. He did not want his Bug Fair used for illegal gains, and the butterfly underworld is rife with amoral opportunists. "Don't kid yourself. Butterflies and bugs are a big business." It's always been so. Wealthy collectors have hired procurers to tramp worldwide seeking rare specimens since collecting began. "Essentially that's what Yoshi is. He becomes a contractor for those people." But Karner doesn't see Yoshi as the ultimate bad guy in the process. "Yoshi is nothing if he doesn't have his marketplace. That's the bottom line of economics. Yoshi doesn't exist, and there is no reason for Yoshi to do what Yoshi does if there isn't somebody buying it on the other end. Is Yoshi the big problem? He's only part of it. There is a marketplace for what he's got. We have to get people to avoid buying the snakeskin shoes and the big butterfly on their wall and the alligator purse. Sometimes when I just sit around at night and think about the world as it is," Brent muses, "sometimes I blame the customers even more. Yeah, Yoshi was doing it and he's the one you can catch doing it. But the person who just quietly sits behind the scenes and buys that animal, and gets away with it . . . ," Karner shakes his head, disgusted.

I ask Karner what question he would like Yoshi to answer. His response comes fast. "Do you actually love these animals, or do you love the money?" Ed Newcomer is sure the answer is just money, not love. But Karner isn't so sure. "The other side about Yoshi that was very interesting is that he had a love for it." I am surprised to hear him say that, and I ask what makes him come to that conclusion. "You can't get involved in something like this if you don't have an affinity for it. You can argue that you could be a poacher just because the money's there." It's an argument Karner rejects. "He did love them. You could see it in his eyes. He came from a collecting background. You could see it." Karner's voice is insistent as I express skepticism. Perhaps Yoshi is obsessed with butterflies, but his grand motive appears to be cash, not collecting. "There was this one beetle that he had been rearing, another illegal thing. He decided to show me some of them. You could just see his excitement. I don't think he was even selling these things. This was just for him. He kept them at home. You don't keep all these things at home if you don't have some interest . . . . " He hesitates. "I can't put it into words. I just knew. Yoshi was a fascinating guy. He'd charm you. His stuff was fabulous, A-rated specimens."

Before we leave the insectary, Brent Karner pulls a plastic container off a shelf and shows off a friend of his, a plump and hairy Mexican Redknee tarantula. He picks up the huge arachnid, rubs its fuzzy belly, and strokes its sharp fangs. No question this Bug Guy loves bugs.

Chapter Seven

DEATH-DEFYING, GLOBE-TROTTING
BUTTERFLY HUNTING

YOSHI KOJIMA IS NO ANOMALY. BUTTERFLY POACHING AND SMUG-gling are global criminal occupations. I learn as I investigate the Yoshi case that nefarious collectors fuel criminal butterfly poachers worldwide. The butterfly trafficking underworld is not unlike other illegal enterprises that move controlled or forbidden commodities from suppliers to consumers: drug smuggling, for example, and other outlaw trading in wildlife such as coral and orchids. In fact, as I cast my journalistic net telling colleagues and informants about my butterfly studies, the Susan Orlean book *The Orchid Thief* is cited back at me as an example of a subculture similar to the dangerous world of butterflies. Collectors seek rare, endangered, and protected butterfly species for the same types of reasons collectors buy stolen art, cultural antiquities, and tribal artifacts that are illegal to sell and buy. They want to possess (and show off) rare and forbidden objects. They enjoy the pursuit of that which is verboten. They appreciate the investment value of endangered species in the illicit marketplace.

"Gangs of professional butterfly hunters organize expensive expe-ditions, sometimes hire local people, and use all possible methods of collecting their target species in large numbers," Vladimir Dinets warns on his detailed Web site dedicated to international butterfly poaching and smuggling.[19] Dinets was born in Russia, trained as a biologist, and moved to the U.S. in his late twenties. As a naturalist he travels extensively and is particularly incensed by what he considers an assault on rare butterflies, especially in the Third World, simply to fuel a continuing appetite in Europe, the U.S., and Japan. "Some of the poachers," he claims, "make special efforts to hunt a species to complete extinction—in this case, the price for each specimen will be astronomical."

Dinets says he's participated in expeditions to the Central Asia highlands to document extreme butterfly poaching. "Professional poachers are tough people, excellent mountaineers, and they try to make friends with local warlords and drug smugglers," says Dinets, who points out that the same strongmen in these remote, former Soviet lands usually are both warlords and drug smugglers. "There is a lot of espionage, electronic bugging, and other James Bond–style activities in this business." Enforcement of laws designed to protect the butterflies in Central Asia is spotty at best, according to Dinets, who tells a story of one arrest that belies any suggestion that butterflies represent nothing but peace and love. "In 1999 we finally got some Tajikistan officials to arrest a group of butterfly poachers (the fact that they were also smuggling opium helped a lot). In a shooting that accompanied the arrest, a few people were killed; others had to escape to a higher elevation, where they froze to death the next night." Dinets reports that 120 kilograms of opium and more than 300 butterflies were confiscated (and subsequently disappeared). In post-Soviet Central Asia police and government corruption is rampant.

When I reach Vladimir Dinets to check on the details of his butterfly chasing, I find him sequestered in Africa working on his Ph.D.; he's studying the mating behavior of crocodiles—it's hard to imagine the fieldwork is more dangerous than butterfly poachers shooting it out with Tajik game wardens and freezing to death.

My continuing search for oddities in the butterfly world led me to a news item with a Czech Republic dateline. A noted Czech entomologist had been arrested in India, charged by authorities with stealing butterflies and other insects from Singalila National Park, just south of Sikkim. The park is in the eastern Himalayas above seven thousand feet, and home to an alluring variety of species of high-altitude butterflies. It's been a wildlife sanctuary since 1986 and a national park since 1992. With an Internet search, I cross checked the entomologist's name, Petr Švácha, against the institute where he worked and found his email address. The news story reported that he was out on bail, and I figured he probably was using email to stay in touch with his supporters in Europe. I flashed him a note, explained my project, and asked him some pointed questions about his case. "Please bear with me," his email from Darjeeling said. "We have the trial just this week and thus I really have no time."

Petr Švácha is hardly the first European to hunt butterflies in Bengal. British collectors were notorious during Victorian times for roaming the Empire and the rest of the world in search of new species for their formal collections. They built elegant, multi-drawer cabinets to house their precious catches. And they often hired mercenaries to prowl the world for them, seeking hard-to-find specimens in dangerous locales. For the bulk of her life Margaret Elizabeth Fountaine personified the Victorian adventurer, except that this Englishwoman defied the mores of the era, traveling the world—alone and with a male companion not her husband—in pursuit of butterflies and love. She left about twenty-two thousand butterflies as her legacy, all pinned and labeled, a collection available for inspection at the Norwich Castle Museum in England. Fountaine also left her highly personal diary, some million words, detailing her love of butterflies and her love life. Fountaine and Švácha were enjoying the same pastime, but lucky for her, Colonial-era collecting was free from the restrictive laws enacted by a democratic India.

Fountaine too headed north out of Darjeeling to add to her collection, but in 1913, long before Indian law protected butterflies ". . . it was a joy in the cool, fine, though cloudless morning, to mount our ponies and ride away, down, down, down through miles of tea plantations which surround Darjeeling," she wrote, "down, down, always down, in the direction of Sikkim, the entomologists' Eldorado." She was suffering a bad cold, she records, but that did not diminish the thrill. "A descent of some 6,000 feet in nine miles brought us down into the Feesta Valley, where the heat was terrific, and the butterflies were wonderful. I caught my first *Kallima* before that day was over, but felt too unwell to dismount again, even at the sight of two lovely pale, blue-grey *Morphos*." She assigned one of the Indians hired to help with the horses to chase the Morphos, and one was netted.[20]

Victorian Britain was prime time and a headquarters for butterfly collectors. The BBC estimates over three thousand serious collectors were at work during Victoria's reign.[21] Amateur collectors from all over the world contributed to the growing database of butterfly knowledge. They were people such as the Pennsylvania sculptor Herman Strecker, who was first to describe and name 251 different species of butterflies and moths in the late nineteenth century. "Amateur" was an understatement when it came to Strecker: When he died in 1901 he left what was then the largest collection of Lepidoptera in the Americas. The over fifty thousand specimens in the collection were bought a few years later by Chicago's Field Museum.[22] In his letters, Herman Strecker referred to his "butterfly mania."

Researcher Petr Švácha told police he did not realize he was in the park because cows were grazing in the vicinity and it appeared the land was being logged. Scientists and collectors seek rare Indian butterflies—there are about fifteen hundred species in India—but so do fashion designers, interior decorators, greeting card makers, and artists who use the butterflies as a medium.

If convicted, Švácha and his traveling companion, amateur entomologist Emil Kucera, faced seven years in an Indian prison. We exchanged email messages just after the two were allowed to post bail and leave the jail where they were held for over a month.

"The room they kept us was about twenty-five meters long and the prisoners slept alongside the walls," the butterfly collector told a reporter for the Czech news agency Aktualne.cz. "They have only blankets. They gave us sleeping bags later on thanks to the Czech Embassy's intervention. There is nothing else in the room. There were roughly thirty men accused of all kinds of crimes, including murder."

When they were arrested, Švácha said, all the butterflies and other insects they collected were confiscated. "They also gave us documents to sign, which were basically clean papers, saying these were meant to be used for the description of the confiscated material. We were stressed out, so unfortunately, we signed them. These documents can now be used against us."

The trial was speedy, and lasted just a week. While Švácha was waiting for the verdict I asked him if he figured the two would be acquitted. He insisted after he was arrested the national park boundaries were not marked and that he was unaware that removing the butterflies from their natural habitat without a permit violated the Indian Wildlife Protection Act.

"I cannot give you any insight," he wrote back, "having none myself." And he followed that assessment with the email happy face.

Academics rallied worldwide to support Petr Švácha, pointing to his long list of published scientific papers dating back to 1985 and his respected position as an entomologist (specializing in Sawyer beetles) at the Czech Entomology Institute of the Czech Academy of Sciences. Indian authorities were unimpressed. National park official Utpal Nath told the Indian *The Statesman* newspaper that the two violated the law "collecting rare beetles and butterflies. They claim that the intention for collection was mainly for research, but there is a serious implication of an import and export business on rare insects." Colleagues from the academy wrote an open letter to Indian authorities insisting, "We know Švácha as a man who is motivated purely by his work. In his case we can fully exclude collection of beetles for other than research." Švácha's boss at the academy, Jan Sula, told Radio Praha Czech, "Petr Švácha is a world-recognized specialist on Sawyer beetle larvae and I think that explains what he was doing there. I think intentional wrong-doing is out of the question." Nonetheless, the Indian authorities claimed he was in possession of butterflies, not just beetle larvae. But it's not surprising if he was collecting some insects outside of his specialty. As long as he thought his activities were legal, why not bring home some other exotic bugs besides beetles?

The photographs of Petr Švácha in the Czech and Indian newspapers make him out to look like a sympathetic figure: he's not just skinny but scrawny, his gray hair is thinning, he's a stereotypically bespectacled scientist.

One deadline passed for the verdict, and Švácha wrote another note to me. "The court session was rather curious—after more than two hours of waiting, we were told that the decision was ready but was so long (and the typist so slow) that it had not been typewritten yet and making the final public decision will therefore be postponed to Monday." He ended the note with "Typical India."

I dropped him a note expressing my surprise at the court's archaic methods. "You are far from having appreciated the whole situation," he wrote back. "The sessions are recorded BY HAND (I mean a ballpoint pen) by the judge, only some important parts are typed on a typewriter that has to be brought from somewhere else (don't know where). There are apparently no computers in the whole court building, at least I have not seen any. Many of the case documents are also handwritten, that's in part why it is so easy to falsify them."

Was he an absent-minded professor who didn't notice national park signs, didn't check a map or study the local laws, didn't check out the local news reports and realize the Gorkhas were once again seeking an independent political entity and it might not be the best time for a foreign-looking guy with a butterfly net to wander West Bengal? His colleagues back home in Prague said yes, but the West Bengal prosecutors and plenty of the *vox populi* were not convinced. Švácha was not in a position to offer evidence to defend himself other than to claim ignorance of the law, no devious motives, and his stellar academic credentials as proof of his decent character.

The *Prague Post* reported his arrest with the introduction: "Bugs are Petr Švácha's life passion." The story was posted on the *Himalayan Beacon*, a blog edited by Gorkha journalist and author Barun Roy. "If bugs are Petr Švácha's life passion, then it is clear that he knew he needed a permit to collect," wrote one offended reader. "Very sad," wrote another, "this scientist coming to our nation and stealing our natural resources." In *The Statesman* Jugnauth Pundit used the Viewpoint page to lash out at the defendants. "The two Czech nationals masquerading as bioscientists who were caught red-handed with rare species of insects from Singalila National Park in Darjeeling must be awarded the severe and exemplary punishment of rigorous imprisonment and a heavy fine so that no other adventurist dares plays fast and loose with the wildlife laws of the country." But Pundit had more to say. "As many as 50 rare butterflies and several species of other insects were found in their possession along with the equipment necessary to catch them. Forest officials allege Švácha had offered to sell butterflies on a Web site and even quoted prices for the contraband. There is enough evidence of mischief and they deserve to be incarcerated." I found no evidence of Švácha attempting to sell butterflies on the Internet, and he vehemently denied such activity.

"A researcher wouldn't need so many specimens," Issac Kechimkar of the Bombay Natural History Society and author of *The Book of Indian Butterflies* told the *Hindustan Times,* assessing Švácha's stash. "I have seen many Europeans collecting Apollo butterflies in Ladakh or employing locals to do it for them." The Apollo is a CITES Appendix II butterfly. In other words, endangered.

Malicious or naïve, Petr Švácha is far from the first non-Indian jailed for chasing butterflies. While researching butterfly poaching and smuggling, I carried on sporadic email exchanges with Maeneka Gandhi, animal rights activist, environmentalist, and longtime member of the Indian parliament, and I dropped her a note while Švácha waited for the verdict.

"There is no doubt in my mind that he was taking them to sell," she writes. "He was backed hugely by 'scientists' in India—most of whom are involved in the same trade. In fact whenever we have raided people who have been selling reptiles, insects, etc. to scientific institutions and museums in the West, especially America, we have found the sellers to be retired scientists from animal departments."

She says it's not just the foreigners who raid Indian wildlife, but also poachers who hire local residents "suborning our own people to go into our forests and get the butterflies out for them in the guise of 'research.'" She expresses frustration at what she considers is a pathetic—or worse—government response, telling me such collecting is "not even recognized as a problem by wildlife officials—many of whom, especially in the northeast, are involved in it themselves."

The Indian news magazine *Outlook* calls butterfly smuggling a "rampant trade" and reports that French, Russian, and other Czech nationals were caught with butterflies within a few years of the Švácha case. Removing *any* butterfly from India without a permit is illegal, says Gandhi, and the cache of some two thousand specimens seized from Švácha and his partner included a Pale Jezebel (*Delias sanaca*), a particularly rare and endangered butterfly according to *Outlook* reporter Shruti Ravindran. My correspondence with Maeneka Gandhi led me to Azam Siddiqui, who carries the intriguing title Master Trainer in Animal Welfare with the Animal Welfare Board of India. The Welfare Board is an advisory body to the Indian government regarding animal welfare and animal rights issues. Siddiqui, whose day job is as a news cameraman for New Delhi Television, studied Indian animal protection laws and veterinary care to qualify for the volunteer position of Master Trainer. "Whatever free time I get from my professional duties," he wrote to me, "I dedicate it to animal welfare." After the Czechs were arrested he organized a counter-petition, urging that Švácha and his colleague be punished severely. "Indian wildlife laws are some of the strictest in the world," he tells me, "and should be respected by every citizen whether Indian or foreign." The petition rejects the notion that Švácha's credentials imply his collecting was benign. "From the common man to the elite scientist, all fall under the same category who are expected to respect and show compassion to India's wildlife whilst in India," the petition pleads. "Therefore we seek the attention of the Hon'ble Prime Minister of India, Shri Manmohan Singh, who has taken special interest in preserving India's wildlife in crisis many times, to take strict action against anyone found guilty of any crimes and offenses, irrelevant of his/her identity." The petition signers wanted Švácha and his colleague jailed for several years both as punishment for their crimes and as a deterrent to others.

In the end, Švácha and his friend were convicted, found guilty of collecting butterflies (and beetles), along with larvae, illegally. "The minimum sentence is three years behind bars," Švácha reminds me after he hears the verdict. "Of course Darjeeling justice is a mafia-like bunch of interconnected interests." I query him about his emotions pending the upcoming judgment. "You asked about anxiety. With time, you gradually get used to being hunted." The hunter understands, finally, what it means to be prey. "We have strong support from our embassy and our home country, so we still believe in some better end." They remained free on bail while they waited to hear their sentences, and Azam Siddiqui was not optimistic that the two collectors would receive a stiff prison sentence. "Fingers crossed," he tells me, but then added, "Sadly the wildlife crime conviction rate in India is abysmally low and stands somewhere around .02 percent. I hope this case serves as a model to both the local as well as the international community. It is very important that the guilty are punished, as this would boost the morale of the forest guards who are mostly illiterate as far as wildlife crime laws are concerned. There is very little that the government has been doing to generate the awareness and motivation of the guards. With just sticks in hands they have to face the AK-47–wielding poacher, and if they die in a gun battle the compensation is at the max around $500."

Maeneka Gandhi checks in with similar sentiments. "I hope they get a million years," she writes to me.

That seems excessive, and I check back with her asking, "You do believe their intent was nefarious and you don't consider there may be any validity to their claims of ignorance of the laws and the park boundaries?"

"Nope," she pounces back. "They have a Web site which offers insects for sale." Not so, declared the defendants. "They knew the laws in India, as they had contacted many 'scientists' before they went in. They couldn't give a toss, as so many foreign people have got off—or so they believed." She makes clear she sees a double standard at work regarding how India is perceived by Švácha and his co-defendant. "Do you think that any country would allow people without permission into their wildlife sanctuaries? Certainly not Czechoslovakia or whatever it is called now. So why would they think that India can be robbed from and poached from so easily?" Her dry dismissal of the Czech Republic is biting. "These are bad men," she insists.

The news comes the next day: Petr Švácha is fined twenty thousand rupees, about $500, but his co-defendant Emil Kucera, who was chasing butterflies without the advantage of advanced academic credentials as an entomologist, is fined three times that amount *and* sentenced to three years in an Indian prison. The court allows Kucera to remain free while he appeals the verdict, but confined to Darjeeling, his passport confiscated by authorities. Indian conservationists complained that the court was easy—as is usual in wildlife crime cases—on the two foreigners.

"Alas, both got off as expected," Gandhi writes, convinced they will jump bail and return to Europe. Siddiqui is not so pessimistic. "Convictions in wildlife cases are very low," he says, "so this is a victory." He sees the case as an important educational tool. "It sends the message that a research visa and a tourist visa are two different things. Every nation should educate their citizens before they embark to India. Indian laws are stringent, and the wildlife is protected and not a playground as some would feel."

"You must be quite relieved," I write to Švácha, "but it must be bittersweet relief given the prison sentence for your colleague."

"Yes," he responds, "I feel very badly for Emil. The differential sentence for the same thing is crazy." He suggested the fight for a separate Gorkhaland state fueled anti-foreigner sentiments against them, but Petr Švácha still insisted they thought they were collecting bugs outside the park boundaries, and consequently were violating no laws, and he firmly denied they were collecting with any intent to sell the specimens.

Jump bail Emil Kucera did, several weeks after the verdict while he was still waiting to appeal his three-year sentence. Once back in the Czech Republic, he told the Indian newspaper *The Telegraph* that he felt forced to flee because the case against him was "absurd," and that he could expect no justice in India. "There are no human rights there." Theories circulating in India about how he managed to escape included slipping across the notoriously porous Nepal–India border on a new passport secreted to him by conspiring Czech diplomats. Kucera told a Czech television station that his girlfriend brought money and a spare passport to him in India.

Animal rights advocate Azam Siddiqui was disappointed but not surprised, writing to me that "the men have now proved that they were not just innocent victims, but instead hard-core smart wildlife criminals who had come with the cruel poaching/trade intentions on insects after full research." He still was pleased they were caught, tried, and convicted, but angry that "they got away in style." A similar interpretation came from his colleague Maeneka Gandhi, who told me, "This man is a criminal and he will continue his criminal activities in other countries. It is a shame he was allowed back into his country." She said bail jumping by those charged with wildlife crimes in India is commonplace. Pleased that his friend was out of India, Petr Švácha remained in Delhi waiting for his exit visa, and dropped me a celebratory note. "Emil, in some way, managed to slip though Nepal. Good work, although I don't know how he did that."

I heard again from Petr Švácha once he finally returned to the Czech Republic, and he still was proclaiming his innocence and insisting that the case against him was fabricated. What strikes me as odd is why he would travel halfway around the world to a foreign country and not protect himself by applying for the necessary permits to collect specimens legally. Was it arrogance and hubris? Did he figure that unsophisticated Indian regulators wouldn't notice his activities? Was he so wrapped up in his studies that it never occurred to him that he might need authorization to practice his profession in West Bengal? Or was he a conniving, lying wildlife criminal? After following his case, and after watching stumbling encounters other scientists have had with wildlife protection laws, I've come to believe that those who study protected animals may often feel that because their work is designed to help wildlife they need not pay close attention to the letter of the law.

I remember several years ago returning to the U.S. from Bolivia. I was in South America working on a story about cocaine smuggling. At the La Paz airport, I struck up a conversation with a fellow at the snack bar while we were waiting for our flight to be called. He was a biologist traveling home to the States after an authorized collecting trip, his bags full of whatever critters he studied. In my bags were souvenirs for my family, including a guitar-like instrument featuring the shell of an armadillo for its body. The biologist was behind me in line as we were checked by Bolivian customs.

The customs man seized my armadillo instrument and said, "You can't take that out of the country. It's restricted because it's made of the armadillo."

I was about to relinquish it when my new biologist friend whipped an official paper out of his pocket, thrust it before the official and said, "He's carrying it for me. I am authorized to take any species I need for my studies."

One of my sons still loves that armadillo guitar, and obviously the congenial scientist I had shared a coffee with was overstepping his authority at the expense of a Third World country's laws with what was a sweet gesture to me.

Habitat depletion is a worse enemy of butterflies than poachers. Lloyd Martin, the longtime curator of butterflies and moths at the Los Angeles Natural History Museum, saw firsthand urbanization threaten Southern California wildlife. After he retired he moved to Prescott, Arizona, where, in 1970, he sat down at his desk and typed out an essay fueled by disgust in which he identified Los Angeles as transiting from "paradise to Hell in 40 years." Martin lived in L.A.

from 1921 to 1969 ("my fortunate or unfortunate experience") and he writes about the drastic changes he witnessed during those fifty years. "With the influx of people, we have destroyed much of our natural environment, and caused problems far greater than we can understand and cope with." He remembers with disbelief collecting larvae of *Agraulis vanillae incarnata* on passion flower vines behind the Ambassador Hotel on Wilshire Boulevard and of *Papilio zelicaon* "on sweet anise on the hill above the old north Broadway tunnel, which no longer exists, due to the so-called progress of man." He remembers Coldbrook in the San Gabriel Canyon as a prime collecting spot. "It would take some time to get there in the old Model T, and the last twelve miles were rough—but, to get a few good specimens of *Papilio indra pergamus*, it was well worth the effort." Martin ends his report on a sad note. "I would say, from what I have seen and experienced by living in the Los Angeles area and collecting butterflies for over 40 years, that most species of butterflies are doomed to extinction, due to man's destruction of the natural environment."

Lawmakers listened to Martin and others who shared his opinion. Three years after his unpublished essay was written, the Endangered Species Act was passed, designed to protect animals on the brink of extinction from their human predators and the habitat destruction wrought by human beings. Its intent is buttressed beyond the borders of the United States by the Convention on International Trade in Endangered Species (recall, it was in CITES-protected butterflies that Yoshi Kojima trafficked). Further enforcement muscle comes from the Lacey Act, which says if poached animals are moved across state or international lines, the transport is an additional crime that can add a charge to wildlife theft.

The first federal case in the U.S. charging violation of the Endangered Species Act for butterfly poaching was decided in 1995, more than a decade before Ed Newcomer sent Yoshi to federal prison. Three rogues, acting as if it were still the Wild West in California and

Arizona, were apprehended by the Fish and Wildlife Service in 1993, indicted for conspiracy to poach and traffic in protected butterflies, and faced five years in prison and $250,000 in fines each.

Remarkable about the trio—Richard Skalski, Thomas Kral, and Marc Grinnell—was not just their butterfly expertise (they were all amateur entomologists) and their amazing inventory of dead butterflies, but the correspondence they exchanged. Detailed letters back and forth established well beyond any shadow of a doubt that they knew for certain that what they were doing violated the law. They apparently never expected to get caught, or figured if they were, they would suffer not much more than a stern warning, or maybe a nominal fine. Even after the case was long over and he returned to his butterfly habit, Thomas Kral denied wrongdoing. "It is an unrefuted FACT," he announced via one of his Internet posts, "that merely collecting insects has no real environmental impact." He complained that he was the victim of a "witch hunt," and that the U.S. attorney who prosecuted the three, Lee Altschuler, is "arrogant and immoral."[23]

It's a hot day in late summer in Palo Alto when I meet with Lee Altschuler, now in private practice specializing in representing defendants of the ilk he formerly prosecuted—those who run afoul of federal law. We eat lunch just blocks from Stanford University, where Altschuler's famous butterfly case began for him. Altschuler fills in the details of the story for me. Richard Skalski worked at Stanford and in a letter to Kral he reports, absolutely free of irony, his job is "a Pest Control Field Representative. No stress and lots of opportunities to use Dr. Erlich and Dr. Murphy's labs," he writes. "Dr. Murphy has consented to let me use their environmental chambers to attempt to break the diapause of my *Papilio* pupa." Skalski earned a bachelor's degree in entomology from the University of California at Davis, and ingratiating himself at Stanford proved the trio's undoing; his Stanford contacts retold stories of the illegal butterfly safaris

Skalski bragged about, and ultimately the tales reached the Fish and Wildlife Service agents who chose to investigate. But back in 1985, when he sent the letter to Kral, the conspiracy was as yet unnoticed. "If I am lucky," Skalski wrote, "these pupa [sic] will emerge late February and thus free my spring to collect butterflies instead of babysitting pupa [sic]."

In neat and controlled handwriting he congratulates Kral on his decision to return to his studies. "I think it is wonderful you are going back to school. I wish I had the 'balls' to go back myself and get my Masters or Doctoral Degree. Presently however, I just cannot imagine putting out the funds and awesome time again towards school. I graduated at age 21 and thus my teens were lost to books and exams. As you can guess, my memories of school are of a lot of hard work with little play time."

Kral had written to Skalski that he intended to spend his 1986 summer traveling and collecting. "I will go to the Grand Canyon & try my luck with," his letter is typed and he carefully underlined the Latin for the type of swallowtail he sought, "P. indra kaibabensis. Will also look for the larvae, in fact that's all I may do as I don't want to get caught with a net in a National Park, I hear the fine can be stiff! Your info & directions are very clear & concise, my only question is how well patrolled is the area where the indra larvae are found? Did you ever have any trouble collecting the larvae & adults without being noticed as Roaring Springs Canyon is within the confines of Grand Canyon National Park." These obviously are the words of an enthusiast who knows he's transgressing, and he doesn't expect to collect just a token sampling of butterflies. "I plan on taking 20,000 envelopes on the trip next summer & using them all up!"

It is sobering to study the letters the trio exchanged. I found the correspondence deep in the vaults of the National Archives Pacific Region depository near the San Francisco airport in San Bruno. Much of the original paperwork from the trial is stored in the secure suburban federal building and I browsed enthralled at the audacity with which the conspirators exchanged intelligence that they gathered in the field. "What can I say about the Grand Canyon National Park?" Skalski writes back, and then breaks from his cursive and prints a large and underlined, "Watch OUT!" Next follows detailed instructions. "Rangers are everywhere as are the spies. The hike down to Roaring is very heavily traveled by tourists and if you stop along the trail to inspect things, these people often become nosy as to what you are doing. Be very courteous to them as if you anger them, you do not know who [sic] they may talk to as to what they think they saw you doing. It would be a real pity if one of these tourists asked a ranger what the man in the red hat was looking for in the rocks along side the trail down to Roaring Springs. I'd bet before you knew it, a ranger would be behind you, saying, 'Good Morning!' Last year, after my trips down, I heard a few collectors without nets were fined for romping in the rocks just off the trail. The law of the parks is very clear," he warns Kral, and then again written large and this time in quotation marks he spells it out: "Don't Touch."

For three pages the specific instructions continue, ending with the line, "Hide Always & trust no one you do not know!!"

Thomas Kral shared his own experiences with Richard Skalski, writing to him, "I myself got caught collecting in Florida's Everglades National Park and twice in Loxahatchee National Wildlife Reserve, but got away with it each time, simply claiming ignorance of the laws." Based on the dates of the letters, the three were in business together a decade before they were caught.

Quick to smile, and looking relaxed in a sport shirt and blue jeans, the "arrogant and immoral" Lee Altschuler picks up the tab for lunch; the former prosecutor is more than happy to talk about the old butterfly days. He was passionate about the case when he framed it for the court with some history: "It was two hundred years ago that there were buffalo on the plains, there were whales in the ocean, and there was an attitude that we can do no wrong." When the Endangered Species Act was passed in 1973, he told the judge, "Congress came to a different conclusion." Over our sandwiches he reiterates his disgust with the poachers. "I loved the butterfly case," he says. "The letters when we first started reading them were astounding." The prosecutor was amazed and delighted as he read the incriminating evidence the three poachers not only sent to each other, but saved.

Atlschuler and the agents worked fast to obtain search warrants for the residences of all three suspects. The fear was that the primary evidence—the butterflies—would be hidden if the three poachers knew the law was on their trail. But the law was not very worried that the evidence would be destroyed.

"Because they loved the butterflies?" I ask.

"Right," he agrees, but with a distinct qualification. "I think one of them had published a piece in a scientific journal, and that might support a suggestion that they had a—quote—love for the butterflies. But what turned me is the excess of the collection, plus the means and methods of the collection. If someone had a love for a butterfly and poached one or two or three, there's an argument that there's sort of a scientific basis for it. I'm not sure I totally believe that, but that's colorable." Altschuler speaks slowly, carefully choosing his words. He is, after all, a lawyer. "I have a very clear recollection of going into the courtroom with cases and cases and cases of these butterflies. They had museum-quality mounting cases."

The three suspects also boasted museum-quality collections, not just cases. One of the more amazing (and valuable) aspects of the case came to light after Fish and Wildlife biologist Chris Nagano and his crew of specialists inventoried the final tally of butterflies seized from the poachers. They were holding many of the North American butterflies then listed—and protected—under the Endangered Species Act, including butterflies that the most important museums in the country lacked. The samples were in perfect condition, labeled with what would be more evidence against the collectors: exactly when and where they were collected, with credit noted for the intrepid collector himself. The final count when all three search warrants were executed was an astounding 2,375 individual butterflies with a commercial value estimated at over $300,000. To accumulate such a collection of perfection, the capture rate must be much higher than the display numbers. Or as Grinnell signed one of his letters to Kral, "Yours in Mass Murder." His gruesome self-congratulation is only exacerbated by the thought of how many butterflies the three caught, murdered, and discarded because they did not meet poachers high standards for rarity and quality.

"It was collection gone wild," says Altschuler. They were not just skilled collectors, they were in business. "The profit motive was awful. They were selling, and trading, and leveraging this excessive collection activity. Perhaps worst of all, they knew what they were doing was wrong."

There was nothing innocent about their activities, but an expert criminal is different from a common criminal. A crook who goes into a bank and sticks up the teller is engaged in a straightforward activity to get the money. There's probably not some kind of deep appreciation for the business of banking and theories of economics, or the architecture of the building. It is a simple, "Here's a gun, give me the money!" exchange. Skalski, Kral, and Grinnell managed to assemble a world-class collection by studying and understanding the habitats and habits of the butterflies they caught. When biologist Nagano, along with Fish and Wildlife special agent John Mendoza, raided Skalski's apartment just south of San Francisco, Nagano was amazed at the amateur laboratory—the factory—they found. Dozens of *Papilio indra* pupae—Swallowtails—packed the bedroom. As soon as they eclosed, Skalski—as did Jane Foulds with her Owls—chilled them to preserve their A+ status. Nagano and Mendoza left with eighty-seven confiscated *P. indra kaibab*, a rare Swallowtail of which they estimated Skalski's collection as the world's largest. By keeping his captive breeding program secret, Skalski was able to take advantage of a market that presumed the butterfly was hard to secure, not propagating in abundance in his San Bruno apartment. Prices stayed high as long as the *indra* was perceived to be in limited supply.

"One of the aggravating factors for me," Lee Altschuler tells me, "was the recognition that in the profiteering they were trading on the rarity." The poachers took them from their protected habitat. "These creatures could no longer be found elsewhere. They were basically promoting extinction by selling or trading specimens unavailable elsewhere and further depleting the resource. There was nothing scientific about it." That Skalski was breeding rare specimens was no mitigating factor for the former prosecutor. "He was manufacturing product. It's like running a factory farm." He was not releasing the butterflies into the wild. "He was the Harris Ranch of lepidopterists," he says, laughing at his odd choice of metaphor—the Harris Ranch is famous for its high-quality beef— but serious about his complaint.

The case did not go to trial, the evidence was overwhelming, and the three pleaded guilty. Richard Skalski was sentenced to five months in a work-furlough facility, five further months in a halfway house, two more years of probation, and a $3,000 fine; Thomas Kral and Marc Grinnell each received three years' probation and Kral the same $3,000 fine, along with mandated community service time. And maybe toughest of all for these three: they were forced to turn over their exquisite collections to the government (which in turn offered them to scientific institutions for study and display). As prosecutor Altschuler said at the time, "The defendants were stripped of their most cherished possessions, the poached wildlife stolen over nine years."

Nonetheless, U.S. District Court judge James Ware listened sympathetically when Kral pleaded that the Endangered Species Act was sometimes ambiguous, and the judge conceded that the law might not always be as clear as it could be,[24] a view from the bench that exacerbated complaints from rogue collectors against the enforcement efforts of the Fish and Wildlife Service and other law enforcement agencies charged with chasing illicit collectors. Typical were the comments of then–Florida Department of Agriculture and Consumer Affairs entomologist John Heppner who railed about the "unconstitutional activities" of the Fish and Wildlife Service and its "nighttime SWAT team raids against butterfly collectors."[25]

We've finished lunch. Lee Altschuler wanders back to his law office, but not before a lingering last thought about his victory against the butterfly bandits. "It's like a stamp collector or a coin collector," he muses, "but dealing with living creatures" (his voice rises), "and illegally. Obscenely. I grew up in L.A. I remember as a kid there were butterflies everywhere. Maybe it's partially because of development and air quality, but butterflies," his voice trails off, "people collected the hell out of them. Most people know you can't shoot birds, even though there are a lot of birds that are kind of a pest. Because there was no protection of butterflies, we're in a world where, other than in camp, my kids have never seen butterflies in the wild. You just don't. To me that's a sad thing."

Chris Nagano's Fish and Wildlife Service office is in a sprawling federal building on the eastern edges of Sacramento. It's an office crammed with golden retriever pictures and memorabilia from his years as an Ivy League–trained field biologist, along with a bumper sticker that reads "The Yale Plot to Ruin America," a *News of the World* front page story headlined "Bigfoot Breakthrough," and a *Seven Samurai* poster in Japanese. "The greatest movie ever made," Nagano informs me, "I watch it every time I can." We meet more than a decade after he worked on that first successful Endangered Species Act butterfly case, but his memories of the astounding illegal collection remain acute, especially the scene in Richard Skalski's bedroom, a scene he described shortly after he and Special Agent Mendoza executed their search warrant and raided Skalski's apartment. "He grew the chrysalis on a paper towel, then cut around it and hung it from the rafters," Nagano said. "When we went in, there were all those chrysalises hanging from the ceiling over the bed."[26]

Skalski's technique for raising A+ specimens for sale was to manage eclosure in the dark, a device that minimized the butterflies' instinct to move around once they emerged from the chrysalises. No movement meant no damage to the product. Just as soon as the wings stretched to a full span, he popped them—alive—into his fridge. When Nagano opened the refrigerator door, piled on the shelves inside were glassine sleeves stuffed with butterflies not yet dead. "They slowly started to move," he said. Warmth and light from the apartment roused them. Their wings secured by the envelopes, the butterflies could only move their six legs. "There were a lot of butterflies," and the macabre sound of those wriggling legs, hundreds of wriggling legs, was "something out of *The Silence of the Lambs.*" The scene was chilling, but it was sophisticated.

The line separating amateur lepidopterists from their professional peers is a thin one and easily blurs. Hobbyists find new species, often named by or for the weekend enthusiast. Research conducted by amateurs expands the overall knowledge of lepidopterists—amateur and professional. Some of those amateurs choose to violate the law, sometimes for the intrinsic value of their collections, sometimes for profit, sometimes both. Kral's university studies, for example, were in business not science. As he told a reporter when he was sentenced, he feared a career in butterflies would wreck the fun and satisfaction of chasing them. "I had seen enough entomologists driving rusty old cars. Very few people are able to make a living in this profession."

"That's something I've always found interesting," Nagano relates to me, "the amateurs are often really the experts. In fact, in our own work here with the butterflies a lot of the information that we use comes from amateurs who have done intensive studies. Their interpretation might not be entirely correct, but their observations are. They have the time and the interest to do these things, and they do it because they like it. It's been like that since butterfly collecting began."

"To me," laughs Chris Nagano, "the personalities are actually sometimes more interesting than the animals." Nagano knows his butterflies. Before joining the Fish and Wildlife Service he was a researcher studying Monarch migration and navigation, a Yale-trained scientist who started collecting butterflies in the fourth grade. "They're easy to collect. They're beautiful. My mom would drop me off in the Santa Monica Mountains and come back a couple of hours later. I'd just go out and collect."

His collecting days are over, but he encourages others to take up the hobby, "obviously not endangered species or in national parks," he adds quickly. "I think there's a real value in collecting, and in enjoying it." Chris Nagano is convinced butterfly species can be collected to extinction, however, and that habitat depletion and destruction are not the only villains. "One of the mantras of some collectors is that you cannot collect to extinction." "Not so," says Nagano, who insists that if voracious collectors assault a species over a prolonged period of time, it will cease to exist.

University of Florida butterfly expert Thomas Emmel, one of the specialists I check with regarding butterfly controversies, disagrees. "No butterfly has ever been exterminated by overcollecting," he stated unequivocally during one of our chats.

"You are convinced it's never happened?" I ask Emmel.

"No butterfly has been exterminated by overcollecting, ever," he repeated emphatically. "In fact, without the enthusiastic collecting of butterflies and moths by collectors through the last several centuries we would have a very poor understanding of their distribution and their biology, and we would be missing a lot of the fascinating facts learned about butterflies."

Collecting to extinction is a concern, University of California at Davis butterfly scholar Arthur Shapiro tells me, and not just for the butterflies. "It is an extremely controversial issue. It's an excellent way to start an argument!" He sees validity in the point of view that voracious hunters can remove a population forever from the environment. "There have been some experiments to indicate that it's certainly possible, and it is especially possible if you have unethical collectors who are collecting for sale and want to get every single animal in their inventory." But he thinks nature works against those who would wipe an animal off the Earth. "Most species do not have highly synchronized emergences." Shapiro responds with a charming combination of inside jargon and street talk. He quickly translates, "Which is to say that catching everything that's flying on Tuesday may not tell you anything about what will be out on Friday." He is much more worried about the toll that habitat loss plays as a threat to butterflies than he is about abusive collectors, especially since butterflies are extraordinarily specific about where they lay their eggs, and larvae are extremely picky eaters—many species limiting themselves to a single host plant, and rejecting any other form of potential nourishment.

Despite the seeming popularity of chasing butterflies with nets, the overall number, Shapiro says, of collectors is not particularly great and always has been small, including all the amateurs—although some three thousand Victorian Britishers roaming the world with nets and straight pins sounds like a pretty crowded field. "The kids with their little green nets are not going to catch endangered species, they're going to catch what the collectors call junk species. In terms of people who are after the real goodies, there are not terribly many of them, there never have been." But Shapiro does not underestimate the damage the predatory collectors can do, especially when they work with sophisticated technology. "The problem is, if they are really unscrupulous, with almost instantaneous communication today, it's easy for a newly discovered population to be advertised online to one's friends and get hit very hard before anybody who is concerned about the biology knows that it is there." And Arthur Shapiro has never encountered a case where nefarious commercial collectors attempt to collect a species into extinction with the goal of inflating the value of specimens they hold as stock in trade.

Richard Skalski was not unknown to the Fish and Wildlife Service prior to the federal conviction that cost him his prized butterfly collection. In one of his letters to Kral he cautioned, "Be extremely careful with collecting endangered species and the mailing of them. Since I wrote to you last, the shit hit the fan and what a bloody mess! First of all, the individual who caught me within the Antioch Dunes did indeed turn my name in to the Department of Interior. I had to hire an attorney. Please disregard the return address on the parcels, they were labeled so as to protect us from the U.S. Fish and Wildlife Service opening the packages." Skalski was caught with a Lange's Metalmark in his net, one of the first butterflies to be listed as an endangered species, a species on the brink of extinction that the Fish and Wildlife Service is struggling to rescue.

"He collected one," Chris Nagano remembers. "He was out there and collected it, and he got caught." I ask Nagano to describe the Lange's. "It's a small, dark brown butterfly with orange spots, and whitish silver spots on the underside. It tends to stay close to its food plant. It has a weak flight; it's not like a Monarch that flies thousands of miles." But with his gentle, soft-spoken delivery, he makes it clear he's fond of the Lange's. "They're very distinctive, and pretty neat-looking animals. Maybe Lange's Metalmark or most of the other species we're protecting—maybe people will never get a rare drug or who knows what out of them, but that doesn't mean we shouldn't protect them."

The man who helped Nagano close down the Skalski, Kral, Grinnell gang—Special Agent John Mendoza—is retired, relaxing on his sailboat, removed from enforcing wildlife protection laws. He no longer wishes to talk about his escapades as an agent. But Skalski's poached Lange's Metalmark figured in the gang's case. Agent Mendoza testified at the trio's pre-trial hearing that Skalski was caught with the Lange's in 1984. "That one turned out to be a female, and it subsequently died." The gender is a crucial question for endangered species; it's the female, of course, who lays the eggs. One male can fertilize plenty of females, but every lost female means a potential loss of critical larvae needed for future generations of butterflies. When Skalski wrote to Kral about his Lange's arrest, he offered detailed advice about backdating specimens caught after the 1973 Endangered Species Act became law. Mendoza told the court, "Skalski indicated that he learned quite a bit about the Endangered Species Act, and one of the things he did learn was that the date the animal was listed was very important and to make sure that all species in Kral's collection had dates prior to 1973." Skalski had written specific instructions to Kral, instructions that made it clear he both knew the law and exercised a specific strategy in his attempt to violate it with impunity. "I suggest," Skalski wrote, "you check your collection and play it safe by not having data labels with dates later than 1973. It is illegal to sell, trade, and/or exchange them by mail or in hand. Thus, be careful with whom you trade and the wording you use and how you do so." The man was thorough, and in fact, Agent Mendoza testified that Kral's collection included a Lange's labeled in Skalski's handwriting as captured in 1964. Kral told the agent Skalski reported to him that it actually was netted in 1984.

The problems created for researchers by mislabeled butterflies are multiple. Attempts to understand species' characteristics, population shifts, and evolutionary changes are muddied if the data from collections are distorted and hence cannot be trusted because they are unreliable. In addition, if dating is fraud-ridden, the provenance of butterflies in legitimate collections may be questionable. Who owned what when, and what exactly is it? Similar questions surround artworks and potentially plague the great butterfly collections on display in museums, along with honest butterfly traders.

Chris Nagano invokes Agent Mendoza's words when I ask him why it's important to save endangered species, even if—as is the case with some butterflies—there's no apparent consequential differentiation between an endangered butterfly and an abundant close relative. "He was trained as a Jesuit. We spent a lot of time working together—on stakeouts and driving all over the country. He's a very learned guy; I learned a lot from him. He'd say, 'It's important just because it is.' Another thing he would tell people is, 'A nation is defined by its laws.' The Endangered Species Act says we value life." Two solid answers.

Chapter Eight

BUTTERFLIES VERSUS
NATIONAL SECURITY

MY TIME FOLLOWING MY NICARAGUA JAUNT TO MEET JANE FOULDS
and her butterflies was not spent only chasing butterflies. I had other
work on my desk, including a study of the crises on the U.S. border
with Mexico, which included drug trafficking, illegal immigration,
and the decision by the U.S. government to build barriers along the
border to deter illegal crossings. It shouldn't have surprised me that
butterflies followed me to the border; I was finding them wherever I
went. Terrorists, drug smugglers, butterflies—an unlikely combination. In sleepy south Texas, down in the Rio Grande delta, just outside of McAllen, butterflies and the post-9/11 Bush Administration's
definition of national security clashed.

The North American Butterfly Association's butterfly park is just
west of McAllen, in Mission, Texas. This is Hidalgo County, home to
more species of butterflies than all the states east of the Mississippi
combined. The more than three hundred species of butterflies native
to the delta bring tourists and their dollars to the region in ever-
increasing numbers as eco-tourism and butterflying gain popularity.
This park differs definitively from places such as Butterfly World in
Florida and the *reserva* created by the Foulds in Nicaragua because
it is not enclosed and not populated with captive-bred butterflies.
The butterflies on display are wild, and come to the park on their
own volition, attracted by the vegetation their larvae eat and the
pollen they like to stick their proboscises into for nurturing nectar.

More than 175 individual species have been spotted in the park. The North American Butterfly Association is proud to exclaim in its literature that the park is "an important pocket of habitat that will be preserved in perpetuity. Its location adjacent to over one thousand acres of state and federal lands assures a healthy pool of wildlife will flow into Butterfly Park." The park is one component of the Lower Rio Grande Valley National Refuge, a ninety-thousand-acre corridor along the river protecting one of the most biologically diverse ecosystems north of the Mexican border. But that's not all. Along the U.S.–Mexico border, 153 miles on the U.S. side is lined with national refuge lands, a total of 1.1 million protected acres set aside as preserved fauna and flora habitat.

Enter the George W. Bush Administration's decision to fortify the U.S.–Mexico border in the name of national security. The White House convinced Congress to fund over seven hundred miles of some sort of reinforced barrier along the borderline. In places it is more of a fence—steel poles stuck close enough together to keep a body from slipping through (although word from the borderlands is that enterprising migrants quickly figured out how to slip old tires cut in half through the bars and build them into an instant and quite portable ladder to climb up the Mexico side and down the other side of the high-priced barricade). In other places it would look more like the Berlin Wall, complete with no-man's-land strips of bare earth and searchlights shining through the night. The cost of the fence/wall is enormous (the DHS estimates $3 million a mile, more when work crews face rugged landscape), and even the Border Patrol's boss acknowledged it will not stop illegal trafficking in drugs and people. "I don't believe the fence is a cure-all," Homeland Security secretary Michael Chertoff told *The New York Times* in late spring 2008[27] "nor do I believe it is a waste. Yes, you can get over it; yes, you can get under it. But it is a useful tool that makes it more difficult for people to cross. It is one of a number of tools we have, and you've got to use all of the tools."

While the Department of Homeland Security was busy plan-
ning and plotting the trajectory and design of the border wall, Sue
Sill was still director of the Butterfly Park. After she retired, I caught
up with her between the trips she leads for tourists who want to visit
the Monarch overwintering grounds in Michoacán.[28] "Of course a
wall, especially if it's a chain-link fence," she makes clear, "is not
going to stop a butterfly from flying." That's not her worry. Even
where the wall is solid, as it was in Berlin, a butterfly can flutter
back and forth over it. "The biggest problem that I see," she tells me,
"is the destruction of habitat. They're going to destroy big swaths
of habitat right smack through all of our national wildlife refuges
and parks." Jim Chapman, president of the Lower Rio Grande Valley
Sierra Club chapter, shares her worry. "We have fought for the preservation of brush along the river for thirty years," he complained
about the Bush Administration decision to build a barricade. "This
is a greater threat than anything else we've faced, and we have no
means to challenge it."[29]

Since the 1970s public and private conservation organizations
have worked together building the patchwork of protected lands
along the Rio Grande River in its delta, and they've worked to rebuild
some of the wild habitat that existed before row crop farming and
urbanization changed the physical character of the delta. Millions of
federal dollars were spent by the Fish and Wildlife Service for its part
of the ongoing project in and around the Lower Rio Grande Valley
National Wildlife Refuge. In an ironic plot twist, the federal conservation work made the land more vulnerable to the fence builders:
it was already owned by the federal government and could be fast-
tracked for fencing. Not that privately owned land necessarily would
be far behind.

As part of the flurry of post-9/11 legislation passed by a politically
fearful Congress, the Bush Administration pushed though the Real
ID Act. That law, hard as it may be to believe, authorized the Homeland Security Department secretary to ignore *any law*—including

laws written to protect wildlife and the environment—the secretary deemed interfered with building the border barricade. Impossible as it may be to believe, Congress further wrote into the law, quickly signed by President Bush, a provision that forbade recourse to the federal courts for anyone who wanted to object to the secretary's decisions. Real ID gave dictatorial powers to Homeland Security secretary Chertoff, and he moved quickly to use them.

On April Fools' Day, 2008, Homeland Security issued a news release announcing it was ignoring and violating previously passed laws once again and quoted Secretary Chertoff as saying, "Criminal activity at the border does not stop for endless debate or protracted litigation. Congress and the American public have been adamant that they want and expect border security. We're serious about delivering it, and these waivers will enable important security projects to keep moving forward. At the same time, we value the need for public input on any potential impact of our border infrastructure plans on the environment—and will continue to solicit it."

The bureaucratic language is easy to translate. *Waiver* means using the irresponsibly passed Real ID Act to ignore laws Congress, states, and local governments passed—laws that remain in effect but can be "waived" by Homeland Security. *Public input* means you can jump up and down all you want, but the executive branch secures the legal authority to do whatever it wants, and it will. *Border infrastructure* means walls.

The April Fools' Day waivers were extraordinarily wide-ranging. The definitions are as broad as the border. "One waiver," reads the official news release, "applies to certain environmental and land management laws for various project areas in California, Arizona, New Mexico, and Texas, encompassing roughly 470 total miles. It will facilitate additional pedestrian and vehicle fence construction, towers, sensors, cameras, detection equipment, and roads in the vicinity of the border."

Certain laws? *Roughly* 470 miles? *Vicinity* of the border? The news release is the missive of an authority above the law.

The second waiver pertains specifically to the levees in Hidalgo County, again with the secretary authorizing his department to violate environmental and land management laws. The levee in question bisects the butterfly park in Mission, just north of the Rio Grande and the international border. "This is land that has been painstakingly accumulated over the decades to add to a wildlife corridor," Sue Sill tells me about the butterfly park and the National Refuge and other protected land marked for fencing. "Butterflies are pretty incidental," she suggests, compared with the other animals on the border. "We've got some endangered cats—the ocelot and the jaguarundi—and their range includes both sides of the river."

Nonetheless, she fears for butterfly homelands with the wall and its no-man's-zone along the levee path. "They're going to cut a swath 150 feet wide straight through all of these habitats. They're going to isolate on the south side of the wall habitat that we've been maintaining and that we've been using for tourism. We're not even going to be able to get to it," she says of the land left in a no-go zone on the south side of the levee. "The biggest threat to the butterflies is the destruction of habitat, of which we have precious little to begin with, and the neglect of the habitat on the south side. Who knows what will happen once it's on the south side of the wall and there's nobody down there to do anything? Who knows what's going to happen about people camping out and trampling and whatever? We won't have any riparian habitat at all," she laments about the butterfly habitat along the Rio Grande. Her frustration spills out. "We have been working in the dark," she says about the efforts to stop the project from ruining wildlife habitat. "We don't know what they're going to do." She's agitated by the blank check Congress gave the executive branch. "They're going to do whatever they damn well please, apparently, without any real consulting of the people here that know the area." She pauses and adds, "I think it's going to be a fiasco. We're building the Berlin Wall right here."

Sue Sill is livid. She loves Mexico and its people, and she is convinced the wall—which officially is referred to with the euphemism Secure Border Initiative—is an artifact of fear: so many Americans have been taught to fear an invasion of Latinos, and they consequently cheer the barrier. She encourages me to find Chris Best, the Fish and Wildlife Service ecologist who spent much of the 1990s and 2000s leading the effort to rehabilitate the Rio Grande delta, to hear from another scientist who intimately understands the delicate ecosystems along the Texas–Mexico border. Best is horrified that Congress gave the Homeland Security Department the authority to override federal laws and regulations, authority that threatens his work rehabilitating the wildlife refuge along the border. "The refuge was not established to create an international barrier," he points out.

"The main obstacle to habitat restoration in that area," Best tells me, "much more so than the semi-arid, subtropical climate with huge variations in rainfall, is the invasive grasses that were brought in. And that ties in directly with butterfly populations." Exotic grasses such as buffelgrass—native to Africa, the Middle East, and Southeast Asia—were introduced in south Texas in the 1950s in an attempt to compensate for lost cattle forage; they replaced the native grasses and herbaceous flowering vegetation. "That's a huge chunk of your butterfly nectar and feed sources," Best says about the losses. With a variety of creative new removal and replacement techniques developed under his tutelage, Best and his crews experienced great success over the years controlling and removing the buffelgrass and other invasive plant species while restoring native butterfly forage. "Some of the best species that had a natural ability to keep the invasive grasses out are also great butterfly species," Best remembers, sitting in his Austin office where he serves as the Fish and Wildlife Service's state biologist. He reels off a list of plants he worked hard to restore to places in the delta where they had been crowded out by row crops, calling them the "number one butterfly food and nectar sources in that region." These butterfly delights include blue mistflower, crucita, amantillo, Mexican Trixis, and Turk's cap. Butterflies thrive on such forbs—low-growing, broad-leafed herbaceous plants that grow in fields and can look to the untrained eye like unimportant weeds.

Chris Best is no advocate of the wall. "Sixteen years of my life is spent trying to make this wildlife corridor, and now its continuity is in jeopardy," he complains as he's explaining the details of his theories and successes to me, "not to mention the money and time, and of course lots of other people made a great effort in this." Nonetheless, Best holds out more hope than Sue Sill regarding the lush delta butterfly life. "I don't think that the border fence or wall—whatever it's going to be—is going to be as disruptive to butterflies as it would be to some of the key mammal species. For most plant species I don't see this as being as big of an impact as for creatures that need to move." But it's not just because he's concerned about seeing the critical habitat rehabilitation ruined that he opposes the wall. "More than I dislike the disruption to wildlife conservation, I dislike the disruption to our relationships with Mexico, and the disruptions of our communities. It's just a huge insult."

Just as Sue Sill sent me to Chris Best, Best sent me in search of Texas Parks and Wildlife invertebrate biologist Mike Quinn, insisting that what Quinn doesn't know about Texas butterflies he'll find out quickly. Quinn agrees with Best, "The greatest negative effect would be running the fence through existing habitat, particularly any of the old-growth habitat. That would be the worst-case scenario." Not that he favors the Secure Border Initiative.

Quinn's roots are deep in the Rio Grande Valley. His great-grandfather bought land along the river; his grandfather cleared this land, and Quinn spent summers there, hand milking family dairy cows. "The Valley is this place unto itself basically. There's always been a high Hispanic population on the north side of the river. People down in the Valley don't see Mexico as any kind of enemy whatsoever. Nobody's for the fence down there from a cultural perspective or from a natural history perspective." But he too is not overly worried about the wall's butterfly effect. "I think everybody acknowledges that the ocelot and jaguarundi—if there are any— are the most potentially negatively impacted species. For birds and insects, if [the fence] is built on the levee and doesn't go through any existing brush, it likely wouldn't have a catastrophic effect. I am concerned. I'd rather not see it. It may be one more nail. But it's not going to be any kind of flipping of a switch and all of a sudden the butterflies are going to be gone."

However, land south of the wall, as Sue Sill makes clear, will be difficult, if not impossible, to tend. Habitat in that strip between the river and wall will be in limbo, vulnerable to invasive non-natives, be they fast-growing weeds or desperate Mexicans heading north unaware of the damage they're causing to the landscape, or running too fast and too scared to worry about butterfly habitat.

Border butterflies are hardy. Mike Quinn is an old hand at creating gardens in the Valley specifically designed to attract butterflies. "It's the only place where, as I was putting the gallon pot into the ground, a butterfly already landed on the plant." The plants thrive in the valley soil and climate as well as the butterflies. "You plant certain fast-growing plants in the ground, you almost have to step back, they grow so fast. You can create good habitat fairly quickly."

Quinn sees the butterflies thriving. "The main factor controlling insect population is rainfall." Long periods without rain dry up the plants that butterflies need for their nutrition. Butterfly larvae are phytophagous: they survive eating vegetation. The Rio Grande Valley is semi-arid, and when it gets so dry the plants are stressed and not thriving, the bugs that depend on them struggle too. But drought years are anomalies, and the delta usually is a butterfly paradise.

Droughts can lead to successful successive generations of butterflies when the harsh conditions reduce predator species and new rains lead to a lush abundance of caterpillar food plants. In such a climate cycle, once the rains come, the ratio of successful egg hatchings can increase markedly. "Even with 95 percent of the Valley converted to row crops and the other catastrophe that has happened to the valley, with the introduction of exotic grasses that are crowding out the forbs that are the butterfly food plants, we still have great butterfly eruptions in the valley, and not just single species," Quinn gushes with enthusiasm. "It's absolutely amazing. You need to go down there in October."

Butterfly eruptions! What an intriguing term and spectacular image.

The summer of 2006 was a prime example of a butterfly eruption. Swarms of Snouts and Yellow Sulphurs darkened the skies. Radiator grills were blocked with explosions of crumpled colorful wings, and motorists were forced to clear off the dead butterflies from their car radiators in order to prevent their engines from overheating. "While driving, we can't dodge the butterflies," Joshua Rose, a biologist at the World Birding Center near Mission, wrote at the time. "We can only aim the car at the parts of the road where the density is the lowest."[30]

Texas highways full of butterfly roadkill. Piles of protein going to waste. Through the ages and around the world, butterflies and moths suffer a history of being served up for feasts. An early European advocate for an insect diet was Vincent M. Holt, author of the now-quaint *Why Not Eat Insects?*, first published in 1885 in England. Holt was an enthusiastic evangelist for the entomophagous (or insect-eating) lifestyle. Don't wash the caterpillars out of your garden vegetables, he advised; instead enjoy the added nourishment they provide. "I could never thoroughly understand the intense disgust with which the appearance at the dinner-table of a well-boiled caterpillar, accidentally served with cabbage, is always greeted," he wrote. "The feeling is purely one of habit, the outcome of unjust prejudice. These delicate, shuddering people, who now, with appetites gone, push away their plates upon the appearance of a well-cooked vegetable-fed caterpillar, have probably just swallowed a dozen live oysters; or they may have partaken of the foul-feeding lobster."[31]

Chef Holt particularly advocates the larvae of the large white cabbage butterfly, *Pontia brassicae,* and the small white cabbage butterfly, *Pontia rapae.* These delicacies he suggests be served not only as caterpillars but also once they become chrysalises, "fried in butter, with yolk of eggs and seasoning." Fry up the cabbage moths too, he suggests, again reminding his readers that all these worms show up unintentionally at home-cooked meals. "Let these minor accidental appearances at table make us acquainted with the flavour of the clean and wholesome caterpillar, and let not the silent appeal be in vain of these martyrs, who invite us to profit by their martyrdom. Let us not, with a shudder, hide the evidence of their sacrifice under a temporary shroud of vegetable, but rather let us welcome these pioneers of future delicacies with smiles and open arms." Ah, the preciousness of the Victorian-era English adventurer.

But Vincent Holt was not just preaching. He tested the recipes, and rhapsodizes about his enjoyment "in both taste and smell, of a fat moth nicely baked. Try them ye epicures! What possible argument can there be against eating a creature beautiful without and sweet within; a creature nourished on nectar, the fabled food of the gods?" He is a pretty persuasive salesman, but I failed his test.

In Oaxaca years ago I was at a business dinner meeting with fellow journalists, me being the only gringo. These *hombres* were hearty eaters and hearty drinkers of the local tequila variant, mezcal. This they drank with a pinch of powder piled on little plates in front of each of us. We toasted each other and I downed my first shot glass full.

"Hey!" the *compadre* next to me pointed to the powder and asked me why I didn't partake.

"What is it?" I asked.

"Ground-up grasshopper," he said with a conspiratorial smile that reminded me of the bandito in *The Treasure of the Sierra Madre*. He insisted I try it.

But I was prepared. I shook my head and explained, "I'm a vegetarian."

"Vegetarian?" He laughed, and the whole bunch joined him. "That's not meat, *amigo*, it's *insectos*."

Farther north in Mexico, in the Copper Canyon of Chihuahua state, the Madrone butterfly—*Eucheira socialis*—is threatened potentially both by excessive logging of its host tree and by the eating habits of the local Tarahumara indigenous populace. The Madrone larvae make themselves into pupae that hang together in madrone trees in pouch-like nests that the caterpillars make out of a silk they spin. The nests protect the larvae, and then the pupae, from most predators. But these clusters of a couple of dozen pupae each are gathered by the Tarahumara and roasted over fire, then mixed with cornmeal. Entomologist Arthur Shapiro observed them in Hidalgo state; Shapiro's colleagues have tramped through the Chihuahua mountains west of the trading post crossroads of Creel, studying the clustering Madrones.[32]

Dr. Shapiro and I had met in his University of California at Davis office where he was generous enough to provide me with an introductory butterfly tutorial, and I thought I was making a joke at the time when I queried him about butterfly consumption—unaware of how close I was to reality.

"Is there butterfly tempura?" I ask. For some reason the image of battered wings came to mind for me, battered and deep-fried to a crisp, golden finish, wings outstretched.

That's when he introduced me to the Tarahumara and their *Eucheira socialis*. "It's one of the strangest butterflies in the world. The pupae are eaten during Holy Week." Shapiro enjoys telling fantastic butterfly stories. "The caterpillars live in nests roughly the size of a football, high up in the trees—big, heavy, rough, papery-silk nests. The adults send the kids out to climb the trees. The kids have machetes and they cut the nests down." Shapiro is a primary source researcher; he's observed the Madrone in the field. "They bring the caterpillars down and feed them until they pupate, because it's the pupae they want to eat. They have special ways of preparing them with special sauces. They eat them in tacos, in Holy Week."

I ask Shapiro if he's tasted a Tarahumara butterfly taco and he looks disappointed as he acknowledges that he's missed the unique culinary treat because his research trips to Chihuahua did not coincide with Holy Week.

"Would you eat one?" I ask.

"Sure," he smiles, "sure."

I suggest that we traipse down to Mexico together and try butterfly tacos during the next Holy Week.

He laughs, "Next Easter?"

"Yeah," I say without owning up to the conflict my vegetarian diet may pose to partaking of a butterfly taco dinner, but we don't confirm the date. I'm sanguine about missing the opportunity to crunch through a taco filled with butterfly pupae, but a trip to the wilds of Chihuahua chasing butterflies and butterfly eaters with Shapiro would be well worth pursuing. Vincent Holt would approve of the culinary practice, of course, especially since the Madrone is a relative—albeit a distant one—of his gourmet Cabbage White.

Down under, Australian aborigines knew the value of a moth meal. Bugong moths were sampled by European explorers as early as the mid-nineteenth century, and identified when roasted on hot ash as sweet and walnut-like in taste. Chroniclers of the time watched hundreds of natives gather for what appeared to them no reason other than a moth fest and feast. Once the wings and legs were broken off, moth bodies were savored freshly cooked off the hot ash. Others were mashed into cakes and smoked for later consumption.[33]

"Moths are a significant component of the diet of certain tribes of Australian aborigines," Shapiro tells me. "They're called Owlet moths, they're the largest family of moths." Many of the Owlets are dormant during summers or winters, collecting in huge masses in caves. In order to survive their long sleep, they build up large quantities of fat in their bodies. The moth eaters "harvest them by the bushel basket full and gorge on them. They're very nutritious." Not that Shapiro recommends a butterfly diet. "A lot of butterflies are not pleasant to eat. Many of them get poisonous chemicals from their host plants and sequester them for their own defense. The Monarch is most famous for this." The milkweed that Monarchs eat is trouble free for them, but the plant makes the butterflies themselves poisonous to predators, predators who learn to leave the red and black wings alone. Such coloring, along with yellow, is a prominent butterfly warning in the wild that means, he says, "If you eat me, you'll be sorry!"

At the University of Tennessee, ecology and evolutionary biology professor Dr. James Fordyce studies butterflies—and enjoys the claim that he won't study a bug he hasn't tasted. Fordyce studies chemical defenses in butterflies, phenomena like the Monarch-milkweed combination. He tells me there is a long history in the field of study for tasting the animals, not just to shock friends and colleagues, but to capture a real sense of how bad they taste.

The Monarch, he reports, tastes very bitter. "I don't swallow it. I just put a little piece of it in my mouth." He tries his research subjects uncooked. "Usually it's the caterpillars, not the adult butterflies. You can tell pretty quickly if something has a bitter taste." And it's not just the caterpillars that taste bitter—a sign that an animal part may be poisonous—there are fellow travelers with which to contend. "With the aphids on the caterpillars your tongue will actually go a little numb for a couple of seconds. They definitely do taste bitter, and foul."

Monarchs make birds vomit; that's one reason Fordyce doesn't swallow his prey. "I don't want to throw up." The larvae are easier to taste than the imagoes—the adults—with their wings. "Butterflies have scales all over their wings, and you don't want to have scales floating around in your mouth because," he is laughing as he explains, "you can't spit that out as easily as a crushed-up caterpillar."

What butterfly tastes the worst? "Pipevine Swallowtails," he says without hesitation. "I ate a very small caterpillar, and it pretty much overwhelmed my mouth with a sense of bitterness that I could not wash out for about a half an hour." Drinking water, chewing gum, nothing helped. "It stuck with me for a really long time. That was the worst tasting of any of them I've consumed." There is no other side of the story; he finds no butterfly delicious. "Usually they taste like gooey plants. If you imagine lettuce that you forget about in the fridge, it gets soggy and brown, that's what caterpillars will taste like if they're just eating a normal plant.

"It's not good to eat too many of them," he goes on to say, "because they are carcinogenic." The aristolochic acid in the pipevine plant, the plant food for the Pipevine Swallowtail, was once used for medicinal purposes, but no longer. It is considered by government regulators too dangerous, and is now illegal to sell as a medicinal plant. The caterpillars and butterflies are toxic because the aristolochic acid accumulates in them as a result of feeding on the pipevine. This toxicity serves them well in the wild. "They are largely avoided by natural enemies, and the more toxic they are, the higher their survivorship out in the field."

Eating the subject matter makes for good cocktail party chatter. "People are like, 'You do *what*?'" I ask Dr. Fordyce if there is any scientific validity to his tasting bugs, or is it his inner Indiana Jones at work. "Oh, no! There's no scientific validity whatsoever." But he's following a longtime tradition in his study of chemical defenses. "I'm certainly not the first chemical ecologist to consume the study organism to get an idea of how bad it tastes. It's an interesting experience to understand how our sensory system responds to these different chemicals."

James Fordyce, despite sampling insects for science, has never eaten bugs cooked up for a dinner. "Does that sound pathetic? I've only eaten the ones you're not supposed to eat, not the ones prepared as a delicacy."

An enthusiastic advocate of insect eating is Zack Lemann, staff entomologist at the Audubon Insectarium in New Orleans. I caught up with him to talk about his reputation as one of the world's preeminent bug chefs, a hobby, he acknowledges, that's out of the ordinary, even for bohemian New Orleans. But it's a hobby he takes seriously, appreciating the protein value of his charges at the Insectarium.

"The problem with crusading for that cause," he says, "is that we have this pretty substantial mental hump to get over, at least Western culture does, with regard to eating insects. But there's no question about their abundance, their nutritional value—at least for most of them—and the relative ease of raising them. If you wanted to be very serious about it and think about ecological and environmental concerns and impacts, insects convert plant matter into edible table food at a much more efficient rate than cattle or pigs do, and so that's certainly something to think about in terms of land use and how much grain we grow and where it goes."

The Food and Drug Administration recommends that we all get fifty grams of protein a day. I asked Zack Lemann to run the numbers with insects. He picked crickets since crickets are food in so many world cultures. His figures indicate that an average house cricket weighs two tenths of a gram and that every hundred grams of crickets is worth about thirteen grams of protein. Using those calculations, if you want to give up steak and eggs, meatloaf and chicken, and get your nourishment from insects, you'll need to chow down about 2,000 crickets a day. Yum.

The gourmet insect demonstration at the Insectarium is called Bug Appétit, an ongoing popular exhibit, and where Lemann promotes grasshoppers. "I think that it would be a great thing if more people ate grasshoppers. I really do. They taste good and they're nutritious." The prejudice many Westerners hold against bug eating is rare worldwide. "There are a lot of places that eat insects out of necessity, but there are a lot of places where they're also eaten because they taste good, whether they're considered delicacies or just snacks. If you've ever been to Oaxaca or other places in Mexico where they have open markets, there are plenty of insects that are offered there." I tell Lemann about shunning the powdered grasshoppers in Oaxaca with my shots of mezcal, pleading vegetarianism, and he laughs. "Depending on what kind of vegetarian you are, you do have to accept the straight scientific fact that insects are animals. Whether you choose to eat them based on your dietary restrictions is up to you. I haven't heard of the ground-up-grasshopper chaser for the mezcal. *Chapulines* are the whole grasshoppers that are served in open markets in Mexico. It doesn't matter whether you're in South America or Africa or over in Southeast Asia—China in particular and Thailand—insects really are consumed by people all over the world."

"What about butterflies, Zack?" I ask him. "Who's eating them and how are they eating them?"

"Oh, we're not cooking butterflies, but we serve caterpillars. Caterpillars in fact are eaten in many cultures around the world."

Caterpillars, crickets, grasshoppers, and beetle larvae are the most common insect foods throughout the world. "The caterpillars we serve the most go by the common name of wax worms. We do Cajun-fried caterpillars. We do a chutney with mango and kiwi and wax worms in it. We've incorporated them into some candy. Sometimes into jambalaya. Really, it's a very versatile bug. The wax worm is actually a pest of commercial beekeepers because unlike most caterpillars, which eat leaves, they feed on the wax that honeybees make their cells out of." Wax worms also make good fish bait, and left alone eventually become moths.

Of course the next question is taste. And Zack Lemann tantalizingly refuses to identify the wax worms as tasting like chicken.

"It's hard to compare insect to something else," he insists. "Just like it's hard to compare crawfish or alligator. A lot of the things that we have here in New Orleans don't have good comparisons. I will say this, if you have not used other textures and flavors and mixed them in with your insect and you really have it *au naturel*, or with very little seasoning, most insects taste nutty. More like a seed or a nut than anything else." But Lemann is a gourmand; he recognizes subtleties "that can range anywhere from peanut to a sunflower seed to a hazelnut."

I'm thinking more disease and dirt than sunflower seeds and filberts when I contemplate eating bugs, but I'm wrong, according to Lemann.

"With most insect cuisine what I recommend is putting the animal, if it's an herbivore, on something like lettuce or an apple, something fairly mild, for at least a day, or starving the animal for at least a day, and this gives them a chance to purge their system of anything that might render them less than palatable." In other words, unlike fish or deer, you don't need to gut and wash bugs, although, he says, "before you cook them it's a nice idea to rinse them with water in a colander and then pat them down." A nice idea, but not necessary.

"I'll be honest with you, there are times when I don't have time to do that sort of thing, sometimes I'm in a rush. I've never, ever had an issue with edible insects, even if I have left out those two steps. They seem to be a really good food source in terms of not having to deal with a whole lot before making them ready for the table."

"Your passion for these disgusting little critters is just spectacular, Zack," I tell him as we say good-bye.

"Watch your adjectives, please," he warns me, ever the champion of his insect charges, even if he does eat some of them.

Entomologist Arthur Shapiro is an endless litany of intriguing butterfly stories. His cavernous office at the University of California at Davis looks like a stage set for the consummate professor: stacks and stacks of books on the floor and shelves, cartoons and notices of past academic conferences on Lepidoptera worldwide stuck to the walls. His salt-and-pepper curly hair and beard look wilder than my own, epitomized by a newspaper clipping stuck on the bulletin board in the hallway outside his office door. It is a photograph of Saddam Hussein at his unkempt worst, shortly after U.S. soldiers captured him in Iraq. Some joker hand-wrote a new caption for the picture, "Professor Shapiro before he was removed to an undisclosed location for interrogation."

One of Shapiro's students is busy with some last-minute research in his office, so he and I convene in a conference room where Ph.D. students suffer their oral examinations. For thirty-seven years Shapiro has been recording butterfly populations at ten specific sites and at frequent intervals from the San Francisco Bay to the east slope of the Sierra Nevada. He's studied butterflies worldwide, written torrents of essays and academic papers on them. It quickly becomes evident to me that he still is infatuated with them. I ask him why, and the answer is bittersweet.

"I think it is a unique artifact of my own childhood, and I have no idea if it can generalize to anybody else. My parents had an unhappy marriage. They fought all the time. I sought refuge from the constant atmosphere of tension in the house by spending as much time outdoors as I could. I got really deeply into nature and explored a variety of things from rocks to reptiles, and ended up in butterflies." When I ask this world expert why he chose butterflies instead of the rocks or reptiles, he says he's not really sure, but he keeps a pat answer handy. "I do it because that's what I do.

"I have to confess to having the same sorts of aesthetic responses to butterflies as a lot of other people," he acknowledges. "I think that's probably a component of why I like them." He takes a breath. "In my research I have to kill quite a lot of them, but I don't enjoy it. I do a lot less collecting than I used to." Collecting by definition means killing the butterflies. "It's not necessary," he says about what he sees now as overcollecting by scientists in the past. "If I had a compelling scientific reason, I would do it." But usually it's enough for him to make photographs, being careful to include a unique landmark in the picture to prove its locale.

Arthur Shapiro's almost-four-decades record of northern California spottings is now one of the two most complete databases in existence of butterfly sightings over time. The project compares butterfly seasonality—when what species are where—to weather. With ever-increasing concerns about global climate change, the project links the effects of weather change to the ability of butterfly species to thrive in regions where they previously were not found. On some trips Shapiro is greeted by an abundance of sightings. At one spot he recorded 115 different species during one visit. But an alarming result of the overall survey is that butterfly diversity is declining precipitously, and some species are becoming extinct. Is the cause habitat loss—or habitat fragmentation—in an urban California that continues to build over its cultivated landscape and its wildlands? Could it also be disease, pests, or pesticides? Is it climate change? Or is it something the researchers have not yet considered? Shapiro is still surveying, and still analyzing his counts.

I continue the conversation with questions about what some call "butterfly magic."

"Is it correct that metamorphosis remains a mystery?" I ask him. I've yet to find an entomologist who claims to fully understand how a caterpillar becomes a butterfly. "Do we know everything that goes on in that soup in the chrysalis when the caterpillar becomes a butterfly?"

"Oh, heavens no! Of course not!" But he's convinced the mystery will be solved. "We're getting there."

"Why don't we know that yet?"

"We're making tremendous progress," he says with enthusiasm. "It was a total black box when I was a graduate student. What's going on is you have a set of genes that are expressed in the early stages. You have a set of genes that are expressed in the later stages. The on and off turning is under hormonal control, and the hormonal control in some cases is specified by environmental inputs to the sensory apparatus, which translates into neural secretion and a whole chain of command."

Here's the best layman's translation I can manage from trying to decode the status of the research: Inside the pupa the cells of the caterpillar break down. New cells—butterfly cells—form making use of adult butterfly cell material that was carried in a latent state in the caterpillar. These cells form the components of the butterfly developing in the chrysalis.

Magic, indeed.

"Is it irritating not to know?" I wonder.

"It's not irritating at all," he answers, scientist that he is, "it's stimulating because it gives us something to strive for. Our future graduate students will not lack for work to do!"

Shapiro is impressed by the toughness and stamina he finds in butterflies. He tells me the story of a stray Queen (*Danaus gilippus*) that he found at his Donner Summit inspection site in the Sierra Nevada, an example of a butterfly thriving far from its usual home hundreds of miles away, likely from the south of California in San Diego or Riverside County. He's intrigued by Painted Ladies that hail from the U.S.–Mexico border flying from dawn until late afternoon for days at a time up to Sacramento, several hundred miles that they can cover in less than a week. Some of the Painted Ladies keep going, as far as Portland and Seattle. "That's amazing," he says with what sounds like an almost parental pride. "There are butterflies on the shores of the Arctic Ocean. There are butterflies in the sub-Antarctic. There are butterflies at sixteen thousand feet in the Andes and perhaps slightly higher in the Himalayas."

"Where are there no butterflies?"

"In the ocean. In absolute desert where there are no resources." If there are no hostplants available for the larvae to feed on, if there is no nectar and water for the imagoes to suck up with their proboscis, there are no butterflies. "Probably in your average Safeway parking lot, although some may fly through from time to time." He smiles. "They're tough little bastards."

Several weeks later I join Professor Arthur Shapiro in the field to catch sight of his "tough little bastards" with his professional guidance. We leave his Davis headquarters on a perfect late summer morning of clear blue skies, the temperature heading toward the high seventies. Out on the freeway we speed east across the Sacramento River, past downtown Sacramento, and out on US 50 toward Lake Tahoe. Just east of the city, in Rancho Cordova, we take the Sunrise Boulevard exit and slide into the urban sprawl—a left turn through a nondescript strip mall parking lot and past its out-of-business end unit, a storefront with a fading sign reading Payless—out into a housing tract for a few blocks to a parking place in front of a generic California tract house.

We walk across a soccer field toward the American River en route to a hike along the river that Professor Shapiro has been taking most every two weeks for the last thirty-one years (along with his nine other site surveys between the San Francisco Bay and the east slope of the Sierra Nevada). His modus operandi is seemingly simple: he walks along the riverbank or on bike paths or atop the endless rock tailings left behind by miners who dredged the river for gold, and he looks for butterflies, scanning the landscape ("Unlike dragonflies, I can't see behind me, but that's life"). When he spots one, he adds it to his tally for the day, noting its species and sex. "I'm looking for motion. You develop a search image. It's not entirely a conscious process. It clicks: THAT'S A FIERY SKIPPER! You don't have to think about why it's a Fiery Skipper."

I'm imposing on what is usually solo time for Shapiro. His routine is to make the study site trips alone. I ask him if he's consumed by the search for specimens, or if the hikes are a time not just for butterfly hunting but also for meditation, daydreams, fantasizing.

"I can't guarantee that I won't meditate or fantasize. What's the conventional wisdom—the average adult male American thinks about sex once every two minutes? But I try to be focused on my data collection. Notice all the yellow jackets," he says, changing the subject. "They are extremely efficient caterpillar-killing machines. They are probably the most important predators of butterflies in most of the north temperate zone, which is not widely recognized."

Walking with Shapiro is like exploring a document dump. He spews endless intriguing butterfly factoids, and details about increasingly rare plants native to California before the arrival of Europeans and the invasive exotics that came with the foreigners. A fighter plane, maybe from nearby Travis Air Force Base, blasts across the sky heading toward the mountains, but Shapiro is looking down and announces, "That was a Fiery Skipper, but I'm not going to count it because I couldn't see it clearly enough to be absolutely certain, but from the motion it almost had to be. All I saw was the motion out of the corner of my right eye." We could not find that individual butterfly again, but we saw other Fiery Skippers, little guys about an inch long and across, the males orange and yellow with brown spots, the females brown with orange and yellow spots.

Dogs bark and birds sing as we stroll alongside the river. Shapiro points out a horehound plant, identifying it as an excellent nectar source for small butterflies with short tongues. Tongues? Why does he call the proboscis a tongue? Why not, the word communicates. He cites a controversy covered in *Science* magazine questioning whether it would be acceptable to use the word fuzz in a scientific paper instead of the technical term, pubescence.

Suddenly there's a flutter!

"What do we have here?" I ask, realizing I'm excited to see a butterfly.

"We have here a Buckeye. It appears to be a female." As is the case with the Fiery Skippers, male and female markings of most butterflies are distinct.

I see something else. "What's that?"

Shapiro dismisses my sighting, "That's a grasshopper." Today we do not care about grasshoppers. But the Buckeye he identifies is not just a female, but a female of the distinct type known as a rosa, "because the underside of the hind wing has a reddish-purplish flush." In a flash, Shapiro sees those specific markings, and makes a stroke in his notebook.

Seconds later he calls out, "Oh, there's an Orange Sulphur male!" We target coyotebrush, one of the late-blooming plants along the river still flowering a couple of weeks before autumn this drought year, and stand directly in front of a patch of it that's as tall as we are; it's buzzing with bees. We don't care about spotting bees any more than we care about grasshoppers. "There we go," announces Shapiro pointing, "right up there, a male Fiery Skipper, that's the one that breeds on mowed lawn." We had seen our first Fiery Skipper of the day back on the soccer field.

The bushy coyotebrush is alive with butterflies. "Here we've got action," Shapiro is enthused. "Male Buckeye," he announces, "look at all the Skippers. That's a Field Skipper, that's another. There's a Buckeye."

I'm impressed; the Buckeye allows me to get close, and I can see its looming eye spots and brilliant orange stripes. "Wow, it's pretty."

"Yeah, lovely," the scientist agrees. "If you look at the underside, you should see the purple flush. And there should be an Acmon Blue here, at least one." After thirty-one years, Shapiro can forecast what he expects to see where and when. "Here's another Buckeye."

The butterflies are busy feeding and seem unaware of—or at least not bothered by—our curiosity and attention to their detail.

"Do you have a favorite butterfly?" I ask.

"Probably the Sonoran Blue. I think it's the most beautiful butterfly in California, but that's purely an aesthetic judgment." The Sonoran Blue is an elegant bright blue with patches of bright orange fringed with a black and white border. It adorns the cover of Shapiro's field guide to butterflies in the region he's been prowling since the early 1970s.[34]

We march on, seeing more skippers, both Field Skippers and Fiery Skippers. The American River glistens blue off to our right, but still no Acmon Blue sighting. We spot a turkey mullein plant. "The seeds are a staple for mourning doves and quail," my mentor for the day explains. "Indians used it as a fish poison and as a detergent. You crush it underwater and it lathers up. It is the host plant of the Gray Hairstreak, which we should see at least one of today, and another component of the pre-European vegetation here. It's one of the most successful at adapting to human occupation because it just loves disturbed roadsides."

Three women on horseback pass us on the path. Otherwise we're alone with the river and the butterflies. It's idyllic.

"When you take this walk every two weeks, you must think you have the best job in the world."

"It's amazing anyone would pay me to do this, yeah."

Shapiro points off to the distance. "See that purplish-brown?" He's pointing to a plant. "That's tall blue verbena. It's a good nectar source and it may still be in bloom." If so, it ought to be full of butterflies. We plod toward the verbena. Most of the bloom is gone, but where the flowers linger we find a Common Checkered Skipper, predictably, given its name, with black and white markings. "And there's a Field Skipper bothering it."

"Why is it bothering the Checkered?"

"I don't know. Maybe one of them is for McCain and the other is for Obama. Oh! A Eufala Skipper, that little drab brown thing there. That's another new species for today." He points to another set of wings, a White Female Sulphur.

I'm thrilled. I'm finding butterflies in the wild I probably would have walked right past without noticing were I not with my local guide. For him, it's a routine day along the transect, void of surprises such as the Queen he saw at Donner Summit. We plod over the cobbles of the mine tailings.

"Someday I'm going to find a two-pound gold nugget here," Shapiro announces, and I realize he looks like a miner, a California Forty-niner, with his grizzled and wild white beard, and his blue jeans and work shirt. Replace his notebook with a gold pan, and he would fit right in amongst the crowds rushing to the foothills in 1849. A day-flying moth flits past us; Shapiro acknowledges it, but adds nothing to his notes. We're counting butterflies, and a moth is not a butterfly.

"Look! There's an Acmon Blue!" It just flew over a patch of deer-weed, Shapiro informs me, but I see nothing. "There's another." I still see nothing. "Follow me. It's a little blue guy." The male is blue; the female is black with a row of orange spots. "There's one, see him dancing?" Yes! I see him, and he is a pretty-looking guy, with a frilly fringe along his wing edges. "You just have to be where the resources are," Shapiro shrugs off my excitement with encountering what is such a routine matter for him. "The butterflies are quite mobile. They will simply follow the resources." Go where their food is located and you'll find the butterflies.

We spot a couple of Buckeyes.

"Courtship," announces Shapiro. "It's a male flying around a female scattering pheromones." He's hovering, patrolling. But she's paying attention to a flower. "She's saying, 'I'm hungry.'" We watch as she eats while he courts. "They are multiple maters, so if he's persistent he might be successful. Almost certainly she's mated before. If it's been awhile she might be receptive, if he's persistent enough." If she's not receptive, it's no go for him. We watch her flutter and stay where he found her. "She's not leaving and she is fluttering, both of which indicate she's interested enough to say, 'Go ahead. Keep it up, I like the smell.' She's not doing anything evasive. If she were very, very uninterested, she would leave." He continues to circle her. "Hope springs eternal. You can watch this sort of performance for half an hour until you finally get fed up and leave." We watch as she takes off and flies a few feet from the flower to a nearby tree and alights on a leaf. "That's a good sign. If she goes up in a tree, that's a really good sign that she might give in, because when they actually copulate they almost always will do it in a sheltered location like in a tree where predators are unlikely to find them." Shapiro smiles as we walk off, with a tip of the hat to Mr. Buckeye, "I think he's probably going to get her."

We allow the Buckeye couple their privacy and head back to the banal-looking streets of suburbia, just steps from the butterfly wilds of the American River banks.

The next day Professor Shapiro sent the results of our survey to me. We saw nine different species and 102 unique animals. Here's our list (in the professor's order):

17 Buckeye, *Junonia coenia*
18 Orange Sulphur, *Colias eurytheme*
13 Fiery Skipper, *Hylephilia phyleus*
33 Field Skipper, *Atalopedes campestris*
3 Common Checkered Skipper, *Pyrgus communis*
4 Eufala Skipper, *Lerodea eufala*
11 Acmon Blue, *Plebejus acmon*
2 Mylitta Crescent, *Phyciodes mylitta*
1 West Coast Lady, *Vanessa annabella*

Plus we encountered a California Tortoiseshell, *Nymphalis californica,* as we walked on the Rancho Cordova streets, but the Tortoiseshell didn't count officially because he was not within the confines of the study site. Compared with past walks, we did okay: not an extraordinary number of different species, but plenty of butterflies.

Just as was the case after my butterfly-spotting escapade with Jeffrey Glassberg in the Greenhorn Mountains, so it is after my walk with Arthur Shapiro along the American River bank. I've been taught techniques for intentionally finding butterflies. I know now where to look for them. Instead of just encountering them by chance, I can choose locales to search where it is likely they will be fluttering and lighting. My eyes have been opened wider with the added expertise.

Chapter Nine

THE BUTTERFLY AS ART

My butterfly brooch came to me unexpectedly in a box of jewelry my aunt was tired of and gave to my wife. Not long after I was enticed by Jane Foulds to write this book, I started wearing the brooch, and it is a remarkable example of the ubiquitous lure of butterflies (and good jewelry design). "Oh, what a beautiful butterfly!" I hear all the time. I wear it on my suit coat lapel or on the pocket of my shirt most days, and sometimes I forget that it's there until I hear another, "I love your butterfly!" It is a great conversation starter.

David-Anderson Norway is stamped on the back. It's an iridescent blue with long, looping antennae, enamel on silver. My aunt chooses nice stuff. I've since learned that the company was founded in 1876, back when Oslo was still Christiana, by the original David Anderson, a gold- and silversmith born in 1843. When his son Arthur took over the company in 1901 following David's death, he hyphenated his father's name to create the company identity. It was David who added enameling on gold and silver to the David-Anderson offerings, and my blue butterfly pin is an enameled piece, guilloché enameled onto .925 sterling—elegant and eye-catching, both because of its size and its sheen. A two-inch blue butterfly is not a common sight adorning an American man's costume.

Guilloché (pronounced gee-oh-SHAY) enameling refers to the process: a repeated ornamental pattern is mechanically etched into the gold or silver (it's been used on banknote printing plates to make forgery more difficult) onto which the enamel is baked. The result makes the pattern seem to float behind the enamel coloring, and is remarkably reminiscent of the compelling veined patterns of butterfly wings.

David-Anderson is still a going concern, still specializing in enameled silver butterfly pins. But they're not the only jewelers supplying butterfly aficionados. Butterfly stuff is everywhere, including other brooches, such as the one highlighted in the Firestone and Parson advertisement in a late summer 2008 issue of *The New Yorker* offering "extremely fine estate jewelry." It's dated circa 1975, and signed by the Paris jeweler Van Cleef & Arpels. The ad describes it as a "yellow gold, onyx, coral, and diamonds butterfly brooch." The price is noted at $27,500.[35]

Butterflies are pervasive in fine art and popular culture; they have been throughout history. In her book rich with full-color illustrations, *The Spirit of Butterflies: Myth, Magic, and Art*, Maraleen Manos-Jones cites Minoan butterflies on the palace wall paintings at Knossos in Crete and other Cretan butterfly images from antiquity, along with butterfly images from pre-Columbian America on Toltec statuary and examples of butterflies decorating pharaohs' tombs in Egypt. Butterflies adorned ancient Greek and Roman Empire coins and appear on furniture, costume, tableware, textiles, tattoos, and, of course, jewelry throughout the ages. It would probably be easier to compile a list of those artists whose work does not use the butterfly as a motif than those who do: from van Gogh to Warhol to Brueghel the Elder to Dürer to Picasso to Escher.

The Barbie Mariposa doll gives little girls (and undoubtedly some boys) the opportunity to size up a Barbie equipped with giant wings that can change from purple to pink with the press of a button—offering a bizarre interpretation of metamorphosis. Mattel, Barbie's manufacturer, marketed the fantasy Barbie-with-wings in 2008 in conjunction with that they called a "butterfly-themed movie" made only for DVD released by Universal and titled, of course, *Barbie Mariposa*. In the late 1990s, Mattel produced a line of Barbie dolls called Butterfly Art. Barbie came complete with a permanent butterfly tattooed on her stomach and a sheet of temporary tattoos that her playmates could affix on her plastic curves to accent her crocheted bikini top and blue jeans short skirt. If you're in a retro mood, you can get a butterfly-tattooed Barbie of your own on eBay for less than ten bucks.

Kjell Sanved and Barbara Bedette roamed the world from their Smithsonian Institution headquarters in Washington, D.C., to collect a full alphabet depicted in the designs of butterfly wings. They now operate Butterfly Alphabet, Inc. and sell posters, books, and customized cards that make use of butterfly wings to spell messages.

Butterflies Are Free was a 1972 Goldie Hawn vehicle based on a play by Leonard Gershe. The movie title comes from a passage in Charles Dickens's *Bleak House*: "I only ask to be free. The butterflies are free. Mankind will surely not deny to Harold Skimpole what it concedes to the butterflies." Steve Schwartz wrote the words and music of the title song for the film. The refrain initially reports the lack of rules for a new love affair, "Butterflies are free, and so are we," but then acknowledges the complications of its ending, "Butterflies are free. Why aren't we?"

Carmen McCrae sings "Poor Butterfly," and it is a classic song based on the *Madame Butterfly* story. But there are many others. Ella Fitzgerald croons "Dark Butterfly." Thelonious Monk plays "Little Butterfly." You can hear "Butterfly" sung by Mariah Carey (from her eponymous album) and "Butterfly Kisses" with Bob Carlisle. But probably the best-known musical butterfly is the title character of Puccini's opera *Madame Butterfly*, relating the sorry tale of the cad

American Navy officer Lieutenant B. F. Pinkerton taking advantage of and scorning the innocent Japanese geisha nicknamed Butterfly. "Butterfly! Butterfly! Butterfly!" he laments as she kills herself.

Butterflies populate mythology worldwide, often playing the role of souls reincarnated. The love story of Cupid and Psyche offers a prime example, in which Psyche, whose name means both soul and butterfly in Greek, gains immortality.

In addition to popular music and film, butterflies populate contemporary literature.

"Ayesha the orphan was nineteen years old when she began her walk back to Titlipur along the rutted potato track," Salman Rushdie writes in *The Satanic Verses*, "but by the time she turned up in her village some forty-eight hours later she had attained a kind of agelessness, because her hair had turned as white as snow while her skin had regained the luminous perfection of a new-born child's, and although she was completely naked the butterflies had settled upon her body in such thick swarms that she seemed to be wearing a dress of the most delicate material in the universe."

In *The Collector* John Fowles creates a crazed loner who collects butterflies and kidnaps a girl, a young art student he holds prisoner in much the same manner as he collects butterflies. "How many butterflies have you killed?" she asks her captor when he shows off his pinned butterflies. "I'm thinking of all the butterflies that would have come from these if you'd let them live. I'm thinking of all the living beauty you've ended. You're like a miser, you hoard up all the beauty in these drawers. I hate scientists. I hate people who collect things, and classify things and give them names and then forget all about them."

The value of poached butterflies is explored in José Manuel Prieto's *Nocturnal Butterflies of the Russian Empire*, and the obsessions of collectors. "Russia has several butterflies, extinct in the West," explains the character who hires a poacher. "There is one type in particular, the *yazikus*, which lives only from the end of May to mid-September. I would give anything to possess it." *Butterfly Stories* is a William Vollman outlet for tales, as he writes, "partly about that most honest form of love called prostitution."

Butterfly imagery circulates throughout language. "Float like a butterfly, sting like a bee," warned Muhammad Ali.

The cantina in Michoacán where the proprietor Simon served butterfly-shaped tart is not the only opportunity to eat butterfly-influenced meals. At the Trieste Café in San Francisco's North Beach, a bohemian headquarters, you can sip a cappuccino and nibble on a sugar cookie cut in the shape of a butterfly, decorated with multicolored sprinkles. Want to make lunch that looks like a butterfly? Check out perpetualpreschool.com, an amazing source for butterfly-themed treats, where teachers exchange ideas. Melinda, for example, suggests a butterfly cake to serve after reading the students Eric Carle's *The Very Hungry Caterpillar*: Bake a yellow cake in a square pan. Cut it diagonally and put the 90-degree points of the triangles together, with a Hostess Twinkie as the butterfly body. Wendy offers a sandwich alternative: Spread peanut butter on toast cut into triangles placed point-to-point to make a butterfly shape. Sprinkle M&Ms on the peanut butter, use a banana slice for the head and pretzel sticks for antennae. From Lynn comes a variant on the theme. Use a carrot between the bread points for the butterfly's body. Spread the bread with strawberry cream cheese or yellow margarine and then arrange Froot Loops and nuts on the cream cheese or margarine to create wing patterns. She uses licorice strips for antennae. Like sushi? Order a caterpillar roll: avocado slices on a bed of white rice to look like the articulated body, strips of cucumber for the antennae, salmon eggs for the eyes.

Innocent fun, valuable science, or an obsessive compulsion—what is the nature of extreme collecting—from butterflies to whatever captivates the collector?

Psychiatrist Werner Muensterberger, a collector himself of African art, studied a wide variety of fellow collectors and came up with his lie-down-on-the-couch style analysis of what motivates collectors to hoard. "They like to pose or make a spectacle of their possessions," he writes. "But one soon realizes that these possessions, regardless of their value or significance, are but stand-ins for themselves." As a shrink, he sees a problem that needs addressing if you're stockpiling stuff. "Their deep inner function," he claims about collected items, "is to screen off self-doubt and unassimilated memories." He thinks collectors, by definition, suffer from self-confidence and self-esteem problems. But collecting can serve a useful purpose, in his opinion, because it can "become an almost magical means for undoing the strains and stresses of early life and achieving the promise of goodness." Nonetheless, he sees butterflies, or any collected items, as "inanimate substitutes for reassurance and care. Perhaps even more telling, these objects prove, both to the collector and to the world, that he or she is special and worthy of them."[36] Harsh words from the doctor, but, despite his qualifications, they are just his opinion.

Relax, cautions Stephen Calloway, a curator at the Victoria and Albert Museum in London and a collector specializing in letters from the 1890s. "Collecting is for most collectors," he writes, "just a reasonably absorbing and largely harmless pastime, looked upon by an uncomprehending world as a kind of gentle madness. For a few," he concedes, "it can become a dangerous preoccupation; its sensations—the breathless exhilaration of the quest, the thrill of capture, the enjoyment of the novelty, the sense of satisfaction and pride in possession—as addictive as any drug."[37] Calloway's analysis may help explain the obsession and compulsion expressed by criminal collectors such as the Skalski, Kral, and Grinnell cabal, the first butterfly poachers successfully prosecuted for violating the Endangered Species Act.

Collecting is a search for immortality, suggests journalist and novelist Philipp Blom. "Every collection is a constant reminder of the very reality it has been created to stave off," he writes. "The greater the value of the collection, the greater the risk of loss that it represents; the greater the will to live on, the more glaring the admission of mortality and oblivion. Objects in rows and cases, arranged along the wall or piled up on the floor, are anticipated headstones and memorials, every one of them the grave of a past desire, or the illusion of having conquered it momentarily, of peace at last."[38]

And you thought your butterflies—or your stamps or quilts or seashells or Hot Wheels—were just a fun hobby.

Foster City does not seem as if it belongs a few miles south of San Francisco on the Bayshore Freeway. Built on landfill around canals, its luxurious houses look like they are in a Florida neighborhood, especially because the horizon is dotted with imported palm trees. The day I show up to visit Steven Albaranes is particularly hot, adding to the subtropical feel. I walk past the open garage and the Corvette parked inside with the personalized license plate reading BUTRFLZ, around the house and down to the floating dock, where Albaranes greets me. We sit on the gently rocking dock; a pleasure craft slides past. A very tranquil scene indeed.

Albaranes practices what he calls the butterfly art business. I first heard about him and his work from Jane Foulds, at her reserve in Nicaragua. He buys butterflies from suppliers like Foulds and mounts them in clear plastic boxes. What started for him as a hobby is now a full-time business. Albaranes makes a circuit of craft fairs, and sells enough "butterfly art" to support his waterfront home and California dream car.

Before the hobby became a business, Albaranes tells me he was paid a visit by Fish and Wildlife Service agents. He figures an informant saw one of his pieces at a fair and was concerned that butterflies with such vibrant colors might be illegal to buy and sell.

"We heard you're buying butterflies," they told him. "We just want to make sure you're doing everything on the up and up." He was. At the time he was buying from dealers in the United States. The onus is on the importer to obtain the needed Fish and Wildlife licenses to bring foreign butterflies into the U.S. for sale. Once the business stabilized, Albaranes decided to cut out the middleman and obtained a license so that he could deal directly with overseas suppliers. Now the burden is on him to ensure that he does not trade in illegal endangered species.

"I pretty much know what those butterflies are." We've barely said hello, and already the conversation is about the dangerous world of butterflies. "First of all, those butterflies [the endangered ones] are very, very expensive and I'm not putting that kind of stuff in my artwork—nobody would be doing that." There are plenty of flashy butterflies that are not endangered. Those are his medium. "I have basically about three hundred species that I've grown fond of that I use in my artwork, and I just use them over and over and over again." He likes the pretty, not the rare. "I've never been interested in the collecting aspect of the real, real rare butterflies. I've been more interested in the art form, the designing and putting together, and then selling my artwork."

Albaranes is a warm and welcoming host. He's wearing a tropical-colored short-sleeved sport shirt, jeans, and loafers with no socks. His life story spills with little prompting. The son of a salesman, he labored for years representing the Italian eyeglass manufacturer

Safilo, working a West Coast route, calling on optometrists and opticians. Life was good. He bought the Foster City house and filled it with the tropical colors that please him still; at the center of his décor was a two-hundred-gallon saltwater aquarium containing swimming fish.

Enter two life-changing events. Number one, Safilo started cutting up his territory, reducing his client base and hence his income. Number two, the 1989 Loma Prieta earthquake struck, with its epicenter not far south of Foster City. The severe temblor knocked down freeways, collapsed the roadway on the Bay Bridge, set San Francisco's Marina District on fire, and shook Albaranes's house—built on pilings driven into the landfill—like a paint mixing machine agitates a five-gallon can at the hardware store. The aquarium was a victim. "All the water came out and the fish died, and it was horrible." A couple of weeks later, Albaranes went to the Academy of Sciences in Golden Gate Park to see a butterfly exhibit. There he saw "a very artistic display—in an acrylic box—of yellow and green and blue butterflies going from the floor to the ceiling. That just blew me away." Albaranes wanted it, but it wasn't for sale. If he could have bought it, he figures he may never have started his butterfly box business. But he was thrilled. "I just loved the colors of the butterflies. I was attracted to the colors of the tropical saltwater fish, and it looked like the same kind of idea. I said to myself, 'God, I don't have to clean it every five minutes.'"

Albaranes bought his first butterflies shortly thereafter. He learned how to "spread" the dead butterflies. He mounted them in acrylic boxes, and he found buyers. I ask the salesman for the sales pitch. What are these things and why would I want one?

"They are real exotic butterflies mounted in clear acrylic panels or clear acrylic boxes. It is just an incredible way to decorate around the house. It's Mother Nature in the house. If you go to a museum, you're going to see butterflies, you'll see a lot of butterflies. But you'll see them independently, all by themselves, spread flat as a pancake, generally with a pin in them." Albaranes offers a different reality. "What I do is I spread them not flat, more of a V-shape. I try to make them look like they're flying and very natural."

I'm trying to understand the appeal. "Yours are dead, but they don't look dead?"

"They look like they're flying. When I mount them on clear acrylic stems and you hang them on the wall, it looks like they're flying up the wall. That's the beauty of it." For him, it's all butterflies, all the time. "I enjoy making money and I enjoy selling my art and I enjoy creating it."

We go into Albaranes's studio, a spacious room just inside sliding glass doors from the dock. It is an awesome sight. I am surrounded by shimmering clear plastic cases filled with sprays of butterflies— and yes, they do appear to be in flight, as flocks of them whirl in place. Some of the cases are filled with butterflies of the same species, others with a variety of sizes and shapes and colors.

"You are looking at some of the most beautiful, exotic, tropical butterflies in the world," he tells me in a voice filled with pride. "Right here." Each encased butterfly is as perfect as the Owls Jane Foulds pulled from her freezer in Nicaragua for me to inspect. "Buying them from commercial breeders, I'm buying butterflies the way you would buy a diamond ring. They already know that I want perfect A-1 quality butterflies. You will not find any rips or tears or smudges in my butterflies. People ask me all the time, 'Are these real?' I understand that question because they look perfect." I'm visualizing Jane's refrigerator again, and the Tupperware box. But Albaranes has another explanation for me. "When the butterfly dies—they only live about two, three weeks on the farms—the workers' job is to pick it up." Three weeks of life with no damage? Hard to imagine. "When the butterfly dies the wings close, but they're still pliable because they had just died. Workers open it up. They look at it and if it's perfect it goes in the perfect pile." Albaranes stops, reaches over to me and grabs at something.

"Let me just take this little bug off you," he says with great courtesy. Here we are, surrounded by dead insects, and at least one live one that found me. He turns my attention back to the perfect butterfly pile.

I'm still trying to justify the A-1 perfect sample with a natural butterfly death. "They die and their wings close," I repeat back to him. "So these guys all died a natural death?"

"Naturally."

It sounds like the beginning of an Abbott and Costello routine. I tell Albaranes about my experiences with Foulds's A-1 perfect Owls, butterflies she refrigerated immediately after they eclosed in order to retain nature's perfection.

"Interesting," he says. "I have heard that some farms will do that. I don't deal with anybody in Central America. I'm dealing with South America. I've never been there . . . ."

"You haven't visited any of your producers to see their operations?"

"Never been to any of them, no. But this is what they've told me," he says about the natural deaths. "I can only go with what they told me."

I ask him if he'd like to make the trip, see the farms, and meet the operators.

"You know," he says to my surprise, "not really, not really. I don't know why. It just never appealed to me. The places I buy from like Papua New Guinea, and Peru, I've been dealing with these people and at times they tell me they can't get in touch with me, they're deep in the jungles doing their thing. I've seen the movie *Arachnophobia* and I've got to tell you, that's how I would come home, in that box, being bit by a spider." He smiles at his confession, and offers an explanation. "I'm from New York. It just doesn't appeal to me, the jungle. I never had that kind of fascination."

"Too dangerous down there?"

"Just not for me. I'm not an adventurous kind of person in that respect, I'm not the Indiana Jones type of person."

"A Corvette goes 180 miles an hour," I remind him.

He laughs. "I don't go 180 in the Corvette."

We're looking at startling and intense iridescent Blue Morphos from the Amazon, butterflies Albaranes buys from Brazil and Peru. Startling because the color is so incredibly rich and deep. Foil-like. Gorgeous. Big ones and small ones, assembled as if in flight. "I've seen on video how they fly, which is beautiful. They're very lumbering. They just kind of float in the air. When they're resting on the tree you will hardly ever see the blue. They will always have their wings closed. The underside is what Mother Nature gave them to protect themselves, because they will look like part of the tree, which is very brown." The contrast is striking.

We walk over to Steven Albaranes's workbench. He picks up a dead butterfly, wings folded.

"I've already relaxed this butterfly."

"What do you mean, 'relaxed him'?"

"Relaxing him is getting him in a state where he is like he just died. The quickest way to do it is to just inject him with hot water, right in the body. After fifteen minutes he'll get pliable. Hot water will do it." He takes the butterfly, holds the abdomen between his thumb and forefinger, and squeezes gently. The dead butterfly's wings magically and slowly open. Once the butterfly opens, Albaranes spreads him on a pinning board he's specially made for the job.

"I guess it's like watching a surgeon work," he tells me as he pulls the wings further open. "When you watch him work, it's going to look easy. But then you try doing it. My father visited me and said, 'Let me try.' He spent an hour and ruined everything that he touched. I ripped every wing when I first tried spreading the butterflies."

He uses a variety of boards with different V angles. He pins the spread butterfly with a pin so thin the hole in the wing is all but invisible. The angle of the board is mimicked by the butterfly wings, which after about twenty-four hours stiffen to appear as they do in flight. He pins the wings of the dead butterfly that he's holding in place, adjusting the fore wing and the hind wing into positions they would be in were the butterfly fluttering in the air. He picks up another butterfly, and squeezes the relaxed body. The wings begin to open.

"This is repetitious work," he says.

I noticed. "Does it get tedious for you?"

"No, never. I just enjoy doing it."

"Now, Steven," I say to him when he's finished showing me how he spreads the butterflies. "Here these guys are, they're all lying here on your table, and they're all dead."

"Yes."

"And you're poking pins in them."

"Yes."

"Is there anything weird about that? For example with your fish, those fish . . ."

" . . . were alive," he finishes my sentence.

"You fed them and you cleaned the tank and they were swimming around."

He's ready with an answer. "These guys already lived their life. I even said the same thing, 'It's awfully sad that God gave them only two, three weeks to live.' Although if you count the caterpillar and the cocoon and the butterfly it's obviously much, much longer, it's like a year. But who am I to say what God gives? I mean I wish we had four hundred years to live. That would have been nicer. I mean sixty, seventy, eighty years, that seems like an awfully short time and once it's gone that's it; we're done. So I don't look at it like that. I'm just offering another way of viewing these things rather than seeing them in a museum."

"They're absolutely gorgeous," I agree. There's no question about it.

"The ones that you give pleasure to outweigh the ones that are not happy with it, hundreds to one."

Handling the dead butterflies day after day doesn't bother him in the slightest.

"I'm getting them already dead. I suppose if I had to have killed them that would be a totally different story. If that were the case I wouldn't be doing this." Once he was given a couple of chrysalises for a present. "That was exciting. One day I get up and they're all hatched and they're flying around the living room. The biggest charge I got was taking them on the deck and letting them go."

The Blue Morpho display I've been eyeing retails for $295. Steven Albaranes tells me that price tag represents a combination of three factors: "One is my time. Another is a petroleum product, acrylic, which is extremely expensive. The other is a collectible item, a butterfly."

"There's a fourth," I tell him, "how you present it."

"Oh, I appreciate that, too. I think that what I do is extremely attractive. You tweak a butterfly here, you tweak a butterfly there, you will change the entire look of the display. It's just like a painter. He has this beautiful scene and then you stick a tree right in the middle of it, I got to tell you, that's going to change the whole look of it. Once I get a particular display to where the butterflies look pleasing, I use that design over and over again with different color combinations."

As I'm leaving his workshop, Albaranes takes note of my butterfly pin, the blue reminiscent of his Blue Morphos.

"I love that. Where did you get that? It's absolutely stunning! I'm just looking at the blue color. That's so gorgeous."

Always satisfying to wow a collector.

When we talked at his University of California at Davis office, ento-mologist Arthur Shapiro described the nature of the colors Steven Albaranes manipulates. "Each wing scale," he explained, "is secreted by a single cell. The scale itself is not alive. The cell deposits one pig-ment in that scale and dies." Most of the pigments in the butterfly world do not fade over the time one of Albaranes's customers would expect one of his displays to last; butterflies in Victorian-era collec-tions still look brilliant.

There are water-soluble colors decorating some butterflies. An example is the Orange Sulphur butterfly, common around alfalfa fields. If the Orange Sulphur gets soaked by a farmer's irrigation sprinklers, the water will wash off some of the pigment, leaving water spots on the wings. "Occasionally you'll pick one up," Shapiro told me, "that's been exposed for several hours to water with the result that most of the orange pigment has been leached out and the wings are translucent." Probably not a good butterfly choice for an artist seeking a brilliant medium.

A film found on the wings and prismatic wing structures both can produce optical effects, which create some butterfly colors. Sha-piro cited the Blue Morpho as a good example of this. "There's no blue pigment there," he said about the flashy iridescent favorite of so many collectors. "It's all an optical effect. If you wet the animal, you see that its actual pigment color is brown." And if you look at the wing from its edge, the color disappears and all you see are the outlines of the wing scales.

Is Steven Albaranes's work art or craft? Others use butterflies and butterfly pieces to make graphic works. Are they artists or ani-mal abusers? I found two well-established artists using butterfly wings as a medium and making works that look remarkably simi-lar. One is internationally famous and sells his pieces for ludicrous sums, the other labors out of the celebrity spotlight, convinced she's been copied. T. S. Eliot wrote in *The Sacred Wood*, "Immature poets imitate; mature poets steal; bad poets deface what they take, and good poets make it into something better, or at least something different."[39]

Above a French café in her Topanga Canyon studio in the Santa Monica Mountains north of Los Angeles (near where biologist Chris Nagano went chasing butterflies with his net as a little boy), artist Lori Precious makes something different. Her sole medium is butterfly and beetle pieces: wings and antennae. When I visit she apologizes for her cluttered studio, but it doesn't look cluttered to me, rather it is alive with works both in progress and recently completed: dazzling, detailed portraits of long-faded Hollywood starlets. Scattered around the studio, piled in drawers, and pinned to the stark white walls are the obituary pages of the *Los Angeles Times*.

"When a starlet dies," she says, pointing to column inch after column inch of details regarding the long life and many movie roles of Virginia Grey, "they'll have an obituary even though she had only a minor role in this world." ("Virginia Grey had everything, except luck," Louis B. Meyer is reported to have said about his longtime contract player.[40]) The obituaries Precious is most attracted to include glamour shots from when the women were in their glory days, and these poses prompted her to move from constructing images of stained glass windows with butterfly parts to making works depicting the prime-time days of the deceased actresses. "I saw them in butterfly wings. I love these," she points at the forever young starlets. "Women, if we're beautiful, are like freaks of nature—in a good way. It's like a flower. There's just that moment." She looks at my gray beard and draws me into her metaphor with a smile. "We're not twenty anymore. You look back and you know there's a time when you were in your youth and in your glory. It's that moment and then it's gone." And it's a moment, she says, that newspapers—especially the *Los Angeles Times*, because of its Hollywood beat—simply cannot resist, because everybody loves a beautiful woman. "They're simply gorgeous," she looks at them with an aesthetic appreciation, "and there's something kind of melancholy about them, too."

Her works are striking, and from just a slight distance it's impossible to read the colors as pieces of butterflies; they appear to the untrained eye as layered paint. The artist walks me to within inches of Virginia Grey and points out how she makes reflections ("which make people alive") in the eyes and lips with pieces of what she calls "a really great White I found." And close up to the pictures the wing scales are clear to identify. Ms. Grey's eyelashes are fabricated with pieces of butterfly antenna. As in classic portraits, the frozen-in-time actresses are framed in oval.

The vibrancy of the butterfly wing hues gives the pieces a Technicolor-like effect, of course ideal for a starlet. Precious sculpts them into images that startle the imagination with a combination of the real and the pretend. They represent the reality of the eight-by-ten glossy publicity photograph while at the same time suggesting the façade that is Hollywood. They convey a sense of uncomfortable disorder to the banal, in much the same fashion that Soviet Realism makes unreal the daily images of workers and factories and tractors. The wings as elements of portraits depicting Virginia Grey, Tamara Dobson, and Anna Nicole Smith accomplish a potent and ideal visual effect: the staged personas fling themselves across the room at me. They tantalize me. They lure me. And yet—is it really necessary for her to use butterfly wings?

I like her work despite a gnawing sense of inexplicable unease regarding the artist's choice of materials. "There are some people who have a problem with it," she understands, and then offers her side of the story. "There is some collaboration I have with them. They're doing it with me; I'm not doing it to them. It's like a second metamorphosis for them. They went from being a caterpillar to a butterfly to now they're in this artwork. My art is about beauty and about a fleeting sense of beauty in particular. So it feels okay. At first it didn't," she allows, "but now it does." She tells me she buys her supplies from butterfly distributors, and that she relies on them to provide her with product from legitimate sources. She says she certainly would not want to use protected species. "That would be bad juju!"

Butterflies became the medium of choice for Lori Precious due to a chance encounter on the streets of Eastern Europe. "I found a crazy old peasant women in Prague right after the Wall came down. She was selling these iridescent butterfly wings out in some square. I had never seen a butterfly that was iridescent, so I bought a number of them for a dollar apiece and I thought, one day I'll do something with these." Not long after, she found herself in Paris, walking up the steps in Sainte-Chapelle, the Gothic chapel on Île de la Cité that's alive with light filtered through its multicolored stained glass windows. "I was enveloped in stained glass windows and I just saw it in butterfly wings." In the early nineties (and the date is critical for the controversy to come), she began work on a series of pieces—eventually totaling about fifty—depicting stained glass windows, and made from butterfly wings.

Precious is not the first to make art out of butterfly parts. Other artists have made use of the butterfly since the mid-1800s. But she may well be the first to use butterfly wings to interpret stained glass windows. In early 2007, Damien Hirst—famous for his dead animals displayed in tanks—hung a show at the Gagosian Gallery in Beverly Hills that included circular works made out of butterfly wings that look remarkably like stained glass windows and remarkably similar to Lori Precious's circular pieces. She was outraged and posted her feelings on the Internet: "This work is exactly like the work I have been doing for the last 14 years of my life! If you are an artist, or anyone who cares about creative individuality, please speak out against Damien Hirst to anyone who will listen!" She signed it, "Lori Precious (who does all her own work, with no assistants)."

Hirst, in fact, showed work he did with butterflies as early as 1991. Precious marks her visit to Sainte-Chapelle as taking place in 1992. But Hirst did not make—or at least exhibit—his butterfly windows until much later.

En route to Topanga Canyon I placed a call to the Gagosian while stuck in traffic on the 405, just south of Beverly Hills. I wanted to reflect on Hirst's work immediately prior to meeting with Precious. The gallery operator connected me with a woman whose Parisian accent flowed out of the earpiece of my mobile phone.

"I'm interested in seeing some of Hirst's butterfly stuff," I told her.

She said nothing was up for show, asked my name and my profession, and allowed that a Hirst butterfly was at the gallery, but in storage.

"I'm a writer," I answered honestly and ambiguously. In L.A.—especially—a writer—arguably—could have a billfold stuffed with enough cash to shop for a Hirst. "I'm stuck in traffic near you, how about I stop by and take a look at it?"

Her next question took me by surprise: blunt almost to the point of crass. But then I was hooked up with Beverly Hills.

"Are you," she asked with her romantic accent, "aware of the prices?"

"Oh, yes," I reassured her. "I'm very familiar with his work."

It was hard not to be that day, unless you were taking a holiday from the news. We were chatting just a couple of weeks after Hirst's record-shattering auction. In September 2008, Sotheby's in London raked in some $200 million peddling his output, including over $15 million for a bull in a tank of formaldehyde. His butterflies did well, too, netting $4 million for a butterfly piece called *Ascended*, and close to $3 million for one named *Reincarnated*.

She cordially invited me to stop by, even when I told her I only had a few minutes to spare. I pulled off the 405 at Santa Monica Boulevard and worked through the stop-and-go traffic to infamous

Rodeo Drive, a block from the Gagosian, and parked. A perky and delightful Cecile Le Paire met me in the gallery, in basic black jeans and a white blouse, the white matching the stark white, all-but-unmarked storefront of the gallery. We briefly swapped Paris stories, and she proved to be a most gracious hostess, escorting me to a basement storeroom where a circular Hirst filled a wall, one of his early—and still shocking—butterfly works: a canvas littered with butterflies stuck in the dried paint.

"He started his first butterfly paintings in 1991." Le Paire and I were chatting while we looked at the big painting, and I asked her to explain it. "The idea was that those butterflies came in cocoons. He put the cocoons on the table and they will," she hesitated and said, "pop up," before adding with a smile, "eclose—it is a French word." Indeed it is, and now incorporated into English, at least among those who fancy insects. "The paint will be fresh, and they will eclose and randomly end up in the paint." There is something quite grotesque about the painting, the canvas littered with a variety of butterflies, their wings and bodies paint-laden with blue, frozen in place where they died, trapped in the paint. It's not a pretty picture, but it is compelling specifically because it is so bizarre.

When the Gagosian show opened, Hirst acknowledged or bragged—take your pick—to the *Los Angeles Times* about the butterfly series, "They're macabre. The beauty of the geometry is more than you would expect, and then you realize that a lot of butterflies died to make it like that. So you are aware of the sort of tragedy."[41] That analysis would not impress Dawn Carr who, as the European director of People for the Ethical Treatment of Animals, called Hirst a sadist, and posed the question, "One has to wonder if Hirst was the sort of demented child who would pull the wings off flies for fun. He certainly has become that sort of adult. Butterfly wings are beautiful on a butterfly, but tearing small creatures to bits is not art, it's sadism."[42]

Hirst first made his stained glass assemblages in the early 2000s, according to Le Paire. Unfortunately, she said, she had none in stock to show me, but Gagosian offers silkscreen prints (absent the diamond dust that decorates the originals) of the stained glass pictures—unframed—for $30,000 each. As we said *au revoir*, Le Paire told me that Hirst had informed the gallery he intends to make no more works with butterflies—leaving the field open to Lori Precious. A few days later she sent a warm email to me checking on my continuing interest in Hirst's work. She attached an image of a round butterfly painting similar to the one I had seen with her in the gallery, except that it sported a green background instead of blue, and—to my eye—featured fewer butterflies than the blue one. Titled *King Midas*, it was for sale through her gallery; Le Paire found it at one of their London outlets. "We are asking US $2,200,000 for the painting," she wrote. I thanked her, saying I would have to pass on *King Midas*. She would not know that, unlike Midas, I did not have that kind of cash at my fingertips.

Cloistered in her studio high in the canyon, Lori Precious is frustrated by the attention (and money) Hirst receives for an idea she is convinced was first hers. "One of the things I most prize is my integrity," Precious says about the controversy, "and my creative originality. I understand that for artists and writers—I'm married to a writer—there can be a *zeitgeist* and they come up with the same or similar ideas, but I don't buy it. He was working with butterflies about the same time I was, except I was doing the stained glass windows at that time. He didn't come up with the stained glass window concept until fairly recently." When she read about his butterfly show at the Gagosian, she was shocked. "I was devastated. When I opened the paper—plus in my own hometown—I've got work in museums and have had solo shows with this work—I felt just completely dismissed. He's a juggernaut. What can I do to fight that? Nothing. It's made me want to not even leave my studio." Her voice is fraught with frustration and sad emotion. "These are my little four walls here, and I'm safe here."

I point to her dazzling and timeless starlets and remind her, "At least he's not doing anything like these." She nods, and I make her laugh when I add, "at least not yet."

Chapter Ten

CREATION VERSUS EVOLUTION

WE AMERICANS LOVE HYPERBOLE. U.S. CITIES AND TOWNS FROM coast to coast, from border to border love to proclaim themselves "The Fill-in-the-blank Capital of the World." Cedar Springs, Michigan, is the Red Flannel Capital of the World. The Cow Chip Throwing Capital of the World is Beaver, Oklahoma. Visit Battle Creek, Michigan, if you want to experience the Cereal Capital of the World and Sheboygan, Wisconsin, for a look at the Bratwurst Capital of the World.[43]

Coconut Creek, Florida, anointed itself Butterfly Capital of the World in 2002 when its city government passed Resolution number 2002–60, and even registered the slogan in all its civic literature. The city hall grounds are landscaped with flowers and trees chosen to attract butterflies. A plaque encourages visitors to watch for Monarchs, Swallowtails, Sulphurs, Skippers, and Zebras. Coconut Creek is home to Butterfly World, the first commercial butterfly enclosure in America, a private park filled with live butterflies from around the world. Butterfly World has been a fixture in Coconut Creek since the late 1980s.

On a hot summer afternoon I stop off at City Hall to greet Mayor Becky Tooley. I want to learn more about Coconut Creek's decision to become the Butterfly Capital of the World. "It's to identify us as a green city," she tells me. "It's a commitment to the environment." Her government teaches its fifty thousand citizens to fill gardens with plants that attract butterflies. Schools and businesses are encouraged to do the same, and if they do it according to guidelines created by the National Wildlife Federation—adequate water, lush shrubbery, and flowers appealing to butterflies—gardens receive certification as butterfly gardens. Even the local Wal-Mart shows off its butterfly-friendly landscaping.

Mayor Tooley carries milkweed seeds around with her, the food plant for Monarchs, and gives them out as a Coconut Creek souvenir. "You can throw those on the ground and they'll grow." She speaks in a low, slow voice as we sit in her office, and I ask her for her theory on the near universal appeal of butterflies. Without hesitation she suggests, "I think it is the calming effect that a butterfly has." She knows from experience. When we talk she is just recovering from knee replacement surgery. After her operation she attached chrysalises to her leg lift, the apparatus she used for physical therapy, and watched them eclose. Using the leg lift was arduous, but the butterflies encouraged her. "Every time a butterfly flew by, I would have to do a leg lift. That's how I rehabilitated myself."

She has yet to find someone who does not like butterflies. "It's a symbol of life, a happy and calming animal. They amaze me, I just like to watch them," smiles the mayor, "they're symbols of renewal." Images of butterflies decorate Coconut Creek buses. The annual black tie Butterfly Festival recognizes citizens' contributions to the community. And if you call city hall and get put on hold, you'll hear advertisements for Butterfly World.

"I'm a Bill O'Reilly fan. That's the only thing I watch on television, Bill O'Reilly. That's all I watch!" Ron Boender, the founder and proprietor of Butterfly World, is showing me through his tropical paradise filled with butterfly eggs, larvae, pupae, and floating, fluttering adults. But we're talking Bill O'Reilly because Boender saw a clip of an interview O'Reilly conducted with me when my book *Wetback Nation* was published. O'Reilly and I debated immigration, and I called for the opening of the Mexican–American border.

I tell Boender about the behind-the-scenes reality in O'Reilly's studio. "O'Reilly introduced himself during a commercial just before we went on the air," I explain. "He said, 'Peter, here's what we're going to do. I'll give you about thirty seconds to explain your point of view and then I'll make fun of it.'"

Boender laughs at the story, but says he was impressed. "The amount of time you got was incredible. Very few people get that much time. For Bill O'Reilly to keep somebody on four or five minutes! And he did not make fun of you, he really didn't. If anything, he was on your side. You both made your points, and I thought it was good. That's been one of his big hang-ups, immigration. I thought you came off wonderfully. I thought, 'Boy, that guy's got guts to go on Bill O'Reilly.' Yeah, I like Bill O'Reilly. I think he does a good job of presenting the other side of the story." Here we were surrounded by butterflies, talking about our common denominator, the antithesis of calm: a screaming television hysteric. But O'Reilly served to bring us together, making it easier for us to stay cordial when we started debating creation versus evolution later during the tour.

Understandably proud of his self-made business fortunes and his self-taught expertise with butterflies and the plants crucial for their survival, Boender shows off *Passiflora boenderi*, the flowering passion vine named for him. He lists a string of firsts for which he takes credit: first commercial butterfly farm in the U.S., first butterfly garden filled with plants specifically chosen to attract butterflies, first U.S. commercial butterfly enclosure—Butterfly World. His love affair with Lepidoptera and his butterfly business started in the early 1980s when he began to fill the enclosure over his home swimming pool with butterflies and the plants that sustain them. "But I kept it a secret." He clearly enjoys the memory of the avocation that he embarked on after an early retirement. "Only a few close friends knew I was raising butterflies. I was ashamed of it. Nobody's ever done this. Am I crazy?" That he really was ashamed seems unlikely, but it makes for a good story these twenty-some years of success later.

Before opening Butterfly World, Boender raised larvae for experiments that Dr. Thomas Emmel was conducting upstate at the University of Florida in Gainesville. The Schaus Swallowtail was dying out in South Florida. Emmel needed a massive amount of butterflies to test his theory that unwarranted use of massive amounts of pesticides sprayed to control mosquitoes was responsible for the Swallowtail's demise. For Boender and his entrepreneurial sensibility, the business opportunity was obvious. He set out butterfly farming on a grand scale, selling to researchers. After a trip to an English butterfly house, he went to work establishing Butterfly World, which he opened to the admission-paying public in 1988.

Just as at Edith Smith's Shady Oak Butterfly Farm, the laboratory at Butterfly World—named for Professor Emmel, the entomologist Boender calls his mentor—is jammed with plastic containers filled with larvae and more plastic containers filled with pupae. Some of the butterflies for the display are raised in the lab's sterile quarters, removed from predators and parasites. Butterflies not raised at Butterfly World are bought from butterfly suppliers elsewhere, farmers scattered around the world, raising butterflies unique to their region. In an enclosure filled with butterfly food plants raised in the on-site Butterfly World nursery, Boender delivers the play-by-play description as we watch one of his *Heliconius melpomene* butterflies start the life cycle.

"Here's a butterfly getting ready to lay an egg." The butterfly crawls back and forth from my finger to a little piece of *Passiflora*—her host plant, what her larvae will feed on once they hatch. "She loves you," he tells me. "She says, 'But I really want to lay an egg.' Go ahead, honey, go ahead," he urges. "They're very fussy. See how she's looking it over? She's got to make sure there are no spiders that can grab her, no ants. She doesn't want her egg too close to any other egg. She's tasting with her front legs and her antennae." The seconds tick past as the butterfly moves around the passionflower leaf, seeming to begin to deposit an egg, and then moving to another spot. "Come on honey, you're so close." Finally, a tiny egg emerges, and then another. Depending on the species, a single butterfly can lay up to hundreds of eggs during her lifetime.

"It all started right here," Boender insists about his Butterfly World locale, and he points out that subsistence butterfly farming in impoverished Third World communities is saving forests because butterfly breeders are learning they can make more money selling butterflies to exhibitors and researchers than by clearing land and raising cattle. "And I get no credit for it," he complains to me, casting a stately and initially reserved figure: tall and straight-backed, silver haired. His low-key façade at first hides his passions: family, God, country, and butterflies—and I imagine, after we get to know each other pretty quickly during the tour, probably in that order.

"You want credit?" I ask.

"Of course!" It was an exclamation of enthusiastic frustration he quickly papered over with a litany of lines. "I don't need the credit, I really don't. What I'm saying is, I *should* receive credit for it. The industry exploded so rapidly, so many other people took my courses and jumped on board and started building these things"—he's talking about live butterfly exhibits, which are not quite as common as McDonald's and Starbucks but growing in popularity—"there are these displays now all over the country. A lot of them are terrible. And the exhibitors don't even know that this is where it all started."

Crowds are slight as we wander the grounds. It's the middle of hurricane season and Florida tourism is taking a battering. Most butterfly species live brief lives as adults. Butterfly World is a zoo that must constantly replenish its livestock. The on-site lab cranks out about 150 adults a day, augmented by the foreigners shipped in from butterfly farms overseas. We walk from the lab through a vestibule framed by screen doors designed to keep butterflies from escaping and, with a whoosh from an air blower attached above the doorway designed to force any wandering butterflies back into the enclosure, we're suddenly outside in a huge screened porch. Butterflies are everywhere, floating and fluttering to the accompaniment of soft, lounge-like piano: Cole Porter's "Night and Day," George and Ira Gershwin's "Embraceable You," and "The Very Thought of You" and others from Tin Pan Alley. The place is lush with tropical plants—deep green leaves and bright primary-colored flowers; gurgling water flows alongside the pathways. The escape is immediate. The butterflies command attention. Some are graceful as ballerinas as they swoon past, while others dart around on flight paths that appear manic. Their vibrant colors, their fearlessness, and their proximity combine to create an immediate and intimate experience. Gorgeous, peaceful, meditative, calming.

Gorgeous, peaceful, meditative, calming until our conversation turns to butterfly politics and North American Butterfly Association founder Jeffrey Glassberg. "He caused a big stir," Boender says with irritation about Glassberg promoting looking for butterflies in the wild as the epitome of activities for butterfly hobbyists. "He was a geek; he was in the software business. He sold his business for millions and millions and millions of dollars, and was bored. He formed the North American Butterfly Association and wrote a couple of books. He was a big butterfly collector and had one of the foremost collections of little Hairstreaks. And he flipped. He did a flip-flop. He went from a collector to the ultimate conservationist. 'You never catch a butterfly in a net,'" Boender mocks Glassberg's new point of view. "'You just look at them.'" But he can't argue with Glassberg's success. "He gained tremendous support because there are so many tree huggers out there. I'm beginning to think the whole world is turning into one big tree hugger. I'm glad I'm as old as I am so I'm not going to see how it ends up."

I tell Ron Boender about my meeting with Jeffrey Glassberg in Kernville a few weeks earlier, and Glassberg's nasty indictments of butterfly breeders as "self-serving, greedy people who don't care about anything—trying to make money lying to people."

"I think a lot of it is show," Boender dismisses Glassberg's harsh rhetoric. "It is promotion, is what it is. The guy is very, very intelligent. He's brazen. He's despicable." He dismisses Glassberg's techniques, too. "To think that with a pair of binoculars you can determine a species of something that's moving is absolutely ridiculous." The two butterfly kings know each other; in fact Boender tells me Glassberg has visited Butterfly World, and he remembers one exchange in detail. "I said, 'Look! There's a Long-tailed Skipper.' And he said, 'That's not a Long-tailed Skipper, that's a so-and-so. You don't know your butterflies very well.'" Boender is irritated by the memory, but it triggers more. "He'll come in here with eight of his people. They've been in the Everglades all day. They're all full of mosquito bites. They all stink; they've been sweating. You can't stand to be near them.

"He came in here one day," Boender is not finished with Glassberg yet, "and he wanted a picture of a Polydamas Swallowtail to finish his book. "He said, 'I've got to have a Polydamas Swallowtail with its wings open.' I said, 'Jeff, there are five hundred of them on the grounds here flying around. Have at it. Have at it, Jeff. Get your picture.'" He laughs, "I knew he'd never get it!"

The enmity in the butterfly world continues to fascinate me. I am fascinated by the butterfly rivalries, but no longer surprised. It makes sense that human nature inflects all our relationships, even those dealing with the miracle of butterflies. "How did you know he'd never get it?" I ask.

"Because you can't get a Polydamas Swallowtail with its wings out. It never stops fluttering." When it alights, it closes it wings. "He spent hours here trying to get it, and he gave up in sheer frustration. I brought him a slide and said, 'Would you like to use this?' It was a perfect Polydamas Swallowtail." Boender is smiling. "He looked at it and said, 'How did you take that picture?' I said, 'It's beside the point. Would you like the picture?' He said, 'Of course. That's what I'm here for.' I said, 'It's yours. Please don't give me credit.'"

"Why no credit?" I ask.

Again he says, "I don't need credit. I'm not in this world for credit, okay?"

Boender ultimately agrees with those who worry butterflies can be collected to extinction. "Walk with a net, but don't collect a butterfly unless you have a reason to collect a butterfly. Look at it and then let it go. I'm interested in the live part of it, the miraculous part of it."

We're surrounded by the miracles. They flutter and glide past us, showing off their brilliant colors. Butterfly World is an oasis of delightful calm amidst the Florida sprawl. It is an ideal spot to re-argue the Scopes trial, and when I found myself asking Boender his opinions regarding the magic that is a butterfly, we ended up in a jocular debate based on the same issues that led to the Monkey Trial. In 1925, at the urging of some friends and colleagues, schoolteacher John Scopes chose to fight the Tennessee law that made it illegal for public schools to instruct students that the Biblical story of creation was not scientific fact and that man descended from a so-called "lower order of animals," as the Butler Act called evolution. Hence Scopes' trial was called the Monkey Trial when he was tried and convicted of intentionally violating the law (a conviction that ultimately was reversed on appeal based on a technical error made by the trial court).

"I'm a Christian and a creationist," Ron Boender announces. "You might as well know that."

"We can disagree and still get along," I allow, happy to hear a creationist interpretation of metamorphosis, especially since science has yet to explain the process from start to finish.

"I believe in a God so powerful that if He wanted to," he snaps his fingers, "in six days He could create all this beauty. Scientific people estimate that there are a hundred million life forms on the face of the Earth today. We don't have a single link that one form evolved into another form. There's not a single link in the hundred million life forms. The fossil record is zero, there's nothing. There are no links; they're still looking for the first link." He's charming, but insistent. "They have not been able to find any intermediate life form between one species and another species. It doesn't exist. And yet we teach evolution as fact in every university and every school in the United States."

"So you're a Sarah Palin fan?"

"You got that right." And with butterflies surrounding us, he looks back to Tennessee and the infamous battle personified by Clarence Darrow and William Jennings Bryan (or Spencer Tracy and Fredric March, if you prefer the Hollywood version). "Do you know that we've been teaching evolution as fact since the Scopes Monkey Trial? And when was that?" he asks.

"In the twenties."

"The twenties, okay. We have been teaching evolution solely now for all these years." Boender doesn't have his facts straight. Turns out, evolution teacher Scopes lost at his trial, and Tennessee didn't repeal the Butler Act until 1967. "You know how many people believe in evolution today, after all this teaching and all this brainwashing?" He answers his question for me: "Sixty-five percent of the people still believe that everything was created by God. Only 35 percent believe in evolution. Those are the latest statistics," he insists.

"Oh, yeah?" I counter. "Then we need to do a better job with our brainwashing."

Boender is a good sport; he smiles, and continues his sermon. "You can't, because it isn't a fact. You have no facts!"

"So where did these butterflies come from?" I find it fascinating to hear an educated and accomplished man, a man who spends much of his time working with plants and animals, reject evolution in 2008.

"God created them. He just said," Boender again snaps his fingers, " 'That's it. That's what I want. I want that beauty. I want that color.' You look at the designs, the paintings, the colors." He points to a spectacular butterfly fluttering near us, a Piano Key. The stark black and white markings on its hind wings resemble piano keys. "It's a *Heliconius melpomene*," the scientific name rolls off his tongue.

"So this is God at work?" I ask. "He wants that butterfly wing to look like a piano key."

"Of course, of course."

"And why did God make Piano Key butterflies?"

"I have no idea." He speculates maybe just to make the world a more beautiful place, but does not presume to second-guess God. "Why did God create the Earth? This all happened from some slime mould or Big Bang theory? It just happened? All these hundred million species just evolved, and we don't have any proof? Yet we teach it? To really believe in evolution, you must also believe in Santa Claus and the Easter Bunny."

"Nothing wrong with Santa Claus and the Easter Bunny," I protest.

"Nothing wrong with them," he agrees, "but you have the same proof for those two as you do for evolution."

"We're straying from talking about your butterflies, Ron, but the same goes for God. You've got no proof."

"Exactly," he smiles with perceived victory. "You've got to have faith that there is a God! And you have to have faith that evolution created all of these things in the world. When it comes to those two things, I am just absolutely astounded that 35 percent of the people still believe in evolution. When you study butterflies you see how absolutely perfect they are—to think that there is not an intelligent design behind our own bodies and everything around us, I find just incredible." Eyes bright and boring into me as he makes his case, he emphasizes his points by jabbing me in the shoulder. His enthusiasm is infectious, even if his logic is faith-based instead of scientific.

⸺

When I met with University of California at Berkeley biologist and butterfly flight expert Robert Dudley, I mentioned Boender's theory of butterfly origin, and he scoffed at the claim we humans enjoy perfect bodies. Perfect "until things don't work very well," he pointed out, "and then you get to go see something called a doctor, and you can spend months in the hospital because the thing is so badly designed! Things go wrong routinely." It was Professor Dudley who introduced me to the works of Bernard d'Abrera—stacks of coffee table books filled with photographic images of butterflies from the vast British Museum's collection. Dudley pulled one of d'Abrera's books off his office shelf and flipped it open to the introduction, which proclaims, "Butterflies remind us of the omnipotence and bounty of the Creator."

I dropped a note to d'Abrera and asked him to expand on his creationist theories as they relate to butterflies. His emailed reply referenced a long list of his books along with the suggestion that I read Ann Coulter's account of the Scopes trial. But he begged off sitting for an interview. "The wonderful quality of Objective Truth," he wrote to me, "is that it just hangs there in front of one's eyes, independent of the person or the vehicle through which it shines. In any case I do not give interviews to self-interested journalists, because I've never yet met one who either truthfully admits to his self-interest, or is capable of telling the unvarnished truth as it is received from his victim. I firmly believe that it is the message, rather than the messenger, that matters in the unfolding saga of man's discoveries about himself, his world and their origins. I have no agenda."

Bernard d'Abrera's definition of what he wishes journalism was sounds more like the job of a stenographer taking dictation than the work of a news reporter. Yet just because of the volume of coffee table–type butterfly books d'Abrera and his self-publishing company Hill House, a well-known publisher of Christian-oriented books, have produced, he is at least a footnote in the butterfly world. A Web site review of d'Abrera's work says, "In his now famous *Concise Atlas of the Butterflies of the World*, the author launched a systematic and scholarly critique of what he sees as the patently unscientific, profligate, and self-serving posturings of the quasi religion of Evolutionism."[44] D'Abrera told me this "is a most accurate paraphrase and synthesis of what I have been saying for the past two or three decades."

University of California at Davis evolutionary biologist Arthur Shapiro has reviewed several of Bernard d'Abrera's books for a variety of scientific journals. While we hiked alongside the American River he told me why. "Attention should be paid to their stupidities, their errors, their pig-headedness, their bad writing. The thing is, as I say in my reviews, they're absolutely indispensable. There's nothing else like them. If you're trying to identify exotic butterflies outside your geographic area, the primary and secondary literatures are so scattered and relatively inaccessible, you're out of hope. Big coffee table picture books are the only way to go. But if you're going to do that," he said about d'Abrera's extensive works, "at least get input from the people in the areas you cover geographically so you don't make an ass of yourself." At that point in our conversation Shapiro pointed to some scat on the path and said to me, "God, there's a lot of dung

around here, look at it all." His comments may have been coinciden-
tal; however, the more I got to know Shapiro, the less I attributed his
remarks, caustic or otherwise, to coincidence.

While the scientific community may scoff at the commentaries in
Bernard d'Abrera's theology-ridden butterfly books, Butterfly World's
Ron Boender is in lockstep with him. "To tell me that I evolved or
descended or ascended from a monkey is the biggest insult you could
ever give me."

"Or the monkey," I propose, and receive a gracious touché from
my debate partner.

We agree to disagree and go back to butterfly watching in what
he reminds me is the first American commercial butterfly house,
and the largest. We wander through rain forest flora brimming with
brilliant flowers offering nectar to the thousands and thousands of
exotic butterflies flitting around us—none of them native to Florida.
Each butterfly is captivating to watch, often fluttering within inches
of us, seeming tame and friendly. The lounge piano music adds to the
surreal environment. The vast size of the enclosure in relation to the
butterflies makes it difficult to imagine them as captives. They show
no signs of distress or a desire to escape. As Boender points out, the
butterflies are living their short lives protected from the predators
that would seek them were they in the wild. There's no question it is
delightful to be surrounded by the fluttering and flapping colors, and
no question they capture my attention and push the petty and grand
problems of the rest of the world out of my mind, at least briefly.

"This is a White Morpho from El Salvador." Boender picks the
butterfly up by grabbing its wings and pinching them together. "This
is the rarest of the Morphos, the Whites." He lets go and the pearl-
colored butterfly seems to float through the air as it flies off.

"Whether it's a creationist miracle or an evolutionary miracle," I offer, watching the White Morpho sail through the air, "it's a miracle."

"Exactly." He picks up a Cairns Birdwing from Australia and puts it on my nose. The legs grab claw-like onto me. It's not a pleasant sensation. Birdwings sport the widest wingspread of any butterfly species. In fact, the Queen Alexandra's Birdwings can measure up to a foot from wingtip to wingtip. The one clinging to my nose is more compact, with a wingspan of about a half dozen inches. Queen Alexandra's Birdwings—the world's largest butterfly—were among the stash Yoshi Kojima sold Ed Newcomer before Yoshi was arrested for smuggling. Yoshi let a pair go for $8,500, but Newcomer told me that on the black market (and there is no legal trade in Queen Alexandra's Birdwings) they can fetch up to ten grand a pair. Boender takes the Cairns off me, places it on his own nose, and poses for a photograph. He releases his grip on it, and it flaps its black and green wings, wings with bright yellow patches that match its yellow body, and lopes on—graceful and gorgeous, mysterious and compelling.

"There's something about the butterfly that epitomizes spirituality," Boender says as we watch the Birdwing float away from us. "The butterfly has a mesmerizing effect on people." In the mystery of metamorphosis, Boender sees a profound metaphor for his own life. "You and I are born as ugly caterpillars," he tells me, "and by the grace of God, if we believe in a savior or if we believe in God eternal, we're going to be metamorphosized into a butterfly—into a beautiful creature someday."

As we talk, butterflies continue cavorting past us, and Ron Boender rhapsodizes about his flock. "The butterfly has this mesmerizing effect on people. The way they fly. Their beauty! They're harmless. They don't spread diseases. They don't bite. They're not dirty." I ask him for his theory of why butterflies exist—they play only a minor role as pollinators and they are not an important food for their few predators—and he offers an answer easy to embrace surrounded as we were with so many of them: God put them here just to make this world a more beautiful place.

The scientist who introduced Ron Boender to the magic of tropical butterflies during a rugged collecting trip to Ecuador is headquartered a few hundred miles north of Butterfly World, in Gainesville at the University of Florida. There zoology and entomology professor Thomas Emmel, one of the experts I've been in contact with during my crash course in butterflies, presides over both the Boender Endangered Species Laboratory (funded by the Butterfly World founder) and the Butterfly Rainforest, a huge enclosure filled with scores of exotic species. The windows along one wall of Professor Emmel's office look out over the magnificent mosaic of butterflies fluttering in the enclosure. In addition, he's in charge of one of the world's largest collections of butterflies, cases and cases of specimens maintained in climate-controlled storage at the university for research and posterity. Dr. Emmel is not even sure how many dead butterflies are in his massive collection, "eight and a half or nine million," he tells me. "So we're probably the largest." Which could mean the Florida Gators surpass the fabled British Museum for sheer numbers of dead butterflies with pins stuck through them mounted on a board for display and/or study.

This is not just an obsessive race for more. There are some 265,000 species of known butterflies and moths, 245,000 species of moths and upwards of 20,000 species of butterflies. Collectors such as Emmel keep millions of samples because there are subspecies and seasonal color variations of the 20,000 to study. Many of the collections kept at the university are of historical note, gathered worldwide over hundreds of years. Studies of all those species collected over time offer insight into evolutionary changes, the effects of pollution, and opportunities to use contemporary genetic manipulation to adapt to other plants and animals phenomena unique to butterflies—for example, the ability of larvae, such as the Monarch's, to thrive eating poisonous plants and then become adult butterflies toxic with the same poison to predators. A sample theory: Take what allows larvae to eat cyanide-laced plants and neutralize the poison, and adapt it to a plant that would grow on cyanide-laced mine tailings and neutralize the poison in the tailings to make the landscape fit for safe use.

Despite the huge number of species living around the world, extraordinary work is done at the university to keep one local butterfly from becoming extinct, work that likely benefits all animals, including human beings.

In 1984, for example, the elegant Schaus Swallowtail population—a native to the Florida Keys—was devastated, down to just some sixty-eight adults left in the wild. Dr. Emmel and his team approached the problem from two perspectives: they wanted to determine what might be occurring in the environment that was killing the butterflies while at the same time they worked to breed Schaus Swallowtails in captivity, butterflies they would release back into the wild in an attempt to stabilize the population. Their research quickly brought them to suspect what was an obvious cause-and-effect relationship: the butterflies began to decline in numbers at the same time Dade and Monroe Counties changed their mosquito abatement procedures. In the Keys, Dibrom was sprayed from airplanes and Baytex from trucks. These are commercial chemical compounds that are designed to be killers (Dibrom is morbid spelled backwards) despite claims from the manufacturer that they are safe—and researchers learned that the applications were much more toxic to wildlife than necessary.

Laboratory tests showed that butterflies are up to four *thousand* times more sensitive to the chemicals than are the targeted

mosquitoes, and that the poisons were being sprayed in concentra-
tions much greater than needed to kill the mosquitoes. "Dibrom was
sprayed at a rate of seven thousand times the concentration needed
to kill mosquitoes," Dr. Emmel says as we watch his butterflies frolic
on the other side of his office windows.

"This was due to ignorance at the mosquito abatement district
offices?"

"Just ignorance. When we asked the district why they were using
that concentration, they said that was what was recommended by
the manufacturer. The Environmental Protection Administration
had been so busy during the Reagan years," he says drolly, "that they
were unable to check more than two of over six hundred new pesticides that had gone on the market during that time, so they depended
on the manufacturer to provide information on the toxicity. Clearly
the manufacturer was instructing use of the pesticide at a rate that
helped them sell more."

"It's like wash your hair, rinse, and wash your hair again," I
suggest.

"Yeah, exactly. The manufacturers were recommending that you
spray Baytex two or three times a day with trucks, and spray at least
twice a week with Dibrom from the air, and they were making a for-
tune. The district was spending $3 million a year on pesticides in
the Keys alone." Emmel still expresses amazement years later at the
expense, and at the $4 million more used to coordinate the attacks
with a fleet of four DC-3s, two Bell helicopters, and forty-seven spray
trucks.

The unnecessary escalation of force was killing not just the mosquitoes but the Schaus Swallowtails, along with who knows what
else. The University of Florida organized a conference and brought
together researchers concerned with the effects of the Baytex and
Dibrom on animals other than those deemed as pests. They found
specialists studying shrimp, saltwater fish, and turtles all reaching

the same conclusion: the chemicals were extraordinarily lethal. The scientists convinced the government agencies involved to change chemicals and tactics. Spraying only at night spares butterflies and larvae the probability of being hit by the toxins since both usually sleep on the underside of leaves. The butterflies immediately staged a comeback, a comeback supplemented with the captive-bred Schaus Swallowtails, a necessary component of the rescue after Hurricane Andrew hit the recovering Schaus Swallowtails and their habitat. A census after the hurricane counted a mere seventeen of the struggling butterflies.

The lesson is clear, says Dr. Emmel. "Study the ecology and behavior of species in the wild before making recommendations about intervention." And before labeling poisons. The university launched a similar project to save the Miami Blue. Tens of thousands of the delicate little butterfly have been raised in captivity and released around Miami. "It's another dramatic success story," says Emmel, "of bringing endangered species back from the brink."

Emmel says he respects the efforts of the Fish and Wildlife Service special agents, such as Ed Newcomer, to protect endangered species and enforce the law, but he's convinced that they err when they chase well-credentialed researchers, targeting them for what may be breaking the letter of the law but not the spirit of the law. He uses an experience of his own as a prime example.

"Los Angeles Fish and Wildlife once tied me up for three hours in an inspection because they were certain I was carrying Birdwing butterflies from Papua New Guinea." Birdwings, I must point out, were among the butterflies Yoshi Kojima was convicted of smuggling into Los Angeles. "I had just arrived from Malaysia. I showed them my passport. I had not been in Papua New Guinea. I had been in Malaysia the day before, flown here."

Emmel acts disgusted as he recounts the tale as if he were talking to the agents. "Here are all the Malaysian butterflies. Here are all the permits from the Malaysian authorities. Here's Form 31–77 U.S. Fish and Wildlife." He then speaks the part of one of the agents. "'We had a secret tip that you were coming in with Birdwing butterflies from New Guinea.'" Emmel says he asked the agent who was the source of the tip and that the agent refused to answer, claiming it was confidential information. But another agent was more forthcoming and showed him a copy of a brochure that advertised a trip to New Guinea with Emmel as guide the same dates as his Malaysia trip.

"I said, 'First of all, that trip was canceled six months ago because we didn't have the permits, and we switched to Malaysia. I didn't go there. If I had gone to Papua New Guinea I would have had all the permits. You guys have been treating me like a criminal here.'

"You know," he looks exasperated, "it just drives you crazy. With all the stuff being smuggled through—live parrots, tortoises in the suitcase, all this other stuff—they want to make an example of somebody with a high profile. Why they want to bring down someone in a museum situation beats the hell out of me. For the next two years, every time I entered the U.S., my name was tagged by U.S. Customs that I had been stopped suspected of smuggling Birdwing butterflies."

In fact, I learned from sources several weeks later at the Fish and Wildlife Service that Dr. Emmel has experienced quite a few encounters with their inspectors. On a trip into Orlando airport in 2002 they found two restricted Birdwings in his luggage and no permits. The butterflies were seized. On another 2002 trip into Orlando, inspectors stopped Emmel with a *Bhutanitis lidderdalii*—a dramatic-looking species with three elongated tail-like features extending from its hind wings and known as the Bhutan Glory—and absent a needed permit. It too was forfeited. That same year he was stopped for bringing forty-five Queen Victoria's Birdwings, *Ornithoptera victoriae*, into Orlando from the Solomon Islands despite a long-standing ban on such imports. In 2008 a DHL package addressed to the scientist was flagged at Los Angeles International and in it were fifty *Troides* live pupae from the Philippines, but not the valid export document needed to bring the chrysalises into the U.S. legally. Inspectors do not think Thomas Emmel is a smuggler, they think he's a sometimes sloppy administrator, and they say universities are infamous for such slips. Some collectors connected with universities don't bother to get permits because they figure that being known researchers and scholars, they simply needn't bother with such details.

Professor Emmel chuckles when I suggest that a quick background check might point out that he probably was not in the smuggling business, that he is in a position to obtain just about any butterfly he wants via legal means. "No, I would not be a likely candidate for the smuggling business. But they said that usually the people who are doing it are the least likely ones, they look like somebody's sweet grandmother." Smuggling must be tempting for those people who know that they can try to rationalize, because of their position, trade in something otherwise illegal to obtain. The controversy over the motives of the Czech entomologist Petr Švácha comes to mind. Emmel wants wildlife laws and the law enforcement agencies dealing with wildlife reformed. He believes the commercial farmed butterflies currently restricted from international trade would substantively reduce poverty in their home countries were they traded without restriction as commodities. Collectors would buy pinned specimens for display, and exhibits such as his university's enclosure would import pupae so that they could fly dramatic and rare butterflies. "Can you imagine a butterfly twelve inches across flying out here?" He points out his window at the butterflies fluttering below his office. His dream continues, "People coming here and being able to see something like that close up on a flower would marvel at it and say, 'I really want to preserve the rain forest in New Guinea. I'm going to give money.' That flagship species would save tens of thousands of other plants and animals" (he's banging on his desk), "because that one exposure to a charismatic species can make all the difference in the world."

⌒

Here's an image of Birdwing collectors that will horrify butterfly lovers. Consider wild-eyed butterfly hunters prowling the vast rain forests of Papua New Guinea—not only without permits, but with shotguns, shooting Birdwings. "The first collectors who discovered them brought some of them down with birdshot because the butterflies were flying above the canopy," Dr. Paul Olper, a senior research scientist at Colorado State University at Fort Collins, told me. He said the gun-toting butterfly collectors were shooting the Birdwings in the early nineteenth century, frustrated that they were flying out of net reach. The ominous-looking Rajah Brooke's Birdwing (*Trogonoptera brookiana albescens*) flies in Malaysia and is Malaysia's national butterfly. It's a CITES Appendix II butterfly, now protected by the international treaty, relatively safe from birdshot.

⌒

The day after I met with Thomas Emmel, he was off to Germany, to pick up and haul back to his university still another butterfly collection he secured for Florida, where the collection is already enormous. How to imagine the millions of butterflies in the bowels of Emmel's showcase building? Impossible. Best to just walk into the massive collection equipped with an ideal guide, Emmel's colleague, research entomologist Andrei Sourakov, the university's butterfly collections manager. Dr. Sourakov takes me first into the four-story enclosure I had been looking at from Emmel's office. "It's been my hobby since I was six years old," he says, with his lilting Moscow accent, about butterfly study. In contrast, Emmel started late, when he was eight.

One after another, the butterfly experts I meet trace their profession back to their childhood fascination with a net, chasing butterflies. We wander through the created rain forest, Sourakov pointing out the exotics surrounding us. The butterflies do not seem confined; they fly around the enclosure without seeking escape against the screened walls.

Weekly pupae are shipped to Gainesville from around the world. They eclose in the facility's laboratory and then are brought in small screened cages into the enclosure for release. One of Sourakov's colleagues comes out with a cage full of butterflies, flips open the lid, and begins releasing a variety of butterflies, including the local favorite, the common Buckeye, alive with color and apparently happy to fly off into the rain forest.

We adjourn to the university's butterfly vault, the temperature-controlled butterfly hold, and enter a long corridor, one of many, flanked by stacks of drawers, all laden with endless butterfly specimens. "The specimens have different levels of importance," Sourakov says when I ask if the gross total in the collection is a defining qualifier of the importance of the university's butterfly holdings. "Numbers are impressive, but I must say the value is not in numbers." In other words, some of the butterflies they accept are nothing to write home about, they are common butterflies or butterflies without information about when and where they were collected. But even those can be of value to primary level students for basic study.

The university takes just about any and all butterflies it is offered, anxious to maintain specimens in a controlled environment where they will last "forever," collections that cannot be replicated because contemporary restrictions forbid the capture of butterflies that in past generations were relatively easy to find, net, and pin.

We stop at a highly varnished cabinet filled with stacks of drawers. "This is a special collection," Sourakov says. "The specimens here are from 1905 to 1920. It is a collection of British butterflies and moths, a Colonial-style collection made by three generations of a family." This is the type of prize that the university will not integrate into its generic stacks of drawers because it is an example of a typical Victorian-era collection—complete with custom-made cabinet. The sociological aspects of the butterfly business are important to the Gainesville operation.

It's impossible to talk butterflies with a Russian and not ask if he was influenced to become an entomologist specializing in butterflies by Vladimir Nabokov and both his writings about butterflies and his work as a lepidopterist. "When I was growing up," Sourakov is smiling at the memory, "I read his books. But they were not officially published." Dr. Sourakov was born in 1968 and grew up in the Soviet Union during the Brezhnev era, before Nabokov's works were readily available in Russia. So he read the *samizdat* editions. "The occupation I was engaged in," he says about butterfly study, "was considered to be a little bit bizarre. I think the fact that Nabokov wrote so fondly and so well about lepidoptery justified in the eyes of the friends of my parents that their son was running all over the world with a butterfly net instead of studying medicine as a good boy should." His laugh is infectious. "He helped somewhat," Sourakov says about Nabokov, "because he writes beautifully. This is great for us because it allows us to publicize the science to the public. I love his writing. You know how you develop friendships with writers? I feel that he and I have a lot in common." Sourakov talks about Nabokov as if he were with us. "Most of my friends have been dead for a long time, for more than a century," he laughs again. Most of his butterflies have been dead for a long time, too.

I leave the University of Florida collection oddly sanguine about all those dead pinned butterflies. They were killed and mounted in another era, and I appreciate Emmel's and Sourakov's point of view: let's preserve them and learn from them. In addition, I can appreciate their cultural value. The well-crafted cabinets custom made—of gorgeous wood with intricate and elegant designs—for nothing other than butterfly collections offer a reminder of a time when society moved at a slower pace than it does for so many of us today, at least for those who could afford it.

Chapter Eleven

BUTTERFLY RESURRECTION

"BUTTERFLIES ARE HOPE," JANA JOHNSON EXPLAINS TO ME. WE ARE walking through the Antioch Dunes Wildlife Refuge after literally cooling our heels in the San Joaquin River, at the headwaters of San Francisco Bay. Johnson is prowling what's left of the riverbank sand dunes, surveying the habitat of the few remaining Lange's Metalmarks, one of the rarest butterflies in California, and one of the first insects to be protected by the Endangered Species Act—it was added to the list in 1976. After watching her successfully repopulate the endangered Palos Verdes Blue in Southern California, the Fish and Wildlife Service—the caretakers of the Dunes refuge—convinced Johnson and her team to try to save the equally endangered Lange's Metalmark, a little butterfly known only to the refuge, with a wingspan of less than two inches, colorful wings of a black, red, and orange background accented with white spots. That it, this Metalmark, creates only one generation a year adds to the challenges faced by those trying to save it.

I had arrived earlier that day at the refuge, a scrap of land sandwiched on the riverbank between massive industrial sprawl and cordoned off from the public with a chain-link fence marked NATIONAL WILDLIFE REFUGE—UNAUTHORIZED ENTRY PROHIBITED. It lies just upriver from the old Antioch downtown, forgotten despite the attempts at renewal announced by banners on the streetlight poles reading "Historic Rivertown District." Empty storefronts compete with Holy Angels Books and Religious Articles, Queen B's Quilt Shop, and the Pueblo Nuevo Restaurant. At the Antioch Armory a Rottweiler growls from inside against the plate-glass front window; an Antioch Police hiring flyer is pasted to the glass. There are bars, two rock shops, a nail salon, and indications of hoped-for gentrification like the poster for periodic special film shows at the otherwise dark old movie theater.

I park at the refuge and seek shelter in the shade of a conifer. It is hot; the forecast is for over a hundred degrees. But the stiff river breeze takes the burn off the late-morning sun. Across the San Joaquin I can see the blades spinning at a wind farm. Nothing much catches my eye on the patch of land known as the refuge's Stamm Unit, fifty-five acres of what were once massive sand dunes rising over a hundred feet from the river. After the 1906 San Francisco earthquake, the dunes were mined for brick making—leaving them diminished to just a fraction of their former height. Post-1906 San Francisco buildings made with yellow bricks may well owe their distinctive façade to Antioch Dunes sand.

It wasn't just the loss of the sand that made life hard for Lange's Metalmarks. A shipyard, a sewage treatment plant, and the Georgia-Pacific gypsum plant cover adjacent territory, and an active freight and passenger rail line cordon off the southern border of the tract. To my as-yet-untrained eye, the Stamm Unit looks as passed-over as the old Antioch riverfront downtown. This is the place where butterfly poacher Richard Skalski nabbed his endangered and protected Lange's in 1984, an act for which Skalski himself was nabbed and slapped on the wrist by authorities. He would poach for over ten more years before he finally was put out of business.

My reverie is soon interrupted by a motorcade. Biologist Jana Johnson and her crew pull up. She is a smiling beach blonde, quick to laugh, and is wearing a T-shirt marked TEAM PVBB—Palos Verdes Blue butterfly. In tow are a couple of other entomologists and a plant specialist. Lange's Metalmarks eat the naked-stem buckwheat, also unique to the Antioch Dunes; the plant specialist has been assigned the task of raising feed for the butterflies Johnson expects to breed. The refuge manager, Christy Smith, unlocks the gates, and we parade onto the site. Immediately the biologists spot their prey.

"Is this your evening primrose?" one of them asked Smith. Another pointed out a wallflower. The Antioch Dunes evening primrose and the Contra Costa wallflower are both endemic to the refuge and are both endangered. Within minutes the dusty swath of land starts to take on a personality for me—it is no longer anonymous blight. "We have a lot of refuges around the bay," Smith told me. "This is our most troubled." She's wearing the badge and green uniform of the Fish and Wildlife Service, and as we walk along the sand she tells me that during her off time she writes mystery novels set on wildlife refuges and starring crazed scientists involved in crimes.

"This is a disaster," Ken Osborne announces. He is the entomologist who was engaged by the project to capture the few Lange's Metalmarks Dr. Johnson will use in her attempts to raise the species in captivity and then introduce the bred butterflies into the wild. "You have to stop being delicate," Osborne told Smith. He mocks our concern as we tiptoe around the endangered plants. "That mentality loses the forest for the trees." He looks around at the degraded, weed-covered land. "This is as bad as it gets." His hay-like long hair and beard are windblown, yet his long-sleeved bright red shirt looks out of place—too dressy—as we tramp around. Osborne advocates radical removal of non-native plants, and shipping massive amounts of sand to the site. He cautions that restoring the dunes to what they were before the Spanish imported the first exotic species to them will be impossible. "It will be perpetual maintenance," he lectures.

Hefting a backpack and sweating in the sun under a safari hat is Gordon Pratt, another entomologist. Johnson worked with him on the Palos Verdes Blue recovery—calling him "the astoundingly gifted

Gordon Pratt" in an email to me—and as we look at the flora and fauna, he and Osborne engage in the kind of rivalry that seems like fodder for Smith's mystery book characters. The language becomes insider baseball between them as the Latin names for species they are stumbling over are invoked, floating out of their mouths effortlessly. I start to hear things like, "Here's the *Erysimum capitatum*," instead of, "Look at the wallflower." And, "There's a flower on this *Oenothera deltoides*," rather than, "Check out this flowering primrose." Each of them tries to be first with such identification and with an analysis of the ecological crisis they are seeing for the first time in person. They are sparring, showing off, and clearly enjoying themselves. But the crisis is real. The last census found only forty-five Lange's Metalmarks, or as Osborne and Pratt would tend to announce it, forty-five *Apodemia mormo lengei*.

It is well after noon and getting hotter. We take a lunch break a few hundred yards downriver at the Red Caboose, a diner built around an old Santa Fe train car. The atmosphere is of the type where the waitress calls all the diners "Hon." She announces the specials: chili dogs "made with those Big Reds" and barbecued ribs. "Anybody want to explain coronary disease?" Jana Johnson asks her colleagues, and it sets the tone for a lunch of jokes as the crew tries to bond for the work ahead. Johnson dumps a half a dozen packets of sugar into her ice tea, and the botanist in charge of growing the buckwheat to feed the larvae in captivity watches, finally questioning how sweet the Texas native is making her drink. "I'm around a whole lot of critters who drink honey water," Johnson tells him.

After lunch we drive over to what's known as the Sardis Unit of the refuge, just a twelve-acre parcel, but the spot where most of the Metalmarks have been found. The Sardis unit is downwind from the gypsum plant. Gypsum dust flies as it's unloaded from ships at the plant's dock. Perhaps that dust is having a deleterious effect on the butterflies, the scientists think, and so tests have been planned to expose surrogates—Metalmarks similar to the Lange's but not endangered—to gypsum samples from the plant.

We hike into a gully protected from the wind, and it is extremely hot. One of the scientists calls out, "We've got a couple of dozen buckwheats over here."

"Yeah, here's some really fresh damage over here!" Damage means damage to the buckwheat leaves caused by feeding larvae.

"There's probably a larva here!" The voice is excited.

"Let me get a picture of that damage," and a camera comes close to a well-chewed leaf.

"Want me to find the larva?" Gordon Pratt starts digging around the base of the damaged buckwheat.

"Will it hurt it?" he is asked.

"No," he announces, and keeps rooting around. "The larva crawled up from down here." Pratt is dripping with sweat. Jana Johnson is down on her knees next to him, looking closely at the freshly turned dirt. Their banter resumes as he digs.

"And I thought going out with ornithologists was bad," Johnson says. "They see a bird and they're off the road."

Pratt keeps digging. "If he's as big as the other one, he might've crawled away," says one of the Fish and Wildlife crew members about a larva they found another day. "We searched a lot and we only found one."

Johnson looks up from the ground at that news, which is new to her. "One?" she says dreamily. "A silver lining!" She smiles, and then Ken Osborne diverts the attention of the pack away from Pratt's digging. He casually points out an adjacent buckwheat plant, about a foot from where Pratt is turning soil, with three Lange's Metalmark larvae on it, and he smiles a victory smile. In this informal entomological bout the score is now Osborne 3, Pratt 0.

"What are they doing up there?" Pratt looks up from the dirt he has been disturbing. There is a hush; the excitement is palpable.

Someone makes a joke in response to Pratt's question. "They breed like rats."

Johnson studies the larvae and exclaims, "Oh, they're gorgeous!"

"Isn't it unusual for them to be out in the heat?"

Osborne, obviously pleased with his find, has the answer with a question. "What's normal?" This is uncharted territory, the contemporary habits of the endangered Lange's. "Who looks for this sort of stuff?"

Meanwhile Johnson is just looking at the prizes, saying, "Fabulous, fabulous."

"Don't bang this stuff around," Osborne instructs the growing crowd around the buckwheat, "you're knocking things around."

"This guy's active," Johnson announces, excited. "He's chewing."

"You're seeing a larva eating?"

"Yes, he's working at it," and she repeated, "fabulous!" As she watches the half-inch-long brown caterpillar chew the buckwheat leaf, she makes the critical announcement of the day. "They're not extinct. They're breeding."

The gang retires to the shade of a nearby oak tree to discuss strategy. Consensus is quickly reached that shortly after the Lange's Metalmarks next emerge from their cocoons, Osborne will capture a precious sample of them—the exact number will depend on how many emerge from the chrysalises (or chrysalides, as Pratt and Osborne may say to each other). If there are only a few, Osborne might be restricted to just a half a dozen butterflies. Half would go to Johnson's lab, the other half to Pratt's. The group will be separated to protect the project against total disaster on the chance that some fatal disease or other catastrophe might occur in one of the labs. Osborne is to capture females, and the expectation is that they will be carrying fertilized eggs. In the lab these eggs will be harvested, and encouraged to hatch. The resulting caterpillars will be fed naked-stem buckwheat, or another buckwheat that proved to be satisfying in tests to Lange's Metalmark surrogates. Even without a hands-on physical examination, biologists and amateur butterfly spotters can often determine the sex of a specimen by its size, its color, the patterns of its scales, and—especially during mating attempts—its behavior.

Pratt is optimistic. He thinks the several larvae we have stumbled upon are an indication that the population might not be as low as was initially feared. "They may have been in diapause last year," he says with some fervor. Johnson tells the group she wants at least one male collected, on the chance that the eggs of one of the few females taken are not yet fertilized—a problem she had experienced in the Palos Verdes Blue lab. Pratt and Osborne dismiss her concerns, and claim such an insurance policy is not necessary.

Butterflies copulate. The male grabs the female with appendages known as claspers and then uses his reproductive organ—his oedeagus—to send sperm into his partner's reproductive system. But the sperm does not immediately fertilize her eggs. She stores it until she locates the foodplant on which her species thrives, and until she locates a spot on that foodplant that she considers prime real estate for her offspring. Once she chooses that ideal place she releases the sperm so the eggs she lays are fertilized. Her larvae feast on the foodplant directly after they emerge from the egg: their home is their dinner.

The Palos Verdes Blue was on the verge of extinction when Jana Johnson became involved in a program to raise them in captivity. In 2006 techniques she developed quadrupled the population of the Blues, and by the next year she was ready to release them into the wild. "Pretty spectacular numbers," she wrote to me before we met about the thousands of Blues in her custody, "considering the wild population has hovered between 65 and 200 since its rediscovery in 1994."

By this time most of us are sitting on the ground; even in the shade it is too hot to keep standing.

Osborne ends the debate, agreeing to secure a lone male when he collects "to humor her," he says, gesturing to Johnson, who noticeably stiffens at the dismissal.

The survey work is over for the day, and we all hike through the brush to the riverbank. In the shade of an alder tree (Osborne and Pratt debate the specific type of alder) we drink water and wade in the relatively cool San Joaquin. Johnson and I move a few yards downriver from the group to talk without needling and commentary from the others.

"I'm obviously the new guy on the block," she tells me with a laugh when I ask about her successful strategies with the Palos Verdes Blue. "You saw me take a couple punches," she says about the "humor her" comment from Osborne. "You have to roll with the punches and head forward because it's a team effort, and I know I'm the new guy on the block."

But she thinks her new guy status has helped her break from the traditional techniques used by experts working to repopulate endangered butterflies. She has chosen to abandon field cages, essentially boxes isolating a bush in the field, because "to know everything that is going on in that bush is impossible." Instead she has moved her larvae and butterflies to all but completely controlled laboratory enclosures of the type favored by Gordon Pratt. And she has gone one step beyond what others have been doing with her feeding techniques. Instead of just providing nectar for the butterflies to find and eat, both she and Pratt choose to hand-feed them.

Johnson soaks toilet paper with honey water, and the blues suck up the sweet liquid. Getting the butterflies they breed to eat is a critical problem; if they do not eat in a timely fashion after emerging from their chrysalis, they quickly die. Pratt uses a pin to unroll the butterfly's proboscis and stick it into honey water, a tricky procedure Johnson wants to avoid. "I'm not comfortable with that process personally. There's a possibility that if they move you stab them through the head," she explains in a matter-of-fact voice, and then laughs. "I was in food service for a long time," she says referring to her pre-butterfly days, "and there are lots of different ways that you can slap down a dish on a table."

Johnson is convinced that ensuring the Blues eat every single day led directly to her successes with them, and food presentation is a major concern as she prepares to work with the Metalmarks, "because if they run out of energy, then you're toast. They're just going to die." The toilet paper technique would not work with the Metalmarks because they sport much longer antennae than the Blues. When they lean over to suck up the honey water, their antennae tend to stick on the paper and they're not able to clean it off. If they try, it gets on other parts of their bodies, and the sticky mess becomes a fatal problem. Johnson has been experimenting with a labor-intensive hand-feeding of the butterflies with honey-water-soaked Q-tips.

In addition to feeding the butterflies, "Breeding them can be really hard," Johnson says. "You can try everything. You can try heating the males and getting them all excited, and fridging the females so that they move very slowly and it's very difficult for them to refuse mating. You can rub the female against the male to make sure the male knows that she is there and ready to go." But in addition to these techniques, she deviated from Pratt's routine by developing a larger enclosure for her captive-bred butterflies when she wants them to mate. She suspended potted plants in the containers and located them outdoors and in the sun. These are containers big enough to guarantee that the butterflies can move around in them. The result? "They're happy. I've had one on one, which is just unheard of. Usually you need between five and ten males to fertilize a female. One on one we put them in there, and a half an hour later we've got gravid females." Gravid females are carrying fertilized eggs. "And that," she smiles at the success rate, "is amazing."

Once the female lays its eggs and the larvae eclose, the caterpillars eat voraciously. Metalmarks remain in the larval stage for about six months. Hence a continuing supply of buckwheat is critical for the project. The caterpillars pupate, the butterflies hatch, and the plan is for Johnson to keep them in a converted greenhouse at Moorpark College while the Fish and Wildlife Service repairs the Antioch Dunes. Maintaining the population safely off the Antioch Dunes site will allow crews to rebuild the dunes without worrying about driving the Lange's Metalmark to extinction.

I ask Jana Johnson what motivates her, what is so important about saving this particular Metalmark when there are other Metalmarks so similar to the Lange's, and why is it important to give such attention to this devastated and blighted, abused riverfront where we sit with our feet in the cool water but are surrounded by heavy industry and its debris. "Abused," she focuses on the word. "That's the key point. I'm not working with anything that got wiped out with a meteor, or some natural event. We did this. We screwed up. And we're the only ones who can fix it. Once you do start to fix it, not only does that fix the one species, but especially with the invertebrates, it's so closely linked to the vegetation that then you're saving the vegetation and the whole community."

The other argument in favor of her work, she tells me, is the Spaceship Earth argument. "Each species is a rivet and how many rivets can you pull out before the spaceship collapses?" She laughs at what's become a cliché and adds, "It's the butterfly effect."

"I have to laugh because it mimics my own freaking life," she says, when I note that she must like her work, the challenge of doing something that seems almost impossible and is an adventure. She has just learned that she will be forced to move out of the house she has lived in for the past ten years and find a new home. She says it makes her feel very close to the Palos Verdes Blues she has raised in captivity and is about to release. They too are going to be looking for a new home. "I can relate to the butterfly. I'd be more concerned if I was working with a common species that was being wiped out. They're not adapted to the punches. I'm working with the scrappers, and the scrappers can take a punch and come back. And I can relate to a scrapper. I'm a scrapper."

The Fish and Wildlife crew are packing up the ice chest, now empty of the cold water we've all been drinking. The day is waning and we have been trekking around the dunes for some five hours. As we head out I ask Jana Johnson about a comment she had made during the day when Ken Osborne and Gordon Pratt were jousting with entomological terminology. She inserted a point into the conversation and then noted to the group that she had lapsed into the vernacular. What was that about? I ask her. She stops her laughs with a serious soliloquy, "We will not win this battle, just the scientists. Can't win it. Can't even try. The cooperative conservation aspect is huge. And that means everybody. That means people who are traditionally viewed as enemies and have absolutely no interest in the little postage stamp butterfly. Getting people to work together means that you can't use an exclusive language, because it excludes them. So I pop into the vernacular frequently. But that also makes the club feel uncomfortable."

"It makes them tend to not want to humor you," I interrupt her.

"True," she says. "So I have to be able to pop back out of the vernacular and get back in the language, and make it clear I can hang with the boys." She catches herself. "Not with the boys, you know what I mean."

As we say good-bye for the day, I ask her if she is optimistic that her efforts would save the little Lange's Metalmark. Jana Johnson looks at me as if I'm crazy. "Optimistic? Absolutely. If you're not optimistic, you're dead from the start. Are you kidding me? Yeah!"

"And finding these guys today, all that larvae?"

She sighs. "I was so psyched. That's the start." Until those larvae were found, it was all preparation work. No one knew for certain the project could proceed because without larvae there would be no butterflies to breed. "To see the larvae, at least we know they are still here. They didn't go extinct."

"So it's a great day?

"It's a great day! Are you kidding me?"

A few months later I join Jana Johnson at her laboratory, a scrap of land at Moorpark College on the grounds of the college's teaching zoo. Moorpark is on the northwest outer edges of the Los Angeles sprawl. Her neighbors include sea lions, hyenas, camels, and a Bengal tiger—all residents of the Exotic Animal Training and Management Program at Moorpark.

She's smiling and excited, her face up against a box of butterflies, as she sings out, "We have sex!"

It's my first look at the famous Palos Verdes Blue, an endangered species thought to be extinct until entomologists stumbled on a few survivors hiding out on the grounds of the eerily named Defense Fuel Support Point in San Pedro, back in 1994. The Point is a maze of fuel storage tanks, pipelines, and fuel loading stations operated by the military and all competing with not just the butterfly but the specific plants it needs for its fuel: types of loco weed, shrubs also called milk vetch, and deer weed. Rudi Mattoni, a UCLA-based entomologist at the time, made the find, as he was prowling around remaining stands of the Blue's food plant. "It didn't register at first," he said then.

Understandable, since he was the last to report seeing a live Palos Verdes Blue over ten years before, and the delicate-looking butterfly was pronounced presumed extinct. Habitat loss was blamed: urban sprawl. It was Easter time when Mattoni came upon a patch of grassland near the Pacific that was home to a couple of hundred hearty survivors. "The sun broke through and there they were," he remembered. "It was a real resurrection for Easter."[45] Mattoni started breeding the Blues, hoping to rebuild sustainable populations around the Palos Verdes Peninsula.

Jana Johnson took over the project, and when I visit, she's ecstatic about its progress, even as greater Los Angeles continues its urban march (Palos Verdes city tore up some Palos Verdes Blue habitat to build a soccer field!). She and her crew have bred and stockpiled over two thousand Blues, using a technique that differs from Mattoni's experiments. Johnson sequesters the process in a closed-off environment: breeding, larval development, pupation, and eclosure all are orchestrated to occur absent outside influences except feeding.

The day I'm at Moorpark—near Easter 2008—Johnson is preparing to release a batch in the species' homeland. Government agencies in charge of public lands and adjacent private landowners work with her offering access to habitat where the Blue can thrive, along with one other needed component to ensure successful introduction into the wilds: complete secrecy. Her mission this day must be void of publicity.

She points into the breeding box. "You can see they're coupled, furthering the species." The prizes are little things with a wingspan of about an inch, gossamer blue and with some accents of charcoal gray for the females. Gorgeous. Boxes of Blues are all around us, over a dozen, filled with butterflies and eggs destined to become more caterpillars, then pupae, and eventually more Blues. Pupae diapause—hibernate—when the crew collects them and stashes them in a refrigerator. When the weather warms, the pupae are taken out of the cold and kept in greenhouses behind netting. As the pupae eclose and butterflies emerge, Johnson's workers keep careful track of which came from where to prevent inbreeding when the new generation of butterflies starts mating.

"I'm trying for the most heterogeneity. That's the key word of the day. This particular species," Johnson says of the Palos Verdes Blue, "we don't know that much about the gene lines that established our colony. We have a grant to start working with UCLA on the genetics and see which gene lines are most valuable. But until then we go with the-more-diversity-the-better theory, and we just try not to breed closely related lines." The day is warm and butterflies are emerging. "As the heat hits we'll have some more pops. We were hoping for a 25 percent eclosion rate, and we're at 50 percent and rising."

It's an incredible number: more than half the pupae are becoming butterflies, twice what the team expected. In the last couple of weeks, over twenty-four hundred Palos Verdes Blues joined the Class of 2008, forcing Johnson's Team Palos Verdes Blue Butterfly to work overtime hand-feeding their charges from wads of toilet paper soaked in honey water—a replacement for the nectar they would suck from flowers were they in the wild.

"It's not my finger you want, it's this," she tells a butterfly as she tries to guide it to the wet toilet paper she's holding. "Come here!" Its proboscis searches for the food it knows is close by because the butterfly is walking on the honey-soaked paper and it walks with its chemoreceptors. "They'll poke you with their proboscis. Luckily it doesn't hurt." She tries to interest another Blue in the ersatz nectar. "Hello. I see you. Not my finger. There you go. He's too busy patrolling. That's patrolling when you see him heading up against the roof. Patrolling for females." Two butterflies start feeding from the same wad of wet paper. "Hi, sweetheart," she says to the newcomer. "There you go. You can see they'll share their food. Not the larvae, the larvae will eat each other."

The pupae that do not eclose are not necessarily duds. They go back into the refrigerator where they can chill for as many as five years and remain viable, and they serve as insurance for coming years that may not be as productive as 2008.

Mated female butterflies—the gravid Blues—are separated from the males, and slated for release south in Palos Verdes after some eggs are collected from them. Once these females are in the wild, if they succumb to a predator before laying their eggs, that gene line is still preserved in the eggs kept at Moorpark that were collected from them before they were set free. The females keep close to their food plant, Johnson tells me, and that improves their chances of not being eaten by a natural predator. With this year's bumper crop of butterflies laying eggs, the potential exists for as many as forty thousand larvae to be introduced to Palos Verdes. The number sounds huge, but introduction doesn't mean a thriving population sticks. Plenty of those caterpillars will become somebody's dinner. But the females released are egg-laden, and sticking close to a plant increases their likelihood of survival. Their duty to future generations is to stay alive long enough to lay their eggs.

"They're very inconspicuous," she says about the females. "Their coloration, as you saw, is more bland." She immediately decides her characterization is a little harsh. "I wouldn't say bland, I think the charcoal gray is gorgeous, but it's definitely not as flashy as the blue."

"No it isn't," I agree. "But the boys look really cool, don't you think?"

"The boys do look really cool. They are an iridescent blue and they will prance. Don't they look proud? They remind me of peacocks. I'd be proud, too. They seem quite impressed with themselves."

"They show a border," I suggest to her, "that almost looks like the piping on a cowboy shirt."

"Oh, yeah. You know I never thought of that before, but yeah. It has both a black and then a white border to it, which really offsets the blue. And they patrol for females. The males will breed as many times as they can. In fact, we do have difficulty convincing them to eat during this time. It's a good life. If you're going to live three to ten days, you might as well make the most of it."

The males patrol, she says, flying around the loco weed looking for females, flashing that attractive blue. She and her team do not want such antics at play for an initial release. Rather, they want the low-keyed, somewhat camouflaged gravid females out in the wild, sitting on the host plants and laying eggs. "They're not going to call attention to predators of any sort, including the unscrupulous who will be looking to net them, pin them, and put them in a collection." Hence the tight security. Johnson is convinced that were the public aware of the exact locale where she and her team release the Blues, there would be thieves on the loose seeking to net them—despite the fact that they are endangered and that such collecting is against the law. Even harassing the Blues is a violation, and harassing includes ignoring the "Please keep on the trail" signs, and tramping through the grasslands where an endangered species is being protected.

On more than one occasion, speaking to public meetings about her work, Johnson has been dumbstruck at the audacity of audience members asking her where the next release would be staged. She remembers one offensive experience when she said as usual, "I'm going to decline to answer on the grounds that collection could really wipe us out." Her questioner responded with the honest follow-up, "My best friend's kids are looking for some for their collection."

She gets agitated just telling the story. "Have you heard of the Endangered Species Act? Are you familiar at all with what an endangered species is? It's just so ludicrous to me. It's like from a foreign planet. It's like somebody saying, 'Where you putting the condor? Oh, good. I'm going to go get my gun.'"

There are purists in the scientific community posing questions about the impact captive rearing may have on wild populations, even under the tight controls mandated by Jana Johnson's Fish and Wildlife Service license, a license she must maintain in order to work legally with an endangered species. But she is sure the benefits outweigh any risks. One of the worries raised is that gene lines are being removed from the wild when at-risk butterflies are captured. Johnson rejects the theory and reminds me of the appearance of the gravid Lange's Metalmarks we collected in Antioch. "You saw them, they were tattered. They were missing parts of their wings. Some of them were missing legs. They were old. There is no argument there because we're not going out collecting young, fresh gravid females. We're collecting the ones who are about to be eaten that have already left their gene line out there."

The battered Lange's ended their days in even worse shape. "We had one of them that was still laying eggs, but she had broken all of her legs. She couldn't stand. We would put food plant underneath her so she could lay eggs while she was on the ground. To feed her we had to hold it up to her proboscis, and sometimes we had to help her extend her proboscis. It was hard. When you're saving a species you've got to take these steps."

I look up Euphilotes Blues in Jeffrey Glassberg's field guide to western North America and find citations for twenty-eight varieties of the beauties (not including the Palos Verdes). At first glance the Dotted Blue looks like a reasonable facsimile to me, as does the Rita Blue and the Spalding's Blue and the Silvery Blue and the Boisuval's Blue and Greenish Blue. I ask Johnson again what I queried her about in Antioch: Why is it so important to save her Palos Verdes Blues when we've got plenty of these other guys? She admits to accepting arguments that there may be redundant species, but she also buys the Spaceship Earth approach. Again she asks rhetorically, "At what point have you popped too many rivets off the spaceship?"

Maybe the Spaceship Earth theory is what makes her susceptible to anthropomorphizing her charges.

"Come on, sweetie," Johnson is nudging a butterfly back into its box from the guarded opening that allows her to stick her hand into the enclosure without the butterfly getting out. "Wrong way. Go the other way. You are not being helpful." It sounds like she's talking with a favorite child. "Oh, get off my hand. I'm not feeding you right now. I'm not. Sorry." She stops talking to the insect and turns to me. "They just have little cerebral ganglia, but that's enough for them to be Pavlovian trained. If there is a hand reaching into the cage, there should be some honey water on it."

"Really? They really do make the connection?"

"Yes, they do. It became abundantly clear last year when we were individually caring for the stock, because our stock was so much smaller."

"Does it work the other way and you start to have individual butterflies with which you develop a personal relationship?"

"This year not so much," she says, because the population is so large. But last year, yes. "I have to say about 07001 from last year, I cried when she died. She was good."

"What was special about her?"

"She always ate when you offered her food, and she deposited so many eggs. I don't have an egg count on her, but she produced over two hundred pupae by herself. And she died with an egg coming out of her abdomen. I felt labor pains for her because I've had two kids. She was the epitome of a good butterfly mother. When she died I was very sad."

"But she never was awarded a real name? Just good old mama 07001?"

"She might have had a name," Johnson acknowledges with a coy smile, and after some prodding allows as how she dubbed her Eve. But she says she makes an effort to avoid referring to the butterflies as if they were people. She tries to call them stock, not Adam and Eve. "That's not very scientific." Blues in captivity, such as Eve, often live longer than their wild brethren, as long as several months—compared with just a few days to a month in the wild. Those kept in the boxes are protected from their natural predators and don't damage themselves flying free in the brush.

The day is getting hotter and Johnson is still waiting for approval to release the waiting butterflies. The holdup is over security: Johnson needs special authorization to release the Blues unannounced; Fish and Wildlife Service regulations require transparency about releases because of the Public Records Act. Johnson is seeking a waiver based on threats she knows the Blues face, were the public aware of their new homes. In this era of hyper federal government secrecy, it's bizarre to learn of the difficulties she's dealing with trying to keep the release site free of poachers. Time is critical. If this generation doesn't get off the Moorpark College campus soon, they'll lay all their eggs at the zoo and die in captivity rather than leave their eggs in the wild and participate in the repopulation of the Blue on the Palos Verdes Peninsula. With over twenty-four hundred ready for release and more eclosing every day, time and place are both critical if the progeny of these gravid female Blues are to hatch in the wild. Johnson must find appropriate and available habitat when the butterflies are at the point in their life cycle when they are most likely to survive without the twenty-four-hour nursemaid attention they receive at Moorpark. She checks her iPhone every few minutes for email updates from the bureaucracy.

Suddenly there's a shout. "Guys! Somebody got out!" A precious Palos Verdes Blue is free of its box, fluttering around the compound. It lights in a tree near the fence that separates the butterflies from the adjacent hoof stock—a Scottish highland cow and a water buffalo. I spot him and point him out to Johnson who jumps on a table and from it climbs up the chain-link fence, straddles it, and manages to grab the Blue in a manic two-handed catch. She climbs back down slowly and carefully, and the escapee is exiled into a box with butterflies lacking a traceable pedigree. It's the mongrel box, full of butterflies with unknown gene lines. (The crisis took seconds and was a momentary diversion from the waiting, but also serious business for Johnson who tells me later, "I feel a need for perfection and this was a less-than-perfect moment. The loss of the stock was minor with our wealth of individuals. The risk was that he would find a mate and introduce genes that don't belong in Moorpark. It was kind of like having a panic attack over planting an exotic plant in your lawn and worrying that it will spread and breed with a native species. Most likely it would have been eaten by a bird, lizard, or spider—but I was relieved to have it in hand again." It was a catch to impress Willie Mays.)

Late in the day all the paperwork finally is processed and Johnson is given the go-ahead to release a batch of Blues. Besides the security issues, it is a laborious process to follow the letter of the law. Fish and Wildlife Service permits are required for each release date and each release site. Property owners—private and government—must agree to accept the Blues, and the regulations for their protection that go along with them. Habitat is being restored on the Palos Verdes Peninsula, and that's where the captive-bred Blues can find suitable homes, places supporting their food plant where the species has a chance of reestablishing. Johnson and her assistants fight ghastly traffic jams across the Los Angeles Basin from Moorpark to Palos Verdes, reaching the Peninsula after dark. With headlights blazing their path, they take 206 Blues—packed into anonymous garbage bags and coolers just on the chance the crew is being watched—and hike to the butterflies' new home. One by one they coax the butterflies onto their fingers and then coax them again onto the wild deer weed where—if all goes well—they will deposit their eggs, the resulting caterpillars will thrive eating the weed leaves, make themselves a cozy chrysalis, and emerge metamorphosed into a vibrant Palos Verdes Blue. "The Blue is flying free!" says Johnson with relief. "Our release site is undisclosed. What an intense day!"

A year after I joined Jana Johnson and her entourage to collect that handful of the last Lange's Metalmarks, I'm back in Antioch with her team and a precious cargo of captive-bred Lange's Metalmarks. Gordon Pratt's colony did not thrive, the factors that led to its demise still uncertain. But Johnson raised a bumper crop of eggs, larvae, pupae, and adult Lange's. It's going to be a scorcher again this summer day. The sun is still low before eight as I arrive at the Stamm Unit. The plan is to release the butterflies—thirty gravid females—before the day becomes an oven, and the transition to the wild could be traumatic. If all goes well, the butterflies will lay hundreds of eggs—which Johnson is confident were fertilized at Moorpark or on the overnight road trip—and the dunes soon will be crawling with caterpillars. More than a hundred other Lange's stayed at Moorpark, breeding stock expected to increase the captive population for release in a year.

On a recent prior visit, to the refuge, Johnson seeded the refuge with Lange's larvae and pupae, and as she walked toward the crop of white buckwheat flowers where she had attached the pupae, two Lange's were fluttering, her first indication that the introduction of insects bred off-site was successful—she was convinced she was looking at Moorpark Lange's settling in the ancestral Antioch homeland.

Johnson and her crew reach into containers and one by one they coax the butterflies to climb onto their fingers, and then from their fingers onto the buckwheat. The idea is to get them eating and laying eggs as soon as possible. The Lange's life span usually is just a few days; oldtimers rarely see as much as a couple of weeks.

"Who has 114?" Johnson yells out.

Butterfly 114 is a special Lange's. Her full name is LMB08114, for Lange's Metalmark butterfly, from 2008, and the 114th bred in captivity. "Number 114 was one of the youngest ladies present at the release," Johnson tells me later. She was just a couple of days old when she moved from the laboratory to the wild. She had been observed breeding the day before the release, so she was carrying fertile eggs. Johnson wants her photographed: she is a perfect specimen, an example of "the beauty of a young adult."

"Brittany has 114," comes the answer from one of her crew. "Do you want 114, Jana?"

"Yes I do, please."

Butterfly number 114 is, as are its sisters and brothers and cousins and friends, in a Styrofoam container of the type designed for take-out food and restaurant leftovers (a bargain bought in bulk from Smart and Final). Holes in the containers and lids are covered with mesh to allow fresh air to circulate while the butterflies stay inside, resting on scraps of buckwheat. Number 114 is brilliant in the morning sun, basking in her take-out container, the colors exploding off her tiny wings. She flutters for a moment, defying the hand-off to the buckwheat, and then lands on one of the bright white flowers.

"She's nectaring!" reports Johnson, excited because eating stimulates the butterflies to lay their eggs. We're tightly focused on 114 as she sucks buckwheat nectar, and it's easy to feel one with nature, out in the wild. A wailing whistle from a railroad locomotive on the adjacent mainline to Chicago breaks that reverie. I look up as the train crosses Fulton Shipyard Road—just the name of the street a reminder of the industrial sprawl that brackets this pocket of protected wildlife. Ashcan School–looking factory silhouettes mark the horizon, steam billowing out of stacks.

"We're kind of putting on a feast," Johnson says. Dragonflies, birds, lizards, and spiders all would enjoy a Lange's lunch. "They're on the diet list for a ton of animals out here and some may be eaten immediately. But they've got to fly free, they've got to feel the wind." She just hopes a healthy number of eggs are laid before the Moorpark batch succumb, whether to predators or butterfly old age. Some of the butterflies laid pinhead-sized eggs on the buckwheat in their containers en route to Antioch. The crew transfer egg-laden leaves into the bushy undergrowth of the buckwheat. All four stages of the butterflies' life cycle have now been imported into the dunes habitat: eggs, larvae, pupae, and adult butterflies.

Fellow entomologist Ken Osborne smiles and congratulates Johnson on the initial success of the operation. He knows the rigors of breeding butterflies in captivity, and the pitfalls that can preclude a successful operation. "We had great trepidations, not so much rearing the larvae and getting to the pupae, but first collecting the adults and getting them to lay eggs in captivity. That's stressful because they have to be happy and in the right condition. You have to feed them every day the buckwheat honey and water mixture that mimics nectar. When you've reared all these larvae and you've got all these pupae that have emerged, it's a whole year's cycle. Are they going to hatch? What if the males hatch much earlier than the females? What if you don't successfully raise enough of them to get a male to meet a female? You have to have big enough numbers, and have them emerge in the same time frame to get them together, and once you get them together . . ."

Johnson interrupts him, "You have to set the mood!"

He agrees, the atmosphere must be right to encourage courtship behaviors. To replicate the natural environment to the extent that the butterflies mate in captivity is "a huge accomplishment." Osborne congratulates her again. He looks around with approval at the patches of naked-stem buckwheat the Fish and Wildlife Service is nurturing on the dunes, and at the attempts made over the last year to clear non-native invasive weeds from the buckwheat habitat. But he is a realist, and these dunes are nowhere near the state they were in before the Spanish arrived in California, and now are home to rapacious grasses that continue to threaten the buckwheat. The sedate San Joaquin River no longer rushes toward San Francisco Bay, rising and falling, depositing sand on its Antioch banks, sand that prior to the river flows being controlled by man would be blown by the fierce delta and bay winds, and pushed high from shore to form perfect terrain for buckwheat, the food and shelter for the enclaves of Lange's that once thrived at Antioch.

"All we're doing is propping up the butterflies," he announces. "This is an epic challenge because of the exotics." He looks at the patches of newly established buckwheat plants. "Ten-foot plots aren't going to do it—we need acres." Otherwise maintaining the species likely will require perpetual captive breeding because there simply is not enough of a rangeland for the Lange's to thrive on its own.

Jana Johnson tells him about the two Lange's she spotted in the air around the buckwheat plants where she left pupae a couple of weeks ago. Osborne cannot help himself; the skeptical scientist seeks proof. He raises his eyebrows when she suggests they were Moorpark adults that eclosed in Antioch, and the next moment Johnson is on the ground, rooting around the bases of the buckwheat, searching for pupa remnants on the plants where she attached pupae. The cuff of her cargo pants rides up her calf, exposing her new tattoo: a Palos Verdes Blue, along with a line from a poem one of her students wrote for her: " . . . and then she flew." I hear a gleeful call. She's found an empty pupa casing, broken open. And she knows it's one she brought to the dunes from Moorpark because it's still stuck to the buckwheat where she superglued it. She snaps the buckwheat, careful to keep the remains of the pupa intact along with her superglue seal, and parades it over to Osborne who smiles and accepts the proof that a captive-bred pupa eclosed in the refuge.

"That's nice," Osborne nods with approval. He is an enthusiastic curmudgeon and later—with a dreamy look in his eyes—half smiles and recites for me from what he says is the last page of his favorite book, W. J. Holland's *The Moth Book*, first published in 1909. I check the source, and he didn't miss a word. "When the moon shall have faded from the sky, and the sun shall shine at noonday a dull cherry-red, and the seas shall be frozen over, and the ice-cap shall have crept downward to the equator from either pole, and no keels shall cut the waters, nor wheels turn in mills, when all cities shall have long been dead and crumbled into dust, and all life shall be on the very last verge of extinction on this globe; then, on a bit of lichen, growing on the bald rocks beside the eternal snows of Panama, shall be seated a tiny insect, preening its antennae in the glow of the worn-out sun, representing the sole survival of animal life on this our earth,—a melancholy 'bug.'"

"My trophy," Johnson is thrilled with the empty pupa casing. "It raises the probability that what we saw was ours. It's a perfect day." She beams about the Lange's revival. "It's never been done before." She and Osborne exchange a high-five. And she's happy for her fluttering freed charges. "How great would that be if I were a butterfly? To come out, sit on a flower; nectar, feel the heat, feel the wind. That's like a perfect day for a butterfly, and she's already gravid, she doesn't have to worry about finding a man! She can just crawl around the plant and lay some eggs. It's all good!"

At least for now, another species is saved from extinction in the dangerous world of butterflies.

EPILOGUE

HERE I SIT IN MY OFFICE AFTER SPENDING THE BETTER PART OF THE
last two years chasing butterflies. Butterfly books line my shelves.
Pictures of butterflies are up on the wall. I've procured sheets of
twenty-four cent butterfly stamps that feature the image of a hand-
some Buckeye to use when I post notes on cards my wife bought me
that display drawings of butterflies dating from the eighteenth and
nineteenth centuries.

My off-hand remark that a book about butterflies would be a
respite for me from serious news reporting was 100 percent off the
mark. I slammed directly into all the elements of a front-page story
with this assignment: species depletion, environmental disaster,
felonious crime, and, best of all, idiosyncratic characters—many of
whom, I'm amazed to discover, I now count as colleagues, and a few
as newfound friends. That's not the norm for me as a journalist. Usually sources remain just that: informants who further the story.

I see butterflies everywhere now, and dissuade friends and family from adding to my growing stash of butterfly memorabilia. There
is an overwhelming amount of stuff out there, from the elegant—
like my flashy brooch—to the tacky (and I promise to refrain from
adorning my body with a butterfly tattoo, no matter how tasteful it
may seem after a few drinks). But I love the fact that I now spot butterflies in the wild and focus on them. Prior to this adventure, as Ed
Newcomer inferred, they were not just insects to me. I considered
them flashier than most bugs, to be sure. I thought them prettier, too,
naturally. Of course they were magical. They doubtless suggested a

counterpoint to war in my subconscious, or I wouldn't have picked them out of the blue as an antidote to the psychic drain of researching and writing a book about the Iraq War. But they were bugs to me then, nonetheless. However a fringe benefit (or liability?) of this project is that I am now sensitized to all insects. Sure, if it repeatedly annoys me, or lights on my breakfast, I'll still swat a fly bloody and dead. But I do it now much more mindful of the miracle that that pest represents.

Now I love butterflies. I watch them flutter into sight and then follow them, trying to keep track of them, not to catch them or even to identify them—just to enjoy them. I watch their flight paths with new appreciation for their purpose. I consider the nourishment they're reaping when they stop off at flowers and extend their proboscises. And I ponder the magic and miracle of the metamorphosis that changed them from one distinct form to another, remembering with curiosity how Edith Smith insisted that she prefers her crawling worm-like caterpillars to her soaring flower-like butterflies.

It's doubtful I'll again join Jeffrey Glassberg and his bands of butterfly huggers for another escapade in the wilderness hunting butterflies simply to spot and add to a list. But I'll always be on the lookout for them when I'm hiking, except in empty deserts and Safeway parking lots—those places Arthur Shapiro taught me were the only sites besides the open ocean that butterflies fail to frequent. I didn't reject evolution following Ron Boender's preaching about the divine origin of the butterflies we watched at his Butterfly World, but I appreciate and share the awe he expressed about their heavenly beauty.

Chasing butterflies instead of the usual suspects we journalists typically confront—wars, natural disasters, corrupt politicians, etc.— calmed me these last couple of years. How nice to be in hot pursuit of a gorgeous creature instead of responding to bad news, especially an animal that brings such happiness to so many of us—and does no harm. It's made me think of the slow food movement as a model. Perhaps it's time to launch the slow news movement (yesterday's news tomorrow?). Which brings me to the question that sent me on this journey and quest.

What's my next book going to be about?

ACKNOWLEDGMENTS

It is traditional to cite family members in book acknowledgments, and I thank mine. My wife, the author and poet Sheila Swan Laufer, is always the critical first editor of my work—frequently salvaging me from myself—and she insisted I grab a flight to Managua without delay when Jane Foulds first invited me to Nicaragua. I very much appreciate the familial support I receive from Talmage, Amber, Ryann (Ri-ot!), Caitlin, and SWLR. I must single out my son Michael, the mathematician, for an extra special tip of the safari hat. Early on in the process he appointed himself managing editor of this project. Throughout the research and writing he offered valuable feedback and brainstorming, along with an appropriate dose, now and again, of cajoling and badgering. He, too, was quick to insist I check out the Foulds' *mariposario*.

My friend and colleague Steven Schragis disabused me from the working title I initially chose for this book. His experiences as one of the founders of *Spy* magazine, the dynamic chief of the Carol Publishing Group, and creative force behind the remarkable One Day University, propelled his advice that I use the one he conjured. University of Nebraska parasitologist Scott Lyell Gardner helped guide me through the morass of butterfly names; we met serendipitously in our relative youth far from home, each doing fieldwork on separate projects, and struck up a lasting friendship. In Nicaragua, my friend and fellow Berkeleyan Nelson Estrada provided gracious and needed hospitality (along with tumblers full of well-aged *Flor de Caña*) while reminding me about us, *"No soy de aquí ni soy de allá."*

Ralph and Toni Jones at their Avatar Community Business Center in Fairfax, California, were most gracious in providing needed back office facilities for me, as was Shona Weir at her Business Services Unlimited in Bodega Bay, California. Kathy Talbert at D-J Word Processing in Santa Rosa, California, provided fast and accurate transcriptions of recorded interviews. Ingalisa Schrobsdorff, the producer of "Washington Monthly on the Radio," the conversation program I co-anchor with Markos Kounalakis, scheduled some needed interviews with butterfly experts. Speaking of *Genossen* Kounalakis, he offered early and hearty encouragement when I first contemplated pursuing butterflies, as did another radio partner, Business Shrink Peter Morris.

Some of the interviews that helped set the stage for this book were conducted during my Sunday current affairs radio show on the station Green 960 in San Francisco. Program Director John Scott is a staunch supporter of its eclectic content, butterfly esoterica included. Another colleague quick to appreciate the intrigue of the butterfly underground was *Aware* magazine founder and publisher Christopher Caen. San Francisco newspaper columnist and boulevardier Bruce Bellingham vetted some early drafts, as did journalist and author Terry Phillips. Further support and consultation came from Alex Roth, Jeff Kamen, Chris Slattery, and George Papagiannis. Thanks to Jana Vance and Ryan Murphy for the use of their sheltered front yard where we staged the Painted Lady release.

The extraordinarily energized Lyons Press publisher Gary Krebs was great fun to pitch when I suggested he publish this book. We were on the floor of the chaotic Book Expo America in Los Angeles, surrounded by distraction. Nonetheless his enthusiasm was keen and he introduced me to his acquisitions editor Holly Rubino. Not only did she favor the idea, she became my editor and we became friends as she skillfully (and usually painlessly) shepherded my draft into its current form.

Over the months following my initial visit to her *reserva* in Granada, I remained in touch via email with Jane Foulds, asking her some follow-up questions, preparing for a return trip. "Butterflies remain my passion," she wrote in one note. In another, following Hurricane Mitch, she assured me the *reserva* survived with no damage. "The butterflies are happy in the cooler rain. We have 200–300 Morphos—the big blue ones—growing, and hopefully they'll live to maturity and prosper." And she signed it as she did all her emails, "Peace and tranquility await you at Nicaragua Butterfly *Reserva*. Come visit us."

When it came time to tell her the book she assigned me to write was nearing completion, my emails to her were uncharacteristically unanswered. I was unable to reach her on the telephone. An Internet search quickly established the sad reality. Jane Foulds died at her dream *reserva* February 25, 2008. "You know when you walk into a theater and they have those big popcorn poppers where the popcorn overflows the top and cascades down the bin? That's what my wife's ideas were like," Gerry Foulds said after her death. "A lot of what happened in our lives was determined by that popcorn popper."[46] After his wife died, he hired a manager to operate the *reserva*, a living memorial to Jane Foulds and her ideas.

That popcorn popper obviously influenced my life. Without her email inviting me to her Granada *reserva* following my flip "butterflies and flowers" remark on CSPAN, it's difficult to imagine I would have surrounded myself with butterflies and written this book.

Thank you, Jane. I miss you.

ENDNOTES

1   http://pestalert.ifas.ufl.edu/butterflies_talk.htm

2   http://jeb.biologists.org/cgi/content/abstract/203/24/3689

3   Nabokov, Vladimir. (1951) *Speak Memory,* New York, Grosset & Dunlap, p. 81.

4   Glassberg, Jeffrey, et al. "There's No Need to Release Butterflies—They're Already Free," www.naba.org/weddings/html.

5   "IBBA's Response to NABA Statements and Opinions," www.butterflybreeders.org/public/nabaresponse.html.

6   Thoreau, Henry D. (1910) *Walden, Or, Life in the Woods,* Cambridge (MA), Houghton Mifflin Co., p. 235.

7   Stang, Wendy, and Richards, Susan. (1967) *Hubert the Caterpillar Who Thought He Was a Mustache,* New York, Harlin Quist.

8   Graves, Robert. (1931) *Poems 1926–1930,* London, William Heinemann.

9   Risling, Greg. "L.A. Man Freed after Decade in Prison," Associated Press dispatch published in the Santa Rosa *Press Democrat,* October 29, 2008.

10   Examples of Elliot Malkin's graffiti for butterflies can be seen at www.dziga.com/graffiti.

11   Throughout the text I refer to the Monarch overwintering grounds as located in Mexico's Sierra Madre, the mountain ranges which encompass the southernmost reaches of North America's Codillera mountain system. The specific neighborhood the Monarchs call home is in the Trans-Mexican Volcanic Belt of the overall Sierra Madre, an important footnote for those who study the

relatively recent history of Monarch research. Robert Michael Pyle—
the author of several books about butterflies including *Chasing Monarchs*—for example, says that Fred Urquhart did not specify the exact
location where he discovered the butterflies his team previously had
tagged north of the border in an effort to protect them from the
expected hordes of researchers and tourists who would follow him.
"Urquhart planted the intentional lie that the sites were in the Sierra
Madre in *National Geographic* back in 1975," wrote Pyle in an email
to me, "to try to throw people off; but it's been well known that this is
incorrect ever since Lincoln Brower and Bill Calvert independently
found them shortly thereafter." Lie or obfuscation, Urquhart's good
intentions failed to hide his butterflies.

12   Urquhart, Fred. "Discovered: The Monarch's Haven,"
National Geographic, August 1976.

13   Berstein-Wax, Jessica. (2007) "Mexico's Broad Plan to Protect Butterfly Habitat," Associated Press dispatch as published in
the Santa Rosa *Press Democrat,* November 26, 2007, Cerro Prieto,
Mexico.

14   Revkin, Andrew C. "Loggers Invaded Butterfly Haven,
Photos Show," *The New York Times,* March 7, 2008.

15   No byline. "Mexico Cites Dramatic Drop in Illegal Logging
in Monarch Butterfly Reserve," Associated Press dispatch, July 2,
2008.

16   Bray, David. "Living with Monarchs: The Uneasy Relationship Between Mexican Peasants and a Migratory Butterfly," *Miami
Herald,* February 1, 1998.

17   Jackson, Derrick Z. "Driving out the Butterflies," *The Boston
Globe,* May 11, 2005.

18   Shoumatoff, Alex. "A Preliminary Report on the Philanthropic Possibilities of Cuba," www.dispatchesfromthevanishing
world.com/dispatch7, May 19–26, 2001.

19   The Vladimir Dinets Web site: dinets.travel.ru/parnassius. htm.

20   Fountaine, Margaret. (1980) *Love Among the Butterflies: The Secret Life of a Victorian Lady,* Boston, Little, Brown and Company, p. 215.

21   www.bbc.co.uk/insideout/south/series1/butterfly-collectors .shtml.

22   www.fieldmuseum.org/butterfly/herman.htm.

23   Williams, Ted. "The Great Butterfly Bust," *Audubon,* March–April, p. 34–35.

24   Romano, Bill. "2 Butterfly Poachers Net Probation, Avoid Prison," *San Jose Mercury News,* August 2, 1995, p. 4B.

25   Williams, Ted. "The Great Butterfly Bust," *Audubon,* March–April 1996, p. 35.

26   Alexander, Caroline. "Crime of Passion: A Glimpse into the Covert World of Rare Butterfly Collecting," *Outside,* January 1996.

27   Archibold, Randal C., and Preston, Julia. "Homeland Security Stands by Its Fence," *The New York Times,* May 21, 2008.

28   Sue Sill serves on the board of La Cruz Habitat Protection Project, Ed Rashin and José Luis Alvarez Alcalá's reforestation organization.

29   McEver, Melissa. "Walling Off Wildlife," *The Monitor,* McAllen, Texas, July 2, 2007.

30   Blumenthal, Ralph. "In Texas, Conditions Lead to a Rabble of Butterflies," *The New York Times,* July 27, 2006.

31   Holt, Vincent M. (1969) *Why Not Eat Insects?,* Middlesex (U.K.), E. W. Classey Ltd., pp. 67–68.

32   Robert Bye and Jorge Llorente-Bousquets at the National Autonomous University in Mexico City along with Peter Kevan at the University of Guelph in Ontario researched the butterfly eating habits of the Tarahumara.

33   Flood, Joseph. (1980) *The Moth Hunters,* Canberra City, Australian Institute of Aboriginal Studies, pp. 61–82.

34   Shapiro, Arthur. (2008) *Field Guide to Butterflies of the San Francisco Bay and Sacramento Valley Regions,* Berkeley, University of California Press.

35   Firestone and Parson advertisement, *The New Yorker,* September 15, 2008, p. 23.

36   Muensterberger, Werner. (1994) *Collecting: An Unruly Passion,* Princeton (NJ), Princeton University Press, pp. 13 & 256.

37   Calloway, Stephen. (2004) *Obsessions: Collectors and Their Passions,* London, Octopus Publishing Group Ltd.

38   Blom, Philipp. (2002) *To Have and to Hold: An Intimate History of Collectors and Collecting,* Woodstock (NY),The Overlook Press, p. 228.

39   Eliot, T. S. (1920) *The Sacred Wood,* London, Methune.

40   Vallance, Tom. "Virginia Grey: Film Actress Who Started in Silents," *Independent on Sunday,* August 7, 2004, London.

41   Haithman, Diane. "New Windows into a Mischievous Mind," *Los Angeles Times,* February 18, 2007, p. F–14.

42   Gibbons, Fiachre. "Hirst Accused of Sadism over Butterfly Collage," *The Guardian,* August 15, 2003, London.

43   Gettings, John. (2007) "Destination Bizarre: Great American Claims to Fame," *Information Please,* Pearson Education, www.infoplease.com/spot/roadtrip1.html.

44   The Bernard d'Abrera review is posted on the Web site learn aboutbutterflies.com, created by butterfly hobbyist Adrian Hoskins.

45   "An 'Extinct' Butterfly Flutters Back to Life," *The New York Times,* April 5, 1994.

46   Roth, Mark. (2008) "Jane Foulds: Children's Advocate, Ran Butterfly Reserve in Nicaragua," *Pittsburgh Post-Gazette,* March 15, 2008.

INDEX

About the Author

When he's not chasing butterfly stories, the news beats of journalist Peter Laufer, Ph.D., include borders, identity, and diasporas. More about his books, documentary films, and broadcasts, which have won the George Polk, Robert F. Kennedy, Edward R. Murrow, and other awards, can be found at peterlaufer.com.